The Essential
Adoption Handbook

The Essential Adoption Handbook

Colleen Alexander-Roberts

TAYLOR TRADE PUBLISHING

Lanham • New York • Toronto • Plymouth, UK

This book is dedicated to my sons,
Christopher and Blake,
and to their birth mothers for first choosing life,
then adoption, for their children.

Copyright ©1993, 1996 by Colleen Alexander-Roberts

Published by Taylor Trade Publishing
An imprint of The Rowman & Littlefield Publishing Group, Inc.
4501 Forbes Boulevard, Suite 200
Lanham, Maryland 20706

Distributed by National Book Network

Designed by Deborah Jackson-Jones

Library of Congress Cataloging-in-Publication Data

Alexander-Roberts, Colleen
    The essential adoption handbook / Colleen Alexander-Roberts.
      p.   cm.
    Includes bibliographical references and index.
    ISBN 0-87833-840-3
    1. Adoption—United States—Handbooks, manuals, etc. 2. Adoption
agencies—United States—Handbooks, manuals, etc. 3. Intercountry
adoption—United States—Handbooks, manuals, etc. I. Title.
HV875.55.A44 1993
362.7'34'0973—dc20   93-7230
                                                CIP

Printed in the United States of America

Acknowledgments

My research for this book began in 1986, one year after we adopted our first child. I envisioned then a book for prospective adoptive parents, a beginner's guide, that would help people through the adoption process and enable them to fulfill a dream—the same dream I once had years ago before I had someone to call me mommy. My desire to write this book was cultivated through the years by the many adoptive families I met. They shared their hopes and dreams with me as well as their frustrations as they tried to add to their lives what so many took for granted. Often I cried with them; their pain became mine.

Over those same years I encouraged and supported many of these families as they worked toward adopting. I also witnessed their joy as they finally brought home their son or daughter. But for every family who brought home a child, there were still so many others trying to adopt. And so I continued to work, both on this book and in my role as founder of Families United for Adoption.

This book is the result of my commitment to helping prospective adoptive parents. But rarely is a book written without the assistance of others. Not surprisingly, when I reached out for help many people came forward and gave generously and freely of their time and knowledge. It is because of all these people that this book was completed and my dream finally realized.

I would especially like to thank Deborah McCurdy at Beacon Adoption Center in Great Barrington, Massachusetts, for editing and offering suggestions in the area of intercountry adoption. Thank you, Deborah, for sharing your expertise, for all of your long hours, and for your support and belief in this project. To my dear friend, Christine Adamec, who acted as a sounding board, offered suggestions and encouragement, and read the manuscript numerous times, thank you. My gratitude to adoption attorney Aaron Britvan, in Woodbury, New York, for offering guidance in the area of independent adoption. To Debra Smith, director of the National Adoption Information Clearinghouse, for always being available when I called and for sharing your expertise, I am grateful. Thanks also to Sally Bartholomew Goligoski and Judith Gilbert, also my dear friends, for your suggestions, support, and for editing parts of the manuscript.

Many others came forward to help, including Ruth Werth, Lutheran Social Services of Indiana; AnnaMarie Merrill and Betty Laning, of International Concerns Committee for Children; Hal Hanna, adoption attorney, Bowling Green, Ohio; Laura Draheim, Lucas County Children Services Board, Maumee, Ohio; Dawn Smith-Pliner, Friends in Adoption, Inc., Middle Springs, Vermont; Valerie Miller, Catholic Charities, Toledo, Ohio; and the library staff at Swanton Public Library, especially Michelle Szabo and Jan Porazinski.

In writing this book, I relied heavily on the experiences of more than 100 adoptive parents who offered their advice and insights. I would especially like to thank adoptive parents Lisa K. Arnold and Sandra M. Cortese for the essays they contributed to the book and Pam and Bob O'Neill for giving me permission to share with my readers their business card and resume, which they used in networking to locate their new infant daughter, Colleen. Other adoptive parents who made contributions include MaryAnn J. Burdge, Debra Graf, Victoria Everett, Lynn Tearney, Bonnie Hickman, Felix Fornino, Lois L. Bush, Shelly Hawkins, Evelyn A. Abernethy, Laurie K. Glass, Linda Pankow, Sabina Seidel, Julia Spann, Marilyn Wistrand, and Nancy Johnson. To the many members of Families United for Adoption (FUFA) who also shared their experiences and encouraged me to continue working on my book, I thank you. And to Cynthia Ungar who especially understood my need to complete this project and willingly took over presidency of FUFA so I could do just that. Thanks Cindy. At Taylor Publishing thanks to my editor Lorena Jones, for her enthusiasm and guidance.

It is impossible to acknowledge all of the agency directors and social workers who graciously answered my questionnaires and shared information on the different types of adoption agencies, programs, fees, and parent requirements. I offer my thanks to each and every one of you.

My wonderful family supported me throughout the years as I worked. To my husband who spent many hours at the computer compiling lists for the appendices—often retyping and reprinting list after list long after I had retired for the night—I am forever grateful for your support, Clyde. My sons, Christopher and Blake, although still too young to realize the magnitude of this project, respected the fact that "Mommy was working to help others adopt" and often let me work uninterrupted for hours at a time. My beautiful "adopted daughter" of several years, Heidi Wymer, took on the responsibility of caring for my children for three years. Thank you, dear Heidi, for loving them as much as you do. A special thank you to my wonderful in-laws, Ruth and Clyde, for helping with the children when Heidi wasn't available. To my parents, Joanne and Stan, for their love and support, I am grateful. And to my father who never stopped encouraging me to write a book, I am proud to say, "Here it is, Dad. Thank you for believing in me."

Colleen Alexander-Roberts
March 1993

Contents

Introduction   xi

1. A Look at Adoption Today   1
2. Adoptive Parent Support Groups   22
3. Gathering Information to Adopt through an Agency   30
4. Understanding Agency Information and Requirements   39
5. Pursuing Agency Adoption   65
6. The Home Study Process   85
7. Intercountry Adoption   107
8. Single Parent Adoption   127
9. Independent Adoption   135
10. Surviving the Wait   166

Afterword   175

Bibliography   176

Appendices   185

    Adoption Attorneys

    Adoption Book Publishers and Distributors

    Adoptive Parent Support Organizations

    General Adoption Resources

    Private Adoption Agencies

    Public Agencies

Index   237

Introduction

The telephone call came on a cold, windy Friday morning. It was totally unexpected, and for minutes after my husband and I were in a state of shock and disbelief. Then slowly the reality hit us and we laughed with joy. We had accomplished the impossible and had beaten the odds. With the help of an agency, we had just become the parents of a beautiful, blond, blue-eyed baby. We had waited only 29 days.

Our son, Christopher, was two days old when we received that phone call and the next day he entered a foster home while we waited for the paperwork for an interstate adoption to be completed and processed. Christopher's birth announcement was received with surprise and some skepticism since we had shared our plans to adopt with family and friends only three weeks before. Many wanted to know where we had found a baby to adopt so quickly. Was there something wrong with him? And what about the agency? Everyone knows there are no healthy babies available for adoption. Why did this agency have one? If adopting an infant is so easy, then why did all of the agencies in town have such long waiting lists? Were we sure this was a legal adoption?

A funny thing happened after we brought Christopher home. Our phone rang constantly. We had the usual congratulatory calls, but most of the calls were from friends of friends, acquaintances, and strangers who weren't sure where they had gotten our name and phone number. They all had one thing in common: They had heard we adopted quickly and wanted to know the secret to our success. Some were just beginning to search for a child to adopt. Others had been attempting to adopt for years. A few were trying to decide if they should pursue adoption or continue with treatments for infertility, yet they, also, wanted to know how we managed to find a baby just in case they decided to pursue adoption.

There wasn't any secret to our success—not in the real sense of the word. There wasn't anything we had learned about adoption that others couldn't learn. We weren't privy to any special information, nor did we know anyone who worked in the adoption field that came forward with a baby. Actually, it was quite the opposite.

When Christopher was twenty months old, a young woman called our home. She was pregnant and wanted to know the name of the agency we had worked with because she was planning to place her baby for adoption. Not being ones to pass up an opportunity, we immediately called our social worker to see if we could put something together. At the time, private adoptions were not allowed in many counties in Northwestern Ohio, including the one we resided in. The first thing our social worker asked was, "How do you keep finding these babies?" Naturally, she couldn't believe the woman had actually telephoned us, but she was beginning to accept the fact that there are babies available for adoption. This particular adoption situation never materialized for us, mainly because we decided we really wanted more than two years between the ages of our children, but the woman did place her baby for adoption three months later.

In the following months, we received many more adoption phone calls. We were astonished that word of our adoption had reached so many people. Ironically, we discovered later that the source was an adoption agency. When people called inquiring about adopting a baby, they would refer them to us. Eventually, prospective parents who were trying to adopt all types of children were directed to us and before I knew it, there was a pile of adoption reference books and a heap of pink message slips from people seeking adoption information.

One day an adoption attorney, Mary, said to me, "Why don't you start an adoptive parent support organization? We need one in this area." And before I could say no, I was in a boardroom at radio station WTOD/K-100 in Toledo, surrounded by adoptive parents, and Families United for Adoption was formed.

Nine months later, after meeting all of these wonderful families and their beautiful babies, we decided it was time for us to think about adding another child to the family. Christopher had just turned four years old, and the time felt right to us.

Our son, Blake, entered this world on a Saturday afternoon about fifteen days after one of those significant birthdays reminded me, once again, that my biological clock was ticking away. We brought this dark-haired beauty home four days later, much to everyone's surprise. A friend acted as the intermediary in this private adoption, and it came together without one complication. (Laws prohibiting private adoption had changed in our area since we adopted Christopher.) Our family was now complete. We had managed to beat that clock with a few years to spare.

When we decided to adopt we knew *nothing* about adoption. I called a few agencies in the area and asked about adopting an infant. "Obviously, you haven't heard there is a shortage of babies available for adoption," one social worker told me. "The women are either keeping their babies or aborting them. If you want a baby, you'll have to find one on your own." The other agencies presented the same scenario. The most frustrating part was that no one could tell us exactly how to go about finding a baby independent of an agency. And again, private adoptions were not permitted in our area at that time.

Next, we called the state social service department in our county. This time we asked about the ages of the children available for adoption. "We have many children over age eight we need to find homes for," a social worker said, "but the problem is that we are understaffed and couldn't begin a home study [a written evaluation of your family, completed by a social worker, recommending you for an adoptive placement] for at least two years. We have twenty-six couples waiting now." Did he have any suggestions? "Well, if you found a child on your own to adopt we could begin your home study immediately," he answered. He suggested volunteering at a shelter for abused children and added, "Some of those children eventually are placed for adoption. Maybe you could adopt one of them."

Six weeks later, after undergoing three interviews and presenting six reference letters from friends, I began my volunteer work only to discover that the children were there for no more than a week or two and that volunteers were not entitled to know anything about the children. From one week to the next I rarely saw the same children, so I never had the opportunity to "adopt" any of them, even as friends.

One day on my lunch hour, I walked across the street to the library and asked for books on adoption. Most of the books were old, but I wrote down a few phone numbers and that evening we connected with a woman in Ohio who gave us the names of several books to read and the address of a national adoption organization, Adoptive Families of America, Inc. (AFA). We ordered the books from a local bookstore and AFA sent us a packet of information and a membership application. We joined AFA, read all of the books and magazine articles we could find, and began writing to agencies across the United States requesting information on their programs.

Within four weeks we had information packets from sixty-six agencies and eleven adoption attorneys. We discovered there *were* babies available for adoption, both privately and through adoption agencies, and we learned how to find one of those babies. We read about other options, such as adopting an older child or a child with special needs and intercountry adoption, but, most important, we learned how the adoption process works and how to make it work for us. Our secret was simply acquiring knowledge about the system and having the ability to organize ourselves.

With the help of this book, you, too, can learn how the adoption process works, from discovering how to effectively and aggressively organize a search for a child to locating a reliable and ethical adoption source to assist you in your efforts. You'll find step-by-step instructions, techniques, and tips for beginning the adoption process and working through the mazes. Also, more than 100 adoptive parents share their thoughts and suggestions on many aspects of the adoption process. The result, you'll discover, is encouraging for all prospective parents.

A Look at Adoption Today

Congratulations! As a prospective adoptive parent you are about to embark on a remarkable journey. This experience will be completely unique because each adoption, no matter how much it tries your patience, brings another story to your family history.

This book has been written specifically to help you begin the adoption process. Many people are very hopeful when they begin that process but soon become frustrated by the system and eventually give up when they are unable to make a connection that would lead them to a child. An adoptive mother, Marissa, from Genoa, Ohio, explains the attitude you must take to successfully cope with the system: "Whatever you do, do not give up. It is frustrating trying to adopt, but it is possible. You have to work at adopting like you work at a job. It is hard work, but persistence pays off."

We will begin with infant adoptions in the United States because most first-time adopters are initially interested in this type of adoption. Those that are not may have lived or traveled in another country or have friends or relatives who have adopted internationally; therefore, intercountry adoption does not intimidate them. If you are a special education teacher or a therapist, you might feel capable of parenting a challenged child, or if someone in your family has a physical or mental disability, perhaps you will feel comfortable adopting a child with a similar condition. Whatever the reasons, we each begin our adoption search by looking for the type of child we think we would feel comfortable with. Often the degree of comfort changes as we learn more about adoption, but I encourage you to always explore your "first choice" initially.

Many people adopt the child of their dreams. Why not you? It's frustrating to hear about those who decide to adopt and have a child before you know it. How did they adopt so quickly? Were they just plain lucky? Did they have an "in" somewhere? For a few, the answer is probably yes, but for most this is not the case. So why do some people manage to proceed through the system with relative ease, while others get nowhere for years? No one truly knows the answer, but in this chapter we will look at the characteristics of people who have adopted in a reasonable amount of time.

CHARACTERISTICS OF PARENTS WHO ADOPT QUICKLY

After working closely with pre-adoptive families for several years, I have discovered that parents who adopted quickly share some traits. First, these families generally began the adoption process *believing* they could adopt the type of child they wanted; they knew they would succeed despite what they had heard from others. They were willing to devote the time and the energy necessary because they truly wanted to adopt at this time in their lives—not five years in the future.

Second, because they desperately wanted to share their lives with a child, they were willing to learn as much as possible about adoption. These people read every book, every magazine article, every bit of information they could find. They talked to others who had adopted and they talked with many of the experts. Eventually, they became experts themselves. Their knowledge put them in the position to search for a source and succeed at adopting.

Third, these people were organized and assertive and were not intimidated by endless writing tasks, record keeping, or telephone calls. They saved every piece of information they received. Every contact call was recorded along with the important details of the conversation. Every lead was followed. They began to know others in the adoption field through phone calls, letters, and fellow adoptive parent support group members. And because they were active and involved, people began to know them too.

Because these parents were so organized, assertive, and fully involved in working to find that connection, they were literally in the right place at the right time. They succeeded because they had so many irons in the fire. Many of these people found their children very easily, often with the help of others they had met while researching adoption.

As you begin your research you will read and hear all kinds of stories. You will hear of people who adopted infants within a few months through agencies, and of couples who adopted two infants in three years through independent adoption. You will also hear of people who decided to adopt from abroad and brought their child home a few months later. These stories are true. Adoptions like this can and really do happen, as the following example demonstrates.

An Ohio couple approached a public county agency for an intercountry home study. They were asked why they were trying to adopt a child from another country when there were plenty of children here in the United States available for adoption. They applied to the county agency and a few months later they were contacted about adopting a two-year-old. This toddler became their son. Three months later the county agency contacted them again. A birth mother had chosen them to be her unborn child's adoptive parents. A few weeks later this baby became their second son.

Of course, you will also hear less encouraging tales of people who have been trying to adopt a child for years, but have never been able to find a source to work with. And there are always the stories of couples who have been waiting on an agency list for five, six, or seven years. Stories like these are also true, but potential adopters should be aware of just how some people manage to put themselves in this position.

There are people, once they are accepted on a waiting list, who wait and do nothing else for years. They do not contact other agencies, perhaps because someone told them there are no children available anywhere with a shorter wait. An agency may compound the problem by implying that they should feel fortunate to be on its waiting list. These people may not be aware of the many agencies and attorneys nationwide that could help them. They do not make an attempt to join an adoptive parent group, either because they are unaware such groups exist or don't realize how helpful other adoptive parents can be. Many of them do not research adoption or even read a resource book. They have simply resigned to waiting for whatever time the agency has estimated, assuming that there will be a child for them someday.

These people are what some adoption professionals call "waiters." Waiters are nice, patient people. But while waiters are patiently waiting, the "doers" are adopting the children the waiters believe they cannot find. Some waiters wait so long that their age disqualifies them for adoption through the agency.

If one were to ask waiters how their plans to adopt were coming along, they would say they have been waiting for four or five years because there are so few children available for adoption. Waiters also seem to attract attention. While they are receiving sympathy and discouraging other hopeful adopters, the doers are actively searching for a child. The irony is that waiters truly believe they are doing everything possible to adopt a child.

Do we ever hear about the singles and couples who do adopt quickly? No, of course not, because their news is not sensational. But there are *plenty* of them—and you'll meet some of them in the chapters that follow.

I am not going to tell you that adopting is easy because it is not. You cannot just telephone your local agency and have a child in your home within a few weeks. Gone are the days when agencies were actively seeking homes for healthy Caucasian infants. Yet, there are agencies seeking adoptive parents for certain types of children of all ages, including infants.

Adoption is possible for those who really want to adopt, for those who will work steadily as if it's a long-range project. Doers do not get discouraged easily. Doers believe they will succeed. Doers are actively involved in finding a promising adoption source. If you have been a waiter, this book will show you how to become a doer.

THE DECISIONS TO MAKE

First you must decide which type of child you want to adopt. Are you thinking of adopting a baby or an older child? A sibling group (two, three, or more children who are related)? A boy? A girl? A child from the United States? A child of the same race? A child from another country?

Next, you must decide if you want to work with an adoption agency or adopt independently with the help of an attorney (if your state permits this). You can find an agency here in the United States that will work with you or, in some states, you can adopt a baby without the help of an agency. (This type of adoption is called an independent or private adoption. See the chapter on independent adoption.)

For an intercountry adoption you can work with an agency in the United States that has connections with other agencies or attorneys in foreign countries. Or you can work directly with a foreign agency, attorney, or orphanage and avoid using a middleman agency in the United States. (See the chapter on intercountry adoption for more information on your choices.) Should you choose to work directly with an adoption source in a foreign country, you will still need the assistance of a stateside agency to complete a favorable home study. A home study is a series of interviews and a written evaluation of your family, completed by a certified social worker. (See the chapter on home studies.)

If you are interested in adopting an older child, a child with special needs, or a sibling group from the United States or abroad, you will generally need to work with an agency. Children with special needs are those who are physically or mentally challenged or have emotional problems. In this country, older children and children with special needs are available for adoption. Many of these children are in state foster care systems. Both public and private agencies can place these children. Adopting children with special needs from outside the United States is best accomplished through a stateside agency, one that works cooperatively with an agency in another country. (Special-needs adoption is further discussed in this chapter and chapter four.)

THE CHANGES

Years ago, people who sought to adopt wanted only healthy infants. In the late sixties and seventies, the situation changed as fewer babies became available for adoption through agencies. For several reasons, women who found themselves pregnant at the wrong time began turning to independent adoption, abortion, or single parenthood. As a result, many agencies went out of business. Those who managed to keep their doors open did so by primarily placing infants from abroad, older children, minority infants, and children with special needs. And many children who were once considered "unadoptable" found homes as agencies began recruiting prospective adoptive parents for them.

Today, some private agencies are still primarily recruiting parents for older and minority children, and those who have special needs or who are born in another country. Others are placing a few healthy Caucasian babies each year. Most Caucasian infants are placed independently, and, despite what you may hear, there are few Caucasian toddlers and preschoolers available for adoption. Women making adoption plans in the United States generally place newborns, not toddlers. In fact, in the United States it is easier to adopt a newborn baby than a toddler or preschooler.

Adoption has undergone significant changes during the last three decades. For years, only childless married couples were adopting. Today single people and married couples with biological children are adopting. Infants are still placed for adoption, but so are older children and children with special needs. Many prospective adopters still seek assistance in building their families from agencies, while other families depend on their own resources to locate a child to adopt.

For years, adoptions were completed with as much secrecy as possible. Many unmarried pregnant women were sent away by disgraced families to have their babies in secret. They were usually expected to "give the child up for adoption" and never speak of the incident again. After the birth, these women rejoined their families and spent years grieving for their lost children in silence. Now, years later, some of these birth mothers have broken the silence and are coming forth to talk about their experiences. They speak and write of the pain they suffered through the years of not knowing where their children were and not knowing if they were even alive. Birth parents, especially the birth mothers, have drawn attention to their plight and are now being heard.

Nowadays, many women who choose adoption demand an active role in the process. No longer are they content to let someone else, like a social worker or an attorney, choose the family that will parent their child. They want to make that decision and some want to meet the adoptive parents they are considering before their child is born. Now, birth mothers write letters to their children and the adoptive parents tuck the letters away until the children are old enough to receive this precious gift. Birth mothers may write to adoptive parents and adoptive parents may write back. Pictures are sometimes exchanged between the two sets of parents, sometimes only once, but often over the course of many years. In some cases, the adoptive parents attend the actual birth of their child. And in other cases, contact may be maintained between the adoptive family and the birth family for years.

Past generations often kept adoption a well-guarded secret. Families commonly announced a nonexistent pregnancy and the couple then returned home with a baby after a lengthy vacation. If neighbors or friends suspected anything, they never mentioned it. If no one spoke about the adoption, where did that leave the adopted child?

Often the child would learn of the adoption from his parents, but he might be told not to tell anyone. If the adoptive parents kept the secret from the child, he would often learn the truth from a relative or family friend, or when a parent's estate was settled. Usually this lack of openness led to a sense of shame and betrayal caused by those the child loved most.

Secrecy is now being lifted as birth parents (or, in most cases, birth mothers) play an active role in more adoptions. Adoptive parents are no longer encouraged to go home and forget about the child's other parents. Now they may go home with a quilt made by their birth mother's mother, photos of the birth parents, or an outfit and a teddy bear or a letter from the birth mother. Adoptive parents no longer wonder if they should tell their children they were adopted. They now wonder how and when to tell them. (For more information write the National Adoption Information Clearinghouse, 11426 Rockville Pike, Ste. 410, Rockville, MD 20852, and ask for their factsheet titled "Answers to Children's Questions about Adoption.")

Today, many an adopted child's baby book holds pictures of both birth parents and adoptive parents and, if the baby was in foster care, pictures of the foster family. We now know that the old method of confidential adoption was sometimes problematic. As a result, confidential adoption is now being challenged across the United States as more birth parents are demanding either an open adoption, with full disclosure of identifying information, or a semiopen adoption, where only nonidentifying information is exchanged.

There will always be birth and adoptive parents who are unable, or unwilling, to participate in an open adoption. That is all right because there is a place for both open and confidential adoptions. But if you are hoping to adopt an American infant and any form of an open adoption frightens you, you'd better prepare yourself. The chances are good that your adoption will be open to some degree.

IS OPEN ADOPTION FOR YOU?

Many people have strong opinions about open adoption. Some vehemently oppose it. Others believe it is the best possible arrangement for all involved. Once they participate in an open adoption, many would not have it any other way. Some who are still considering it walk the middle of the road, unsure of open adoption yet not totally convinced confidential adoption is the best choice for them either. Only you can decide what's the right route for your family.

In an open adoption, the birth parents choose and meet the adopting parents with full disclosure of information. Their relationship will be ongoing, so that all members of the adoption triad (birth parents, adoptive parents, adoptee) will have access to each other throughout the years. In some open adoptions, the birth parents, and sometimes the extended family of the birth parents, are incorporated into the adoptive family.

The definition of open adoption has changed over the years. No longer does a one-time meeting between birth parents and adoptive parents, or an exchange of letters and pictures over a few years constitute an open adoption. Arrangements such as these are now called semiopen adoptions.

In a semiopen adoption, the parties may exchange only nonidentifying information (they disclose their occupations, but not their places of employment; the cities they live in, but not their complete addresses). If the parties meet in person, they generally do so without disclosing their identities, although first names are usually exchanged. Parties involved in a semiopen adoption may exchange photos and letters through a third party, once or for several years. Many professionals and potential adopters who are not comfortable with the full disclosure of information that occurs in an open adoption may be untroubled by semiopen adoption. To learn more about current thinking on open adoption, refer to the book *Children of Open Adoption*, by Kathleen Silber and Patricia Martinez Dorner.

Ideally, the parties enter an open adoption with a working agreement based on a joint decision by all involved. Clearly not all open adoptions are the same. The terms differ, as do the people involved. But they should be spelled out clearly, and agreed upon by all, so no one feels forced into a situation he or she cannot honor.

"Even when the parties involved agree, those terms will change as time passes," says an adoptive father from Indiana. "The child grows older. The birth mother becomes less involved or more interested, depending on what is happening in her life. At first, our birth mother wanted to visit once a year, near our son's birthday, and that was fine with us. That worked until his third birthday. Then, four weeks later, much to our surprise, she knocked on our door on Christmas Day with several gifts for Robbie. It was an awful shock for our guests, especially the grandparents."

The adoptive parents and the birth mother later met and implemented some changes. "We negotiate much like divorced parents do when changes need to be made regarding visitation rights," says Robbie's dad. "We expect this to be an ongoing process of change. It was something we hadn't given thought to in the beginning. Nothing ever stays the same."

It is not always the birth mother who requests changes in the terms. Often the adoptive parents change their minds about the pattern of visitation or other terms. Says one adoptive mother, "We did not mind our son's birth mother visiting the first two years until our older child began to question why *her* birth mother never visited. Our daughter's adoption was closed and she became visibly upset every time our son's birth mother came to the house. So after several conversations with the birth mother we all agreed it would be best for now to meet elsewhere without our daughter present."

It is also important that adoptive parents consider the birth parents' feelings. If you agree to yearly visits from the birth mother, or to exchange pictures and letters every six months, it is imperative that you keep your end of the agreement. While it is true that agreements you make with a birth parent may not be enforceable (at this time) by law, you have a moral obligation to keep your promises. As prospective parents you should never agree to terms that you have no intentions of keeping, no matter how much you want a baby. Unkept promises will cause great anguish for the birth parent and may, in the end, hurt your adopted child.

The rules of adoption are rapidly evolving because birth parents increasingly request or demand that they take an active part in choosing the people who will parent their children. They have the right to do this. The child is legally theirs until the final papers transferring parental rights have been signed.

Most agencies, and many adoption attorneys, are responding to birth parents by honoring their requests. Those agencies that do not participate in some form of open adoption are often the ones with five- to eight-year waiting lists and few babies to place, since the birth mothers may choose to go elsewhere.

According to open adoption advocates, open adoptions sidestep some problems that are inherent in confidential adoptions. For instance, secrecy can promote the notion that adoptive parents and birth parents are natural adversaries and can maintain an unhealthy

The Benefits of Open Adoption

☐ Honesty and openness about the birth mother's circumstances and her feelings toward the child
☐ All parties share in the design of the adoption
☐ Adoptive parents usually feel immediate entitlement to the child
☐ A past to share with the child
☐ Solid answers to questions the child may ask
☐ No fear of an unknown birth parent
☐ No need for a child to search in later years

atmosphere of fear. The importance of background information often is underestimated, and the information that is gathered is often censored to "protect" parties from each other. Since the information is collected behind closed doors, it is often incomplete and difficult to update.

Another concern is power, and who has it. When an adoption facilitator insists on retaining control of the adoption process, power is taken away from the birth and adoptive parents, leaving them no control over this important life-altering event. Those professionals, who insist on maintaining control, usually believe the birth parent lacks the proper training to choose an adoptive family.

WHAT ABOUT THE PROBLEMS?

Education and counseling are the key ingredients in a successful open adoption. It is imperative that both the adoptive parents and birth parents receive counseling and education when they plan an open adoption, because the issues they will face together are unique. The parties involved must understand each other's position. On one side you have the birth parents making an adoption plan for the child—a decision that takes a tremendous amount of courage, love, maturity, and foresight. By choosing an open adoption, the birth parents terminate their parental rights, but do not sever the ties with their child. They are choosing to maintain contact with their child and the adoptive parents. They recognize that they will never be their child's parents in the full sense of the word because that role will belong solely to the adoptive parents. Counseling should prepare the birth parents for the child's birth, and the subsequent adoption, and should educate them about the role they'll play in the child's life.

On the other side are the adopting parents. They are eager to be parents and feel they can provide love, warmth, a nurturing environment, and a secure future for a child. Counseling and education should prepare them for adoption by explaining the pain that birth parents experience, and presenting the realities of adoption—the most important being that their child will have two sets of parents. The prospective adoptive parents will meet and get to know the birth parents, and together they will make their joint decisions concerning the arrangements before and after the baby's birth.

Sometimes, after giving birth, a birth mother may decide to parent the child herself. If this happens, in a counseled open adoption plan the birth parent stays to support the couple through the grieving process.

Without counseling and education, the birth parents and the adoptive parents may set themselves up for conflict because the open adoption plan may fail, no matter how good the participants' intentions. Roles must be defined and agreed upon. Honesty and trust must prevail. The parties making the agreements must be open to changes as people mature and lifestyles alter. They must also be able to adapt to the ups and downs inherent in human emotions and relationships.

All must be secure in their roles and flexible in their attitudes to make an open adoption work successfully.

Is open adoption really as good as it sounds? With proper support, education, and counseling it can work. Even so, there are certain risks. A birth mother, for example, may become too dependent on the adopting parents for emotional support especially if she is immature and lacks family support. "Assess the emotional stability of a birth parent as much as possible before moving ahead with an open adoption plan," says an adoptive mom from Michigan who is involved in an open adoption.

Another possible negative of open adoption, especially without adequate counseling, is that the birth parents could interfere in the lives of the adoptive family so much that they may need to move and cut the ties. The birth parents' relatives, especially the child's grandparents, may not be ready to let go and may insist that they be included in the life of the child on their own terms. (Some agencies wisely include grandparents in counseling sessions.)

Parents eager to adopt have been known to breach trust with birth parents as well. Adopting parents may agree to terms they are unwilling or unable to meet because they are desperate to become parents, which may cause birth parents to question their choice and lose trust in the adoptive parents. Adoptive parents may never fully trust the birth parents and may withhold information from them over the years. One birth mother was led to believe that her son was growing up as an only child, when, in reality, he had two brothers (born later) to the adoptive parents. This birth mother lost trust in the adoptive parents, not because they lied, but because they withheld the truth.

Adoption professionals are the first to admit they do not know how open adoption will affect the children. It is too early to tell. But, open adoption may very well be the logical choice in the future. If so, it will be a return to the old days, the years before the 1940s when adoptions were generally open and the word "confidential" was yet to be paired with "adoption."

Problems that May Occur
with Open Adoption

☐ Birth parents become intrusive
☐ Birth parents agree to the open adoption thinking it will be "easy" to place their child
☐ Child becomes confused by having two sets of parents
☐ Adoptive parents agree to terms they are not comfortable with because they desperately want a baby

THE NEXT STEP

If you will be attempting to adopt a baby in the United States, talk with parents involved in both open and confidential adoptions. If you are not already a member of Adoptive Families of America (AFA), write or call them at 3333 Highway 100 North, Minneapolis, MN 55422, (612) 535-4829, for membership information and ask for their free booklet for prospective adoptive parents. AFA is a national adoptive parent support group with 15,000 adoptive and prospective adoptive parent members. It is the umbrella organization for more than 350 adoptive parent support groups nationwide. AFA promotes both U.S. and intercountry adoption. The membership fee includes the bimonthly magazine *Adoptive Families.* The magazine's People-to-People department is an excellent way to locate individuals who can help you. As a member, you can write to this department in care of Adoptive Families of America and ask other members who've coped with similar concerns and questions to contact you. Membership dues are $24 per family per year. The magazine regularly carries stories on all forms of adoption.

Read the many excellent books available on open adoption and understand their inherent bias toward open adoption. Do not accept an open adoption or be pressured into something that feels wrong for you. (Check the recommended reading list at the end of this chapter.) As with any other adoption-related issue, learn as much as you can. Do not overlook the drawbacks in this relatively new type of adoption. Then, if the opportunity presents itself, you'll be able to make an educated decision about whether an open adoption would be right for your family.

WHAT IF OPEN OR SEMIOPEN ADOPTION ISN'T FOR YOU?

Not all prospective parents and birth parents want to participate in an open or semiopen adoption. Most still prefer the traditional, confidential adoption. An adoptive mother of a two-year-old says, "We did not want the birth mother involved in any way and we are thankful she didn't want any contact with us. The birth mother has no right to ever interfere with our lives. However, if our daughter wants to search for her birth mother at an appropriate age, we will help her. But that is our daughter's decision to make, not her birth mother's."

One woman, a 22-year-old mother who was attacked and raped, says she never considered abortion because the baby was part of her, and "an innocent child who had no choice in the way he was conceived." She opted for adoption. "I chose the adoptive parents, but wanted no contact with them, not even a letter or a picture. I wanted only to be assured that he would be accepted and loved and I feel confident I made the right choice for him. I hope he never decides to search for me."

According to several agency directors, birth mothers who are emotionally unstable, or who are substance abusers, are usually advised to place their babies in a confidential adoption. (This does not mean that a birth mother is unstable if she opts for a confidential adoption!)

Now that semiopen and open adoption are becoming popular, what should you do if you do not want to participate in this type of arrangement? First, be sure the agency or attorney you are working with understands your position. Agencies and attorneys do work with birth mothers who want anonymity. Second, there are still agencies and attorneys who oppose an open or semiopen arrangement. If possible, try to find one of these sources to work with. There are sources that continue to place infants with the next couple on the waiting list and only the necessary information is exchanged. Third, realize that your wait may be longer than the couples' who are willing to be involved in a semiopen or open adoption.

Just as birth parents and adopting couples used to be left with no choice but a confidential adoption, some professionals are concerned that the opposite is beginning to happen today. It is important for birth and adopting parents to know they do have a choice about the type of adoption they become involved in.

INFANTS AVAILABLE FOR ADOPTION IN THE UNITED STATES?

Yes, there are American infants available for adoption! Do not let anyone try to convince you otherwise—not friends, family, agencies, attorneys, magazine articles, or television programs. There are babies available. There is not an overabundance of babies, but if you truly want to adopt a baby, it is certainly possible. It may take you six months, one year, or three years, and you may adopt independently when you said you would only adopt through an agency, but if a baby is what you want, do not give up.

As the founder of an adoptive parent support organization whose members have primarily adopted infants from the United States, I can tell you that I have witnessed couples adopt the infants they wanted independently and through agencies without a long wait. A year or less has been typical for most. Others have adopted in eighteen months or less than two years. However, your wait may be longer so don't give up if you have not adopted within two or three years. Continue looking for an adoption source.

One woman called me early one Saturday morning. She was in tears. She and her husband had worked with a birth mother who in the end had decided to parent her baby. "This is the twelfth birth mother we have lost in less than a year," she said with despair in her voice. "What are we doing wrong?"

Now obviously, Linnea and her husband had worked very hard over the past year. Twelve birth mothers do not just appear. They weren't doing anything wrong. In fact, they were doing everything right! They just had not connected with the right birth mother yet. Two weeks later, Linnea telephoned again. "You'll never guess what happened. We brought a baby home from the hospital last night," she announced with great excitement.

Marissa and John arranged for a nondenominational agency in Ohio to conduct a home study for them for a promising out-of-state agency. When the agency in Ohio opened its list in January, Marissa and John decided to apply and submitted their pre-application. They were invited to attend an orientation meeting in March with about seventy-five couples. In April, they were asked back to the agency to attend a smaller meeting with about ten other couples. "At this meeting, we turned in our completed application, the results of our police check and our physical exams, a list of our references, our marriage certificate, and a copy of our autobiography," says Marissa. "The autobiography was submitted to be shown to birth mothers who wanted to choose the family who would parent their baby." (The fact that the agency already had the couple's home study on file may have been one of the reasons they were accepted on the waiting list.)

After that meeting Marissa and John did not hear again from the agency until mid-June. When the agency contacted them they were told that there was a birth mother who was very interested in them. The agency asked if they would consider a conference call with the birth mother who wanted to interview them. Marissa and John readily agreed and the phone call was scheduled for the next day.

"We were so nervous," recalls Marissa, "and so afraid we would say the wrong thing. She asked us all sorts of questions and it seemed that over and over we kept saying the same thing—'We would love to have your baby, but we want what is best for you.' Somewhere in the middle of our conversation, she said she wanted us to be the parents. John and I kept saying, 'Are you sure? Are you sure you want us?' By that time we were all crying."

Two and one-half weeks later, Marissa and John brought home their four-day-old daughter. From beginning to end, it took them seven months to adopt their baby. But the story does not end here. A year and a half later, they applied to the same agency for a second child. Not long afterward, they brought home a newborn son, and they have since opened their first adoption. (Please remember that when working with agencies that allow birth parents to choose the adoptive family that your wait may be short—as was Marissa and John's—or much longer.)

TRANSRACIAL ADOPTIONS

Thousands of Caucasian couples have adopted African-American and Caucasian/African-American babies, but they have done so despite much controversy. In 1972, the National Association of Black Social Workers (NABSW) took a strong stand against transracial adoptions, insisting that these children should not be placed in Caucasian homes because there are African-Americans who want to adopt them. They insisted that the adoption system works against African-Americans the way it is now. Agency fees and insufficient recruitment of African-American families were cited as the barriers preventing placement of these children in African-American homes.

It should be noted that NABSW does not represent the views of all African-American social workers. Many African-American and Caucasian social workers favor transracial adoption because there are simply not enough African-American homes known to agencies.

Because of NABSW's strong opposition to transracial placements, thirty-five states now have laws or policies that favor the placement of children in same-race families. Most agencies and national adoption organizations favor same-race placements and will always try to place African-American children in African-American homes first. When they are unsuccessful the children are generally placed with Caucasian families, which is preferred over having them grow up in the foster care system.

There are many issues involved in Caucasian families adopting a child of another race and no family should make this decision lightly. If you are interested in this type of adoption, by all means discuss the option with your adoption agency. You will be reassured by the results of recent studies, which show that adopted children placed transracially do just as well, in all respects, as children placed in same-race homes.

The adoption of American Indian children is limited and regulated by the federal Indian Child Welfare Act. It is difficult, and often impossible, for a non-Native American to adopt an American Indian child born in the United States. Your agency can advise you on the regulations. If you or your spouse are of American Indian descent, be sure your agency knows it because those who're registered with a tribe are allowed to adopt these children.

UNITED STATES INFANTS WITH SPECIAL NEEDS

Dixie Lawrence is the director of Adoption Options of Louisiana, located in Gonzales. She can tell you about the large number of minority newborns, older infants, and young children, with or without disabilities, waiting for homes. "We have ten thousand profiles on file right now, and we receive twenty to thirty profiles each day. We have children, many children, and we need families."

The babies, says Lawrence, "are usually referred to us by hospital social workers or agencies who cannot or will not work with the birth mothers. After the baby is born, the birth mother usually tries to find a local agency to take the surrender [child] and they won't do it so we get the refe ral. We network with licensed agencies, attorneys, and hospitals nationwide.

"We also place many Down syndrome babies and we are always looking for families for Caucasian Down syndrome newborns. I have some waiting families, but I can always use more. I let the birth parents choose the adoptive family and they are usually looking for a specific type of family."

Many agencies that place infants born in the United States are also faced with finding homes for certain healthy babies. A baby, like an older child, may wait for an adoptive family merely because of his skin color. A healthy African-American infant, for example, is often hard to place because most agencies do not have African-American couples waiting to adopt. A Caucasian/African-American, and occasionally a Latino infant, may become hard to place for the same reason.

There are many reasons, other than skin color, that identify an infant as a child with special needs. Maxine Chalker, director and owner of The Adoption Agency in Ardmore, Pennsylvania (which also has offices in Delaware and New Jersey), says, "Many of these babies are born with noncorrectable handicaps or disabilities. A child born with Fetal Alcohol Syndrome or Down syndrome would be considered a special-needs infant. A child born with a missing finger may, or may not, be hard to place. Some prospective parents will consider adopting a child born of a manic depressive parent, but a child born of a schizophrenic parent is usually more difficult to place." If you are considering adopting an infant with special needs, be sure to let your agency know so they can discuss it with you. Always ask an agency for its definition of special needs.

Chalker says her agency uses a four-page questionnaire that lists a range of emotional and physical problems and asks prospective parents to check those conditions that are acceptable or unacceptable to them. The form also allows prospective parents to note backgrounds of birth parents that may be unacceptable, such as a history of drug or alcohol abuse or cigarette smoking.

Adoption Options of Louisiana places children nationwide. They sometimes place healthy newborns, but concentrate on placing children with special needs including biracial and minority newborns, infants and children with major and minor disabilities, older children, and sibling groups. They also have intercountry programs.

The agency works with younger and older couples, singles, physically disabled parents, and families with many children. "We actively search for handicapped parents. We recently placed a biracial infant with white adoptive parents . . . the adoptive mom is completely blind," said Lawrence. "And we placed a biracial infant with a white woman who is fifty-seven years old. The baby was their fourteenth child. They had been rejected by several agencies because of their ages and the number of children they have. The birth mother selected them though. It was her choice. We ignore age. It's ridiculous not to, especially when you cannot find homes for these children. And we also ignore race. We will place black babies with white couples . . . look at the black kids in foster care. These children need families."

Almost every agency I've contacted needs parents from minority groups for their programs. Healthy babies and babies with special needs can be placed within a few days to a few weeks. Most agencies do not have minority group families waiting to adopt. So if you are a minority family or a mixed race family, do not let anyone tell you these infants are hard to find. Just about any agency should be able to help you, or at least direct you to another source.

WAITING CHILDREN IN THE UNITED STATES

There are literally thousands of children in the United States waiting for permanent homes, for "forever families." Most are older, over the age of seven, and some have physical, mental, or emotional disabilities. Some wait because they are members of sibling groups; they are brothers and sisters that need to be placed together. Others wait simply because of their skin color. These "waiting children" may be registered with state, regional, and national adoption exchanges. Adoption exchanges and many agencies have pictures with descriptions of waiting children that prospective parents can look at.

ABOUT THE CHILDREN

Parenting an older child or a child with special needs is not for everyone. Those who decide to follow this route to adopt a child must be flexible people without preconceived ideas of how a child should act, behave, talk, think, or even dress.

Older children and children with special needs—due to environmental or biological factors—usually arrive with a prior history of experiences. Unfortunately, their histories may include negative circumstances, such as abuse (physical, sexual, or both) and neglect. It would be wonderful if these children only needed good homes, committed parents, and lots of love to thrive. But the truth is that these things alone cannot always heal the many scars caused by countless abuses.

Even in a wholesome new environment, some children may, for example, continue to lie, steal, and act inappropriately for at least some time. Parents must be willing to work with their child at home and with her teachers at school. They must also be willing to seek and accept the help of professionals. In some cases, a child may need ongoing counseling or physical therapy weekly, monthly, or for years, in addition to frequent doctor visits.

Parenting a child with special needs can be an exhausting and stressful challenge. It can also be fulfilling and gratifying, especially when you see your child's progress. If you are considering adopting an older child or a child with special needs, learn as much as possible about the child beforehand and talk with other parents who have adopted a child much like the one you are interested in. While you can never fully know what the road ahead will bring, you can learn from other peoples' experiences and prepare yourself to an extent. Children waiting for permanent homes need to be adopted by families who are willing to make a lasting commitment to them. When times get rough, you must be there for your child no matter what. All children deserve that commitment from their parents.

If you are contemplating adopting a child with special needs, the following organizations can give you information on specific disabilities:

National Information Center for Children and Youth with Disabilities, 1-800-999-5599

National Information Clearinghouse for Infants with Disabilities, 1-800-922-9234

Library of Congress, Handicapped Hotline, 1-800-424-8567

Federation for Children with Special Needs, 1-800-331-0688

Keep in mind that no matter what type of child you adopt—even an apparently healthy newborn—he may have undiagnosed medical problems that may surface later. Recent studies have shown that adopted children in general appear to be at risk for learning disabilities and attention deficit hyperactivity disorder. It is important to realize that, as with a biological child, there are no guarantees in life.

INTERCOUNTRY ADOPTION

Many prospective parents are interested in adopting children from other countries. Many private agencies in the United States will work with pre-adopters toward this goal. Fees in intercountry adoption can be substantial, but usually the waiting time is much less than it is for adopting within the United States. Children ranging in age from infancy to fifteen years old are available from a number of countries. As in the United States, these children may be healthy or have special needs.

Before deciding to adopt a child from abroad, you should know that the United States Immigration and Naturalization Service (INS) requirements are very specific and all conditions must be met before a child may enter this country for the purpose of adoption. To adopt a child from another country, you must also meet the requirements set forth by your agency (if you are using an agency), your state regulations, and the requirements of the country you are seeking to adopt from. The good news is that nearly all couples and single applicants are able to meet these requirements; patience and persistence will get you through the paperwork.

Many say the safest way to adopt internationally is to use a licensed agency in the United States to locate the child and assist with procedures. However, others have chosen to work directly with a reputable agency or an orphanage in a foreign country. They use a stateside agency's services only to complete their home study and for follow-up supervision after placement. (A home study is required for all intercountry adoptions, and some states require postplacement supervision by a licensed agency as well.)

Another possibility is to locate an adoption attorney in the United States who networks with lawyers, or other facilitators, outside of the country. Adopting independently—that is with the help of attorneys in place of agencies at both ends—occurs more frequently these days, but is not legal in all states. The fees for this type of adoption usually exceed the costs of a licensed stateside agency. Prospective adoptive parents who are considering this route need to be smart consumers. They should talk with several attorneys before committing to the first one they find. (Options will be discussed further in the chapter on intercountry adoption.)

Prospective parents must give thought to the many emotional and social ramifications of adopting a child from a different culture or race or both. Adopting a child born in a foreign country is not for everyone and the decision to adopt internationally should not be made lightly. You are not just adopting a child. You are adopting a child from a different background. Are you willing to preserve your child's heritage and encourage him to feel pride in his birth country?

Even if you can accept parenting a child who is "different" than you, will your parents, friends, and community be as accepting? Once you have adopted internationally, your family may "stick out" in the eyes of others and strangers may ask you personal questions. Are you willing to learn how to cope effectively with situations like these if they occur?

Your child's skin coloring may be much lighter or darker than yours. Can you accept this? Now, picture who your child will date. Picture the person your child will marry. You must be comfortable with that image because that spouse will become family and any children born of that marriage will be your grandchildren. Adopting a child from a foreign country is a wonderful choice, but only if you can fully accept that child's culture and race.

WHERE TO START

Before beginning your adoption search, there are several knowledgeable sources to contact for adoption information. The first resource is Adoptive Families of America, Inc. (AFA). (See the section on infant adoptions in the United States earlier in this chapter.) Membership in this national organization is essential for anyone attempting to adopt. Once you review the group's free information packet you will understand why.

Another source is the National Adoption Information Clearinghouse (NAIC), which was established by Congress to provide easily attainable information on all aspects of adoption to interested people. Debra G. Smith, NAIC's director, notes that they have an excellent packet of information for prospective adoptive parents and says it's "very helpful for someone just starting to explore the possibilities of adoption." There is no charge for this packet of information.

NAIC will give prospective parents information on educational adoption programs in their area and referrals for adoption agencies and adoptive parent support groups. NAIC also provides valuable factsheets on adoption, one of which is titled "Adoption: Where Do I Start?" Some of the other factsheets are "Intercountry Adoption," "Adopting an Infant," and "Adopting a Child with Special Needs." The Clearinghouse will also send you a list of the materials they offer that may be helpful to you.

"NAIC also has an excellent collection of writings on hundreds of adoption-related topics for families who need help after adoption or [for] professionals working in the field," says Smith. Abstracts are also available on hundreds of adoption topics such as open adoption, the adoption home study process, and subsidized adoption. Contact the National Adoption Information Clearinghouse at 11426 Rockville Pike, Suite 410, Rockville, MD 20852, or call (301) 231-6512 and ask for their information packet for prospective parents.

An indispensable resource for those considering intercountry adoption is the annual *Report on Foreign Adoption,* available for $20 from the International Concerns Committee for Children, 911 Cypress Drive, Boulder, CO 80303. This book includes outstanding articles on adopting from overseas, as well as descriptions of dozens of international placement agencies—including information on their requirements, types of children, and fees. You'll receive monthly updates from February through November, including descriptions and pictures of children who have one last chance at adoption. (These "last chance" children will soon turn fifteen years old and will no longer be eligible for adoption.) Some of these children already have siblings in the United States.

If you are interested in adopting from Latin America, contact Latin American Adoptive Families (LAAF), 40 Upland Road, Duxbury, MA 02332. The organization was established in 1986 and has over 600 member families, all who have adopted or are waiting to adopt from Latin America. The association also publishes the *LAAF Quarterly,* a forty-page magazine/newsletter, which includes many features related to Latin American adoptions and is mailed throughout the United States and Canada. *LAAF Quarterly* also contains articles for prospective and adopti 'e single parents. With a one-year membership you receive four issues of the magazine, one edition of the LAAF membership directory and one update, announcements of LAAF events, and an opportunity to participate in group activities. Membership fees are $16 a year for individuals and families, and $32 a year for adoption agencies. LAAF also networks in Canada.

RESOURCES

There are many books written on all the aspects of adoption, from informational books to those that recount actual couples' stories.

Although adoption is a popular topic today, some bookstores do not seem to stock many books on the subject. If you are fortunate you may find a book or two, but if you really want to learn about adoption you are going to have to hunt for more on your own. Ask your bookstore to print out a list of available books on adoption. Check the appendices in this book for the names of publishers or distributors that handle adoption books. Request a list of the books they carry.

Tapestry Books is one of the largest distributors of adoption and infertility books. Contact them at P.O. Box 359, Ringoes, NJ   08551, or call 1-800-765-2367 or (908) 806-6695, and request a copy of their catalog.

Check your local library and read every book on adoption you can find. If it does not have the books you are looking for, the library can often borrow them from another library. If not, ask the library to purchase them—many libraries will.

While you are at the library, search for magazine articles. Consult the *Reader's Guide to Periodical Literature* for the titles of articles and the magazines they appeared in. This guide is updated monthly. Articles are often followed by the names and addresses of agencies and parent support groups, all additional sources for you to contact.

The National Council For Adoption and the North American Council on Adoptable Children (see appendices for addresses) can provide you with a list of books they sell. Adoptive Families of America reviews current books in its bimonthly magazine and you can also purchase books for adults and children through AFA.

Reading for Prospective Adopters

Adamec, Christine A. *There ARE Babies to Adopt: A Resource Guide for Prospective Parents*. New York: Pinnacle, 1991.

Feigelman, William and Arnold R. Silverman. *Chosen Children: New Patterns of Adoptive Relationship*. New York: Praeger, 1983.

Gibbs, Nancy, Mary Cronin, Elizabeth Taylor, and James Willwerth. "The Baby Chase." *Time* 134, no. 15 (October 9, 1989): 86–89.

Hallenbeck, Carol. *Our Child: Preparation for Parenting in Adoption*. Wayne, PA: Our Child Press, 1988.

Johnston, Patricia Irwin. *Adopting After Infertility*. Indianapolis: Perspectives Press, 1992.

Sorosky, Arthur D., M.D., Annette Baran, and Reuben Pannor. *The Adoption Triangle: Sealed or Opened Records: How They Affect Adoptees, Birth Parents, and Adoptive Parents*. San Antonio: Corona, 1984.

Wirth, Eileen M. and Joan Worden. *How to Adopt a Child from Another Country*. Nashville: Abingdon Press, 1993.

Wooley, Suzanne. "When It Comes to Adoption, It's a Wide, Wide World." *Business Week*, June 20, 1988, 164–165.

Intercountry Adoption

Erichsen, Jean Nelson and Heino R. Erichsen. *How to Adopt Internationally*, 1992. Available from Los Niños International Adoption Center, The United Way Building, 100 Lake Front Circle, Suite 130, The Woodlands, TX   77380.

Register, Cheri. *Are Those Kids Yours? American Families with Children Adopted from Other Countries*. New York: The Free Press, 1991.

International Concerns Committee for Children. *Report on Foreign Adoption*. Boulder, CO: ICCC, 1993.

Sheehy, Gail. *Spirit of Survival*. New York: William Morrow, 1986.

Open Adoption

Arms, Suzanne. *Adoption: A Handful of Hope*. Berkeley, CA: Celestial Arts, 1990.

Caplan, Lincoln. *An Open Adoption*. New York: Farrar, Straus and Giroux, 1990.

Gritter, James L., ed. *Adoption Without Fear*. San Antonio: Corona Publishing, 1989.

Lindsay, Jeanne Warren. *Open Adoption: A Caring Option*. Buena Park, CA: Morning Glory Press, 1987.

Rillera, Mary Jo and Sharon Kaplan. *Cooperative Adoption: A Handbook*. Westminister, CA: Triadoption Publications, 1985.

Severson, Randolph. *A Letter to Adoptive Parents . . . On Open Adoption*. Dallas: Cygnet Designs, 1991.

Silber, Kathleen and Patricia Martinez Dorner. *Children of Open Adoption*. San Antonio: Corona Publishing, 1990.

Silber, Kathleen and Phylis Speedlin. *Dear Birthmother: Thank You for Our Baby*. San Antonio: Corona Publishing, 1983.

Older Children and Special-Needs Adoption

Dorris, Michael. *The Broken Cord*. New York: Harper and Row, 1989.

Dunn, Linda, ed. *Adopting Children with Special Needs: A Sequel*. Washington, DC: North American Council on Adoptable Children, 1983.

Jewett, Claudia L. *Helping Children Cope with Separation and Loss*. Boston: Harvard Common Press, 1982.

_____. *Adopting the Older Child*. Boston: Harvard Common Press, 1978.

Sheehy, Gail. *Spirit of Survival*. New York: William Morrow, 1986.

Adoptive Parent Support Groups

Across the country adoptive parents come together to share their experiences, express concerns, socialize, and offer support to adoptive parents and prospective adopters. Adoptive parent groups are composed of singles and couples who have adopted, prospective adopters just beginning the adoption process, those waiting for referrals or placements, and others who are considering adoption but want to learn more about it first. They organize in large cities, rural areas, and in the suburbs. Collectively, they are known as adoptive parent support groups.

Support groups are formed around different issues. A group may be a collection of parents who have all adopted healthy same-race infants and are drawn together by this common bond. They may organize after adopting older children or those with special needs, having now become advocates for the placement of all children waiting for permanent families. Or maybe they have all adopted children from the same foreign country or different countries. The ways groups are formed and the issues they devote themselves to vary. Whatever the agenda, the primary goal of all groups is to provide support for adoptive and pre-adoptive families.

HOW THE GROUPS WORK

Adoptive parent groups are one of the most valuable resources available for prospective parents. Whether you want to adopt in the United States or from abroad, support groups can provide you with information on how to proceed. Most adoptive parents love to talk about adoption and are eager to share what they have learned—and their firsthand experiences are well worth listening to. Much of the information they have, especially if they adopted internationally, cannot be found in adoption books or is more up to date than what you will find.

Group members can often advise and assist you on everything from finding a good adoption attorney in your area to locating a child to adopt in another country. They can provide a list of invaluable contacts, but you will have to do the work. "Members provided us with information on special issues concerning children from abroad, bonding, extended family adjustment and cultural retainment," says an adoptive couple from Cedar Rapids, Iowa. "And they also know the ins and outs of many of your local adoption agencies and your state adoption laws."

Members sometimes know of new agencies with no waiting lists (or short lists) and can tell you who to contact to have a home study completed quickly. They can refer you to agencies placing the babies or children you want to adopt—whether that child is a Latino baby, an infant with special needs from Brazil, a sibling group from your state, a toddler from India, or a healthy baby from the United States. Many groups designate an Adoption Resource Person whose job is to write for information from new agencies. It is not difficult to locate new agencies as long as you have a large contact base, and many people in support groups have contacts all across the United States.

Realize that those who have completed an adoption carry a wealth of information with them. Many adopters do plenty of research before they bring a child home. Most are willing to share that information. An adoptive parent from Brooklings, South Dakota, recalls, "Our group gave us answers to all the questions we had." And certainly, people just beginning the adoption process have many questions.

You will also be able to compare notes with other prospective parents. There is always the possibility that someone has come across an adoption agency with an open list that just might be the lead you need. "Our group helped us locate a child," says Barbara from Ten Sleep, Wyoming. "It took us only six months from the time we identified our child to the date of her arrival." One couple, while on vacation, learned of an attorney in Kansas who handles independent adoptions. After they adopted their son, they shared the attorney's name with others in the group. About eight couples now have children as a result of the first couple's lead.

Support group members sometimes hear of prospective birth mothers looking for an adoptive family for their unborn children. Groups may be contacted by an attorney, a social worker from a public agency, or a birth mother herself. Sometimes a birth mother may have specific or unusual criteria she wants the adoptive parents to meet (such as a family who lives in a town where the population is under 4,000), and no family on their waiting list is eligible. What better place to look for a family than an adoptive parent group?

Kay and Steve are parents today because of their membership in a group, and their willingness to meet their son's birth mother. "We were contacted by the president of our support group. He had a lead on a birth mother who was due in a few weeks," says Kay, "and asked if we were still interested in adopting." In this case, the birth mother wanted a childless, college-educated, Catholic couple, and a stay-at-home mother. She also wanted an open adoption with the right to visit the baby after placement. Kay and Steve met the criteria and brought home their son a few weeks later. A few days after that their birth mother stopped by to visit the baby—a happy ending for all. While contacts like these do not materialize every week or every month, it does happen.

As support group members, you can also learn about adoption situations outside the United States. Parents who have completed a parent-initiated intercountry adoption often hear from their sources about other babies or toddlers waiting in orphanages or foster homes for an adoptive family. With a lead like this, couples or singles who already have the paperwork completed for an intercountry adoption can sometimes bring the child home within a few months. Support group leaders may even receive phone calls from other support group leaders who are looking for adoptive families for babies or toddlers waiting in a foreign country or for babies in the U.S.

Support groups usually hold monthly or bimonthly meetings. Some are more formal, with scheduled guest speakers such as agency representatives, adoption attorneys, psychologists, birth parents, adults who were adopted, social workers, and other professionals. Consequently, a support group meeting may be a great place to meet agency personnel, attorneys, and social workers in your area. Meeting these professionals at a group function gives you a chance to introduce yourself and ask questions about procedures in a relaxed, friendly atmosphere.

Some adoption professionals work closely with support groups and know the active members. If you have tried unsuccessfully to be placed on one of their waiting lists, you may be invited to fill out an application once you get to meet and know each other.

Ann, president of a support organization in the Midwest, worked very closely with an adoption attorney in her community. "At any given time I knew how many couples were on his waiting list, how many birth mothers he was working with, and when he placed a baby," says Ann. "I resisted the temptation to ask if he would put our name on his list because ours was a professional relationship. One day I just received an application in the mail from him." Ann and her husband brought home their second child, a daughter, about three months later. "I know our daughter was the result of my commitment to the group and my visibility in the community as an adoption advocate."

Other groups may be less formal; families socialize at monthly meetings and have a speaker once or twice a year. Many groups encourage families to bring their children to meetings by providing a play area and babysitters, while other groups limit the number of meetings children may attend.

Some groups hold morning coffees, some have play groups, and others may have subgroups of prospective parents who all meet once a month and share experiences. One adoptive mom of two children living in Brookfield, Wisconsin, recalls, "After placement I attended monthly morning coffees for moms and children, and met others with adopted children. This gave me someone to talk with about adoption, medical issues, and naturalization."

If being around children is painful for you, you may want to ask whether children will be present before attending a meeting. On the other hand, if you want to adopt from another country, a support meeting is the best place to meet children that may be like the child you want. All groups host activities or events, such as family picnics and holiday parties, for the children. Members want their children to meet other adopted children, and these gatherings encourage that.

Group members are there for each other. They will encourage you while you search, support you as you wait, and when your child finally arrives, they will rejoice with you. "Shortly after bringing our baby home from the hospital our doorbell rang. When we opened the door, about half of the support group members were standing there with balloons and champagne. We were overwhelmed," says adoptive parents, Don and Shelley, from Ohio.

Well-established groups may run an adoption helpline number, have a small lending library for members, provide information packets, and publish newsletters. Groups may also lobby for adoption bills at the state and federal level; send financial aid to an orphanage overseas or a particular child in need; or actively promote adoption awareness in their community through a speaker's bureau, for instance.

If you think adoptive parent support organizations are small, think again. The Open Door Society of Massachusetts, Inc. (ODS) boasts a membership of more than 1,400 families, according to Betty Laning, chairman of ODS's adoption information committee. Founded in 1967, Laning says that ODS presents the Annual New England Adoption Conference, one of the largest adoption conferences annually. "ODS supports a network of seventeen chapters throughout Massachusetts, publishes *ODS NEWS,* hosts adoption information meetings for prospective adopters, monitors developments in Massachusetts adoption laws and practices, promotes projects to aid children waiting for permanency, and much more." Membership is $15 a year. Contact ODS at P.O. Box 1158, Westboro, MA   01581, for more information.

Families Adopting Children Everywhere (FACE) is an even larger adoptive parent support organization (membership is nearly 4,000 families). Based in the state of Maryland, the organization publishes an excellent magazine, *FACE Facts,* operates a helpline number, and holds its annual Adoption and Foster Care Conference. FACE presented its first Family Building through Adoption course in 1975 and FACE chapters in Maryland and Virginia continue to offer courses. Many families from Maryland, Virginia, Delaware, West Virginia, Pennsylvania, and the District of Columbia participate in these courses. Write FACE, Inc., at P.O. Box 28058, Northwood Station, Baltimore, MD   21239 for more information, or call the FACE helpline number: 410-488-2656.

Once you've joined an adoptive parent support group, become involved in adoption by volunteering to work at your support group's fund-raising events. Prospective birth mothers have been known to approach members at bazaars and garage sales. Be the member who volunteers for the speaker's bureau. Go to the high schools and churches in your area and talk about adoption. Become an adoption expert and make yourself known in your community. You do not have to be an adoptive parent to become an adoption advocate.

Other benefits of belonging to a local group include:

- Referrals to adoption books, newsletters, and other resource materials
- Conferences, or mini-workshops, sponsored by the group for pre-adoptive families
- Support through a "soft shoulder" or "buddy system" program, whereby an adoptive family becomes a friend to a prospective adoptive family
- Keeping abreast of the most current information and trends in the adoption field

FINDING A SUPPORT GROUP

A few adoptive parent groups can afford to maintain a listing in the phone book. The number may ring into someone's home, be picked up by an answering service, or ring directly into the support group's office. How do you locate a group in your vicinity? Check the yellow pages under the heading Adoption Services. You may find a listing. If you know the name of the group, also check the directory's business pages.

If you are unable to find a listing, contact local adoption agencies, adoption attorneys, or the adoption division of your state's social service department. If a group exists, someone will know about it. Newspapers often devote space to support groups in an area, listing them every few months. If your city has a locally published magazine, investigate that source. In this case, it's better to call than write because you will get a response more quickly.

Groups may be affiliated with a particular agency or attorney. While these groups are helpful for people on their waiting list (or for adoptive parents who have worked with the agency or attorney), try to find an independent group. Members of an independent group will have much more information to pass along because they are not affiliated with only one source.

Many groups are members of national adoption organizations like Adoptive Families of America, Inc. or the North American Council on

Adoptable Children. These organizations, and the National Adoption Information Clearinghouse, can refer you to groups in your area.

An adoptive father from Brooklyn, New York, offers these suggestions: "Join a parent group. Talk with people and listen. Follow the instructions of those who have been successful. Partake in meetings, activities, and attend the workshops provided by your group." This is great advice for prospective adopters, even if you're not one to participate in support groups and their activities.

CONTACTING AN ADOPTIVE PARENT GROUP

There are hundreds of adoptive parent support groups in the United States that can give you adoption information. Nearly all adoptive parent groups are volunteer organizations. Newsletters, handout materials, and information packets have been prepared and produced for prospective and adoptive parents by members who freely give their time.

When calling a group member for information, please be considerate. These contact people are also volunteers, and almost all numbers are home numbers. Many of the volunteers who welcome calls at home have small children, so when calling, ask if this is a good time to talk. (If it is mealtime, bedtime for children, or if you hear screaming or crying in the background, it is probably not the best time.) Be polite. These people are trying to help others, like yourself, adopt. This is not the time to become defensive or argumentative about information they give you. Should you need to request information by mail, include a self-addressed envelope and a postage stamp or two because letters are answered by members and postage is often an out-of-pocket expense.

Packets of information are often available to those who contact a group. While there generally is no charge for this material, you may want (or be asked) to make a small donation to cover postage and printing costs. Usually a few dollars is sufficient. Your donation will be gratefully accepted because groups operate on membership dues and money raised through small fund-raising projects. Should you decide to join the group, just mail in the membership fee. If you write to a group with specific questions and receive a handwritten or typed response, know that someone took the time to write a reply. A short thank-you note would be a nice gesture.

ORGANIZATIONS THAT WILL HELP YOU FIND A SUPPORT GROUP

When contacting resources, keep your letter short and to the point. Ask to be referred to a support group in your area. Be sure to ask them to send any information on adoption they may have available. (Copy the following pages for your records.)

Adoptive Families of America

3333 Highway 100 North   Date contacted _____
Minneapolis, MN 55422   Mail contact ____ or Phone ____
(612) 535-4829   Date information received ____

The North American Council on Adoptable Children

1821 University Avenue   Date contacted _____
Suite N-498   Mail contact ____ or Phone ____
St. Paul, MN 55104   Date information received ____
(612) 625-0330

The National Council For Adoption

1930 Seventeenth Street, Northwest Date contacted _____
Washington, DC 20004   Mail contact ____ or Phone ____
(202) 328-1200   Date information received ____

National Adoption Information Clearinghouse

11426 Rockville Pike, Suite 410   Date contacted _____
Rockville, MD 20852   Mail contact ____ or Phone ____
(301) 231-6512   Date information received ____

If you are single, contact:

Committee for Single Adoptive Parents

P.O. Box 15084   Date contacted _____
Chevy Chase, MD 20815   Date information received ____

More Support Group Sources

☐ Check the appendices
☐ Check your telephone directory
☐ Call local adoption agencies or adoption attorneys
☐ Call your state's social service department (see appendices)
☐ Check your newspaper or locally published magazines

Parent Group Contact Sheet

Phone and Mail Inquiries

Date _____

Name of Group _____

Address _____ City _____ State _____ Zip _____

Contact person _____ Phone Number _____

Main Focus of Group:

_____ International, children all from same country

_____ International, children from several countries

_____ Children from all countries with special needs

_____ United States infants

_____ Minority children from the United States

_____ A mixture of adoptive families representing all kinds of children

_____ Single adoptive parents

_____ Other: _____

Dates of Meetings _____

Time(s) _____ Meeting Location _____

Information Packet Available?   _____ Yes   _____ No

Date Packet Received _____

Summary:

Gathering Information to Adopt through an Agency

Should you decide to adopt through an agency, you may find your search to be an exciting yet frustrating project. But you must believe that there is a child out there for you. **All of the prospective adoptive parents I have known who truly worked at adopting now have a child.** You can do the same if you do not give up.

As explained in chapter two, you must first locate and join a support group before you begin your search for a child. If you have already located a group, keep in touch with the members. If they are unable to help you, try to find another group, preferably in your state. Make finding a group your first priority. Your search for a child could be speeded up at this point if group members direct you to an agency or another source that will work with you.

The group(s) you contact can give you some suggestions or a list of agencies to call or write for information. While you are working on that project, you will want to get organized. Fairly soon you will be bombarded with all kinds of adoption information and will need a system to keep your notes and papers together.

CREATING A WORK SPACE

Today, adoptive parents must rely on themselves to find a child. They must find their own information sources and be knowledgeable in all kinds of adoption procedures. They must be able to keep track of phone calls, letters mailed and answers received, who has been contacted and who needs to be contacted. An organized space with organized files will make your search much easier and more effective. Create a work space in your home that can be used specifically for pursuing adoption information and sources. However you structure your work area, you will need the accoutrements of an office because it will eventually feel like you have taken on a part-time job.

The reference books you will need can be purchased (often they must be special ordered) or borrowed from your local library or, possibly, from your parent support group's library. The following titles are highly recommended for anyone searching for an adoption agency to work with. These books have state-by-state listings of agencies:

Adoption Choices: A Guidebook to National and International Adoption Resources, by Ellen Paul (Detroit: Visible Ink Press, 1991). Check library or bookstore.

The Adoption Resource Guide: A National Directory of Licensed Agencies, by Julia L. Posner with James Guilianelli (Child Welfare League of America, 1990). Check library, bookstore, or order from The Child Welfare League of America, 440 First Street NW, Suite 310, Washington, DC 20001.

National Adoption Directory, edited by National Adoption Information Clearinghouse. Order from NAIC, 11426 Rockville Pike, Suite 410, Rockville, MD 20852. The cost is $25.

Report on Foreign Adoption can be obtained from the International Concerns Committee for Children, 911 Cypress Drive, Boulder, CO 80303. A $20 donation is requested for this publication, which is updated ten times a year.

There ARE Babies to Adopt, by Christine Adamec (New York: Pinnacle, 1991). Check library, bookstore, or order from Tapestry Books, PO Box 359, Dept. K1, Ringoes, NJ 08551.

Be sure to also check the state-by-state listing in the back of this book.

THE NEXT STEP

For a complete listing of licensed agencies in your state, contact the adoption division of your state social services department by telephone (you may wait weeks for a written reply). Write or call agencies in your state also.

Next, check the listings in your reference books. Decide which states you want to contact first. Base this decision on such aspects as the population of the state, the number of adoption agencies, and whether private adoption is permitted. Agencies in states that do not permit independent adoption (there are several) often do not work with out-of-state clients who want healthy Caucasian infants because of the number of local pre-adopters who are also trying to adopt these same babies. They may, however, place infants with special needs and older children through their American program, or have an intercountry program open to out-of-state residents. For information on states that don't permit independent adoption, you may want to order a copy of *Adoption Laws: Answers to the Most-Asked Questions* from the National Adoption Information Clearinghouse.

Check the yellow pages for various cities across the United States under Adoption Services for additional adoption resources. Many couples and singles do this routinely when traveling through new areas. But you do not have to be traveling to search the yellow pages. Most libraries have phone books for major cities nationwide.

You may come across people who will tell you not to bother contacting agencies outside of your area or state. Some may also tell you to avoid specific religious agencies. Ignore these people. Find out for yourself which agencies will work with you. Many agency directors warn that their programs change and the information they provide is current only at that time.

THINGS TO REMEMBER

The suggested reference books and the list in the appendices, will give you hundreds of agencies to contact for information on their programs. As you call and write these agencies, be aware of the following:

1. Agencies listed as a source for intercountry adoptions sometimes have U.S. infant programs even though it may not be printed in their brochures. Be sure to ask. Agencies placing U.S.-born infants often limit placement to within their county or state, but some agencies place infants nationwide. If you want to adopt from the United States, contact an agency even if it appears to focus on intercountry adoption, or vice versa. Consider all agencies as possible sources until you learn otherwise. More than one prospective parent has found the words "local infants available from time to time" handwritten on a brochure. In this case, telephone the agency and ask about their infant program. They may tell you they really do not have a full-sized infant program because they only place a few infants a year, but ask if you can submit your application anyway.

One couple, Mike and Joan, did adopt a baby this way. When the agency found themselves with a birth mother who was due within two weeks, and every couple on the waiting list was in the process of an intercountry adoption, they called Mike and Joan because their application was on file and their home study was completed. "We were shocked since we were so sure nothing would ever come of our application. It was a long shot," says Mike. "The next few weeks were a whirlwind for us but we brought home a baby boy."

2. Do not let the name of an agency prevent you from contacting them. If the name includes a specific religious denomination or faith (such as Jewish, Methodist, Lutheran), this does not necessarily mean the agency only works with families practicing that faith. Years ago, many religious-oriented agencies were founded to serve the needs of their members. Now, many of these agencies serve people other than their members. Always ask an agency what programs and services are available to people of different faiths.

3. You may work with any agency anywhere in the United States as long as the agency is willing to work with you and the state you reside in. Many people assume they can work only with agencies located in their state; that simply is not true. All states are members of the Interstate Compact on the Placement of Children (ICPC). The ICPC enables families to live in one state and adopt from another. It is illegal to move a child across state lines for the purpose of adoption without first meeting the requirements of the ICPC.

To meet these requirements, it is necessary to send specific papers to the Interstate Compact for approval. Those documents include:

- the adoptive parents' home study
- the child's birth information, including any correctable or non-correctable handicaps or other pertinent health information, regardless of the child's age
- biological information on the birth parents
- relinquishment or termination documents from the birth parents

All documents must be approved by Interstate Compact officials in the state where the adoptive parents reside and the state where the child resides. Once approval is given, the child can be placed with the adopting family.

Your state department of social services (which may also be called the department of human services or social welfare) may be able to provide a list of out-of-state agencies to contact. The agencies on this list are not necessarily approved or recommended. It is always your responsibility to check an agency's reputation, no matter who gives you the referral.

4. You can and should check the practices of any agency you are considering working with. Do not be afraid to work with an out-of-state agency for fear there is no way to verify whether the agency is legitimate and ethical. Agencies' reputations can be verified by contacting the Better Business Bureau in the city the agency operates in, the state attorney general's office in the agency's state, the court that oversees adoptions in that area, and the agency that supervises adoptions in that state. Unless you have other valid reasons for not wanting to adopt from an out-of-state source, your willingness to work outside of your state, when an in-state agency cannot meet your needs, will increase your chances of adopting the type of child you want. Just remember that the responsibility of checking an agency's validity is yours. Never depend on someone else to do this for you.

ESTABLISHING A TIMETABLE AND PLAN OF ACTION

Some people begin their adoption search at full speed. They live, breathe, and think adoption. They devote much of their free time to searching for a child and it works; these people usually adopt quickly. But most people work at their search for awhile, back off for a time, and then start again. Others just seem to work steadily on the project until they adopt.

You may want to consider working steadily on a timetable. Many people swear this method works. Begin by checking your calendar and deciding which days or evenings are best for you. A preferred schedule would be one day a week, say a Tuesday, and one evening, a Thursday. If you work full time from eight to five, a full weekday is not feasible, so reserve two evenings a week to do paperwork and reading, and make phone calls on your lunch hour. Note your schedule on your calendar and if, for some reason, you are unable to work on your designated day, reserve another day and time immediately and jot it down on your calendar. The nice thing about this approach is there is little risk of burnout, since you set your own schedule.

If you hope to use an agency to adopt, you are now ready to begin a letter-writing campaign requesting information on programs from various adoption agencies. The theory is that the more information you receive, the more you will learn about adoption agencies and the process, making your experience something you can actively participate in. The more agencies you contact, the earlier you will find an agency to work with and the knowledge you gain will give you the opportunity to play an invaluable role in this life-altering experience.

A mother who adopted two children from Japan gives this advice: "Write, write, write. Write to agencies, organizations, and friends, and make copies of every paper that crosses your desk." This family adopted their first child in less than ten months.

Gathering information from many agencies will give you a good idea of what's happening in the adoption field across the United States. After receiving several responses you will know which agencies may be able to work with you, the types of children that are available for adoption, the costs involved, which international programs are open, and the waiting times involved for different adoption programs. You will also learn about the requirements you must meet to work through agencies. You may find you are too old to be eligible to adopt a baby in the United States, but just the right age to adopt an infant from another country. Or, your heart may be set on adopting a baby from a particular country only to find, that at age thirty, you are not quite old enough to meet their adoption requirements.

Adoption is confusing, but as the agencies' information begins arriving the puzzle pieces will start coming together. Tempted to call the agencies instead of writing? Certainly you can call, but the best way to approach an agency, unless it's in your local area, is by letter. By writing you can keep your expenses down to a minimum. Call later after you have studied their information packets and have specific questions.

Dear Sir or Madam,

    My spouse and I (or "I") hope to adopt. Please send us information on your adoption programs. Thank you for your time.

Sincerely,

John and Jane Doe
123 Main Street
Anytown, Any State 12345
(111) 555-1234

A typical letter to an agency requesting information on its adoption programs should be brief, much like the one presented above. You may even want to use this letter.

It is not necessary to send a letter detailing why you want to adopt. If you are interested in adopting a minority infant, an older child, or a child with a specific medical condition, mention this in your letter; agencies usually need parents for certain children. State this simply in the first sentence, by writing something like, "My spouse and I are interested in adopting an African-American infant (or a biracial infant, a Latino infant, or a child with Down syndrome)." If you are specific, your letter may be relayed to the right person immediately.

Once the letter is typed, make 100 or 200 copies. Begin by addressing envelopes to agencies in your state because the easiest way to adopt through an agency is to work with one in your state for both the home study and placement.

Keep an updated list of the agencies you have written (or called) so that you do not contact them again in a future mailing. Once your letters are in the mail, you can expect responses to begin arriving within a week's time. Others will take weeks or even a few months to respond. A small percentage may never answer.

Sometimes an agency that cannot work with you will enclose a list of other sources you may want to contact. Says Carol, the mother of a two-year-old adopted from Chile, "One agency sent a nice letter saying they could not work with us and included a two-page list of additional sources for us to contact. I finally wrote to them a few weeks later. That's how we found our agency. It was a new agency and they were looking for clients to work with." Always follow through immediately on any leads another agency gives you.

There are always a few sad stories circulating about people who have contacted an agency and just assumed, when they did not get a response, that the agency was considering them for a placement. **The adoption process does not work this way.** Never assume an agency is considering you for a placement unless you receive confirmation to that effect. It takes more than a query letter to adopt a child.

SETTING UP YOUR FILES

While you are waiting for responses, set up separate files for the following information:

- International, U.S.-based Adoption Agencies
- Foreign-based Agencies
- State Public Agency
- U.S. Private Agencies
- International Parent-Initiated Resources
- Agencies with International and U.S. Adoption Programs
- Dead Ends (for agencies you are unable to work with for a variety of reasons)
- Pursue Further (sources you want to learn more about)
- Adoptive Parent Support Groups
- Newsletters
- Newspaper and Magazine Clippings
- Books
- Things to Do Next

The last file, Things to Do Next, should hold the names of other agencies you want to contact and the names of individuals that may be helpful to you. Start with this file on your next working day.

It is important to keep accurate records when contacting agencies. Keep track of every phone call you make, every agency you contact, every bit of information you find. Date everything. If an agency tells you to contact them again in two months, mark that on your calendar. If you are accepted on a waiting list and told to call every other month, mark that also. It is imperative that your records always be in order and that you follow through at the appropriate times.

You will eventually come across individuals who have been extremely helpful—people you will want to keep in touch with. Keep their names and addresses in a safe place. You may never need to call on them for help again, but when you mail your adoption announcements send one to each of them along with a brief thank-you note. They will appreciate knowing they were of help.

THE HIGHS AND LOWS OF SEARCHING

Some people begin their search with great enthusiasm and then find themselves backing off. Or they stop working completely. This is not unusual. We all reach a point with any project (even an important one) when we just need to remove ourselves temporarily. Sometimes, pre-adopters can point to an exact conversation or a negative response to a letter as the reason they stopped searching, but often other commitments like the holidays, summer activities, and vacations get in the way.

"High and low days were common for us," says one adoptive mom named Gail. "We would find a new lead, make a few excited but anxious phone calls, only to discover they could not work with us, or the program was not one we were interested in. Or worse yet, we couldn't afford the fees. Once we had a lead on a woman who was looking for adoptive parents for the baby she was carrying," Gail continued. "We contacted her attorney and sent a résumé to him. He promised to telephone us either way. For days I sat at home and waited for his call. It never came."

Depression can halt or slow down efforts for weeks or months. Although the process of adopting is not easy for most people, perseverance and determination are needed to succeed. "If you feel down and just cannot seem to find the energy to continue your search, think about asking your spouse or a friend to take over instead of abandoning the project for any length of time," says 31-year-old Nikki. "My husband and I changed jobs. I was writing the letters and following them up with phone calls. He was doing the research. The change was just what I needed to keep me going."

Single mom Stacy asked a friend to continue her mailings when her first and second letter-writing campaigns failed to find an agency she could work with. "Annie just took over and the only thing I had to do was wait for the mail each day. After a few weeks I was ready to start again, but I didn't have to. One of the agencies Annie wrote had just the program I was interested in and the agency was able to begin working with me almost immediately."

If you abandon your search and can't bring yourself to return to work for an extended period, you may be suffering from severe depression. If you experience any symptoms of depression for two weeks or longer, you should seek counseling.

No matter what you think or feel, discontinuing your search for whatever reason does not mean you are unprepared to be a parent or incapable of parenting. Those who have already coped with infertility may experience many of the same feelings when agency searches are unsuccessful. It is important to understand that this can happen to anyone.

Just as you wondered why you could not conceive, you may question why you cannot find a child to adopt. You may feel you were not meant to be a parent, or that you did something terrible to deserve this.

While you search and wait, remember that others have faced the same thoughts and feelings. This is why it is so important to be around other prospective and adoptive parents during this time. These people understand how it feels to be unable to conceive or find a child to adopt when they desperately want a child.

Checklist of Things to Do
(Copy this checklist for your files.)

☐ **Join a support group**

    ☐ Let members know the type of child you hope to adopt

    ☐ Ask about adoption sources members have used

    ☐ Ask for help

    ☐ Become a visible member

    ☐ Ask questions

☐ **Prepare a work area in your home**

☐ **Purchase supplies**

☐ **Purchase, or borrow, the following suggested books for state-to-state listings of adoption agencies**

    ☐ *Adoption Choices* by Ellen Paul

    ☐ *National Adoption Directory* compiled by the National Adoption Information Clearinghouse

    ☐ *Report on Foreign Adoption* compiled by the International Concerns Committee for Children

    ☐ *The Adoption Resource Guide* by Julia Posner with James Guilianelli

    ☐ *There ARE Babies to Adopt* by Christine Adamec

☐ **Write agency form letter**

    ☐ Copy letter

    ☐ Address envelopes

    ☐ Complete first mailing

    ☐ Maintain list of agencies contacted

☐ **File information received**

☐ **Prepare a second mailing, if needed**

☐ **Select agencies you are interested in**

☐ **Compile a list of questions you have for each agency**

☐ **Call these agencies to learn more about their programs**

Understanding Agency Information and Requirements

Making it past the first hurdle is one of the most exciting times in the adoption process. For many people that first hurdle is overcome when they begin receiving adoption information in the mail and see the initial results of their own hard work. Jeanie, a prospective parent from Tennessee, summed up the feelings of many pre-adopters at this stage when she said, "I never imagined there were so many agencies with so many types of adoption programs available. Now we feel like we really have several options to consider."

As you begin sorting through the information you receive you will quickly notice the differences from one agency to the next. Their application and adoption fees, waiting times, and parent requirements may all differ. Agencies must meet the requirements of their state's laws, but all may add additional parent qualifications. Since state laws and international regulations vary, this is one reason requirements are different. Another reason is there are two distinct types of agencies in the United States: public and private. The whole adoption process becomes much easier to understand if you know how agencies work, the kinds of children public and private agencies place, and how the type of agency influences the expenses that are passed along to the adoptive parents.

PUBLIC AGENCIES

Public agencies operate under their state's social service department and are commonly referred to as county or state agencies. Adoptions completed through a state agency often require no fee, or a very modest one—a major plus for families who cannot afford to adopt through a private agency.

Years ago public agencies played a major role in the placement of infants, especially Caucasian infants, but today many of these agencies no longer have infant programs because very few pregnant women turn to state agencies for assistance. For those agencies that have a program for Caucasian infants, waiting lists may be as long as ten years and, in some areas, five years for a home study. However, a public agency is still a possible source for infants, especially minority infants and toddlers, crack/cocaine babies, children with special needs and older, school-age children.

OLDER CHILDREN AND CHILDREN WITH SPECIAL NEEDS

Your public agency should be the first place you check if you are considering adopting an older child or a child with special needs because many of these children are waiting to be adopted in the United States. Public agencies are prepared to find homes for waiting children. If you live in a state where the social service staff is committed to locating homes for such children, you should be able to adopt a child in a year or less.

A child is classified as a "waiting child" when an agency considers that child hard to place (usually because the agency has no families waiting to adopt that specific child). The agency may have a waiting list of families seeking to adopt healthy Caucasian infants, but no families waiting to adopt, for example, a healthy six-year-old or fourteen-year-old, or a biracial baby. Children classified as waiting children may be:

- biracial
- cocaine babies whose future developmental outlook is unknown
- physically, mentally, or emotionally disabled
- mentally retarded
- a healthy ten-year-old
- chronically ill
- a sibling group of two or more who must be adopted together (a sibling group may be classified as such only because it is often difficult to find a family willing to adopt several children at the same time even if they are all healthy)
- a sexually and/or physically abused child
- a healthy infant who just happens to belong to a minority group
- a child born in another country who is past infancy

Many adoption professionals hesitate to classify healthy sibling groups and healthy children of minority groups as "waiting children" or even "special-needs children," but many adoption agencies classify them as such because of the lack of adoptive families waiting to adopt them.

Children who're waiting for adoptive homes come from all backgrounds. Some remember their birth families and others do not. Some children were removed from their homes because their parents were unable to be good parents. Others may have been released for adoption at birth, or years later, because of physical limitations or developmental disabilities. Some have been physically, emotionally, or sexually abused. These and other children may have been caught up in the foster care system for years and carry their own emotional baggage. Often they have been moved around from one foster home to another, and because of this they carry the scars of never having had one person to depend on and bond with. All would benefit from having a family and a place to call home. Without a doubt, special people are needed to parent these children.

If you think you might be interested in a waiting child, contact your county or state agency and ask for an application. Study parent requirements (which often are more flexible than those of a private agency placing infants). Review their materials, jot down your questions, and then call for more information. Find out exactly what is required to adopt a waiting child.

Laura Draheim, adoption supervisor at Lucas County Children Services Board in Maumee, Ohio, suggests asking the following questions when telephoning your county or state public agency:

- What is the actual adoption process through your agency?
- How long does it usually take to adopt a child from start to finish?
- How much does it cost?
- Exactly what do you mean by "special needs" or "waiting children"?
- What about financial support to help care for the child?
- What psychological and medical services are provided?
- Do we pay for these services?
- How long before the agency can begin the home study?
- How long will it take to complete the home study?
- What will happen after the home study is completed?
- Once the home study is completed, how long before a child is placed with our family?

Try to determine how committed an agency's workers are to finding homes for waiting children. Are children, that you're interested in, available in your county? Is your social worker willing to send your home study to other county agencies in an attempt to locate a child? Does he have access to children in other states? Is he willing to search out of state for a child for you?

State agencies usually provide information sessions for prospective adoptive parents. At these sessions you will have the opportunity

Sample Public Agency Application

APPLICANT
Name *(Last, First, Middle)*

Birthdate	Place of Birth
Race/Ethnic Background	Social Security Number
Occupation	

APPLICANT
Name *(Last, First, Middle)*

Birthdate	Place of Birth
Race/Ethnic Background	Social Security Number
Occupation	Maiden Name

Address *(Street, City, Zip Code, County)*	Telephone Number

Completion of this application will begin the process of acquainting you with the children in Ohio who are legally available for adoption and with the agency services that will assist you in making this very important commitment. The following information will begin to help you and the agency determine your desires regarding an adoptive placement.

ADOPTION INTERESTS

I am interested in adopting a child with the following characteristics *(check all that apply)*:

RACE OF CHILD
- ☐ White
- ☐ Black
- ☐ Biracial
- ☐ Hispanic
- ☐ Asian
- ☐ American Indian
- ☐ Other _____

AGE OF CHILD
- ☐ 0-2 Years
- ☐ 3-5 Years
- ☐ 6-9 Years
- ☐ 10-12 Years
- ☐ 13-15 Years
- ☐ 16-18 Years

INTELLECTUAL FUNCTIONING OF CHILD
- ☐ Above Average
- ☐ Average
- ☐ Slow Learner/Borderline
- ☐ Moderate Mental Retardation
- ☐ Severe Mental Retardation

PHYSICAL CONDITION OF CHILD
- ☐ No Physical Impairment
- ☐ Moderate Impairment
- ☐ Severe Impairment

NUMBER OF CHILDREN
- ☐ One Child
- ☐ Sibling Group
  Specify Maximum Number _____

SEX OF CHILD
- ☐ Male
- ☐ Female

EMOTIONAL FUNCTIONING OF CHILD
- ☐ No Emotional Problems
- ☐ Moderate Problems
- ☐ Severe Problems

Additional characteristics or comments: _____

_____

_____

_____

This section of the application tells the agency some basic information about you. Please complete all items as applicable.

OTHER MEMBERS OF HOUSEHOLD				
Name *(Last, First)*	Birthdate	Sex	Relation to Household Head	Race/Ethnic Background

(Use reverse side if necessary)

Date of Marriage	Licensed Obtained *(City, County, State)*

COMPLETION OF THIS FORM IS REQUIRED FOR THE AGENCY TO PROCEED WITH YOUR ADOPTION APPLICATION PROCESS.
DHS 1652 (Rev. 8/90)

Source: Ohio Department of Human Services.

Has either applicant been married before? ☐ Yes ☐ No If divorced, when and where was the divorce obtained and identify which applicant. _____

_____

Has either applicant been convicted of a criminal offense? ☐ Yes ☐ No If yes, what was the offense? _____

Have you ever applied to or adopted a child from another agency? ☐ Yes ☐ No If yes, what agency and when? _____

Previous address(es) you have lived during the past five years: (Approximate dates)

Address	Dates	Address	Dates
Address	Dates	Address	Dates

List four references who know your home life well:

Name	Address *(Street, City, State, and Zip Code)*
Telephone	Relationship
Name	Address *(Street, City, State, and Zip Code)*
Telephone	Relationship
Name	Address *(Street, City, State, and Zip Code)*
Telephone	Relationship
Name	Address *(Street, City, State, and Zip Code)*
Telephone	Relationship

I understand that this document is only an application and that additional information and documentation will be required.

I have received a copy of the agency's adoption policy and understand the eligibility requirements and timeframes involved in completion of the homestudy, and placement of a child in my home.

I understand that a homestudy approval does not guarantee that a child will be placed in my home, but that the agency will work towards this goal.

If I desire to withdraw this application for any reason or if there are any substantial changes affecting health, marital status, residence, household composition, or employment, I will notify the agency promptly.

My signature below authorizes the agency to contact references regarding the adoptive placement of a child in my home.

Adoptive Applicant Signature	Date	Adoptive Applicant Signature	Date

AGENCY USE	
Date Application Received	Agency Determination of Applicant's Special Needs Status ☐ Yes ☐ No
Continue With Application? ☐ Yes ☐ No	Date of Notification to Applicant Regarding Continuation

to ask questions and learn more about the adoption program, meet staff members, see pictures of children who are waiting for homes, and talk with parents who have adopted through the agency. Attendance at these group meetings is usually required.

Once you have submitted an application and have been accepted, a social worker will conduct a home study. During your home study, your caseworker will talk with you about the type of child you are considering and whether that child will fit well in your family.

You should have the opportunity to attend social functions and meet the children available for adoption or—at the very least—view videos of the children. Although agencies do their best to find homes for waiting children, it often takes a determined, assertive family to put an adoption together. If, after six months, you have not yet met a child through your public agency, take a more active role and begin to search on your own.

BECOMING MORE ASSERTIVE

If you feel you must take a more active role in finding a waiting child to adopt, ask your support group for the names of other area agencies with an adoption program for waiting children. Or, contact the adoption division of your state social service department and ask for a list of agencies serving waiting children.

Contact all the agencies you learn of. Inquire about the type of children they have waiting for homes. Visit agencies and look at their state and regional exchange books. These books list descriptions and photos of waiting children. Ask about national exchange books. These books often list children who have not been placed after having been listed in their state and regional books for a certain time.

You can help an adoption materialize if you can locate a child on your own. Continue to look through the exchange books because they are updated and new children are added bimonthly or monthly.

Many waiting children are in the custody of their state foster care system. Others are in the custody of private agencies in their home state. Exchanges do not have children in their custody. Instead, they accept referrals and try to facilitate a match between a child and the adoptive family. There is no charge for their services. You can help yourself further by registering your family with a state or national adoption exchange. Your family will be listed in the exchange book, along with a description of the child you hope to adopt (age of child, sex, race, intelligence level, and acceptable disabilities). You may need a social worker to register you, but frequently you can do this on your own. (See the appendices for a listing of regional and national exchanges.)

The Adoption Information Center of Illinois (AICI) is among the state exchanges that use a computer system to match children and registered families. The AICI computer system is linked with the

National Adoption Exchange in Philadelphia, Pennsylvania. AICI also maintains photo listing books from several other states in its office. Families are welcome to visit its office and look through these books. Many states have similar programs. AICI can be reached at 201 North Wells Street, Suite 1342, Chicago, IL 60606 (1-800-572-2390).

The Rocky Mountain Adoption Exchange is a regional exchange that has been connecting children who wait and families hoping to adopt for over twenty years. "The Exchange is not an adoption agency," says Dixie van de Flier Davis, president. "When an agency in the Rocky Mountain region is unable to locate a family for a waiting child, the agency uses our services to find a family." The Rocky Mountain Adoption Exchange (925 South Niagara Street, Suite 100, Denver, Colorado 80224, (303) 333-0845) serves Colorado, Nevada, New Mexico, South Dakota, Utah, and Wyoming.

Contact national adoption organizations also. Gloria Hochman, director of communications for the National Adoption Center, says the center "promotes adoption opportunities for children throughout the United States, particularly children with special needs and minority children." According to Hochman, the center "operates a telecommunications system that links adoption agencies around the country and permits a child in California, for example, to be placed with a family in Illinois." For additional information contact the National Adoption Center, 1500 Walnut Street, Suite 701, Philadelphia, PA 19102, 1-800-TO-ADOPT or (215) 735-9988.

Children Awaiting Parents (The CAP Book, Inc.) is a national photo-listing service for children who need additional exposure to find adoptive families. *The CAP Book* registers children from agencies throughout North America. Social workers who register children with CAP must be willing to place the child outside their states. Query letters and phone calls to the CAP office from prospective adopters are directed to the child's caseworker and agency. (Always telephone if you're inquiring about a specific child.) The book is available by subscription for $75 a year and is updated by mail twice a month. For more information contact The CAP Book, Inc., 700 Exchange Street, Rochester, NY 14608, (716) 232-5110.

The International Concerns Committee for Children (ICCC), 911 Cypress Drive, Boulder, CO 80303 (303-494-8333), also maintains a listing service. "The service is for children still in their birth countries whose placing agencies are seeking adoptive homes," says AnnaMarie Merrill, publications coordinator for ICCC. "These children may be infants to fifteen years old; be siblings of any age that want to stay together; or have correctable or noncorrectable medical conditions (often very minor) and occasionally healthy infants whose agency does not have a family ready. A few of the children are already in the United States and have experienced disruptions." About 800 children are listed with ICCC. It asks for a $25 annual donation for the listing and updates it monthly.

Other resources you may want to contact are:

AASK Midwest (Adopt a Special
   Kid)
1025 North Reynolds, Suite 201
Toledo, OH   436315
(419) 534-3350

(Not an agency. AASK helps
connect families with waiting
children.)

Adoptive Families of America, Inc.
3333 Highway 100 North
Minneapolis, MN   55422
(612) 535-4829

(Provides information on
waiting children and their
bimonthly magazine carries
pictures of both American and
foreign-born children waiting
for adoptive homes.)

Council of Three Rivers
200 Charles Street
Pittsburgh, PA   15238
(412) 782-4457

(A service that helps bring
together Native American
families and children who need
adoptive homes. Ask about the
organization's Rainbow
Project.)

REQUIREMENTS FOR ADOPTING WAITING CHILDREN

The parent requirements for those considering an older child or a child with special needs are ordinarily much more flexible than the requirements for adopting a healthy newborn at a private agency. All agencies have different requirements, but usually parents applying to a public agency can be married or single and range in age from at least twenty-five to fifty, or even older depending on the age of the child they are interested in adopting. Couples must be legally married a minimum of a year or two and do not need to have parenting experience—although it is considered highly beneficial. Adopters need not be infertile. It is not necessary to own your own home or have a separate bedroom for each child. Usually, agencies try to place children with families of the same race and cultural background because they believe this is in the best interest of the child, but exceptions are made in some cases.

A public agency will conduct a home study for you if you are trying to adopt the type of child in its custody or a child listed in the state exchange book. Usually there is no fee. (Public agencies occasionally will conduct a home study for an intercountry adoption or a United States independent adoption. There may be a fee.) A private agency that has waiting children in its custody may charge a fee for its services but usually the fee is reduced.

There are families who attempt to adopt a waiting child but become lost along the way. Do not let this happen to you. Learn as much as you can. Ask questions. Keep in contact with your parent support group, your agency, national adoption organizations, and national adoption support groups. Continue to check the listing books at the local, state, regional, and national level. There are over 36,000 children in the United States that are legally free for adoption and waiting for a family. (See the chapter on single parent adoptions for information on adoption subsidies.)

PRIVATE AGENCIES

There are two types of private agencies: denominational agencies, which have a religious affiliation, and nondenominational agencies. As you look over the agency information packets you should be aware of the differences between the two.

Denominational Agencies

There are many denominational adoption agencies in the United States. Some of them may be familiar to you. The more well-known ones are Catholic Charities, Jewish Family Service, and Lutheran Social Services. Agencies with these names are located in almost every state. There are other religious agencies that are less well known.

Denominational agencies were originally formed to provide social services for the members of their religious groups, adoption being one such service. Today quite a few religious agencies work with applicants of any faith, or even unaffiliated applicants in some cases. However, you will not know if an agency will work with you unless you contact them.

Every denominational agency has different requirements, and religious requirements may also differ within the same agency depending on the types of children it places. However, an agency that only places children with families of a specific faith usually offers other services to families of different faiths. For instance, most Jewish and Lutheran Agencies conduct home studies for Catholic families.

If you wish to adopt through a religious agency, usually you must be a member of a church or synagogue and be actively involved. "Actively involved" does not mean as a child. You must be actively involved now, as an adult, and be able to provide a reference from your minister, priest, or rabbi. Ruth Werth, adoption specialist for Lutheran Social Services in Griffith, Indiana, says that the agency wants to know what church prospective parents belong to and whether they attend church, or plan to do so once a child is placed. But she stresses that she "merely collects the information and is not passing judgment on the applicants." You may want to ask a denominational agency to explain its religious requirement before deciding you do not qualify.

Many denominational agencies require applicants to their Caucasian infant program to be members of a specific faith or denomination. Betty M. Wallin, adoption caseworker for the Baptist Family Agency in Seattle, confirms this, saying, "We are a Baptist church-related agency and so for the most part, it is Baptist girls we work with who desire their child to be placed in two-parent Baptist families."

According to Paul McFerron, foster/adoptive coordinator for the Missouri Baptist Children's Home in Bridgeton, "Prospective adoptive parents [of Caucasian infants] must be active members of a Southern Baptist Church within the Missouri Baptist Convention and live in the state of Missouri. For black, biracial, or special-needs infants, we will place with Christian families in the United States. For older children, over ten, we will consider any Christian family."

At a few Christian agencies, applicants must have what agencies call "a personal faith and living relationship with Jesus Christ." Applicants must be willing and able to respond appropriately to questions, both verbal and written, regarding their personal relationship, and its development, with Jesus Christ.

As you review agency packets, you should be able to determine just how important a personal religious commitment is to an agency by reading the questions it asks. Agency information packets sprinkled with Biblical quotations are clearly religiously oriented. These agencies will undoubtedly expect you to answer questions regarding your spiritual life and religious beliefs. Even if you meet all other requirements of the agency, do not try to misrepresent religious beliefs.

With the help of a friend, one couple managed to complete their application to the satisfaction of the agency. They were invited to visit the agency. "When we were questioned about our faith it became immediately apparent we had no idea what we were talking about. We were both very embarrassed," remembers the husband.

A few agencies require a pro-life agreement. One such agency is The Light House in Kansas City, Missouri, where a letter from your pastor expressing your church's position on abortion is needed. The Light House Adoption Agency works with "committed Christians who are both actively involved in the same Bible-believing, pro-life church," says Shirley Gibson, L.M.S.W., director of adoptive services. "The agency usually places newborns and most placements are Caucasian, biracial (black/white), or black."

Many religiously affiliated agencies have been in existence for decades. They tend to have excellent reputations and to be traditional in their approaches. Fees may be unusually low since these agencies often operate with money from their members and receive contributions from charities. Often services for the birth parents are donated. Maternity clothes and housing for the birth mother, for example, may be provided by church members.

Fees paid by the adoptive parents will vary from one agency to the next, but it is still possible to adopt an infant at some denominational agencies for around $5,000. Many of these agencies are willing to work with prospective parents with limited incomes and may base their fees on the parents' ability to pay. In 1993, James Balcom, executive director of Children's Homes, Inc., in Arkansas, quoted a fee of $5,000 for a newborn adoption. According to Balcom, $4,500 is the adoption reimbursement fee and $500 is the home study fee. The agency places with applicants who are members of a Church of Christ and reside in Arkansas.

Denominational agencies may limit their Caucasian infant program to applicants who are:

- Childless or have only one child
- Infertile, or have health reasons why they should not conceive
- Married three years or more
- Active members of a church or synagogue
- Between the ages of about 25 and about 40
- In good health
- Financially able to provide for a child
- Plan to have one parent remain at home after the baby arrives

The lower fees of many religious agencies make them very attractive to prospective adopters. Unfortunately, because of the many applicants interested in adopting healthy Caucasian infants and the small number of such infants available through most denominational agencies, the result can be a wait of several years. Some agencies also have infants with special needs and older children to place. The waiting time for these children is shorter, and often fees are lowered or waived.

Nondenominational Agencies

There are hundreds of private agencies that have no religious requirements. Like all agencies, they are looking for stable, secure, loving families who will provide a stimulating environment in which a child will have the opportunity to grow and reach her fullest potential. But they place little, if any, emphasis on religious commitment.

One major difference between denominational agencies and nondenominational agencies is the latter will place children with a wide variety of families as well as families of all faiths and those who're not members of an organized religion. Many work with singles, previously divorced couples, older couples, and families with other children. Their upper age limit for an infant, if they have one, may be forty-five years of age or higher. Some agencies have a unique arrangement. The ages of the husband and wife may not exceed a combined number of years, often 90 years.

Some agencies have no set age requirements. Phoebe Dawson, director of New Beginnings Adoption and Counseling Agency in Columbus, Georgia, says, "The agency does not have an age restriction.

Since the birth mother selects her family, she makes the decision regarding an acceptable age range." Darlene L. Zeigler, adoption coordinator at Adoption Services in Camp Hill, Pennsylvania, says, "There are no age requirements [imposed by our agency], but persons age forty-seven years or older can be more difficult to place with because birth parents tend to request younger parents."

On the other hand, being older also has benefits, which can be very attractive to a birth parent. Many older couples are well established in their careers and tend to have higher incomes than many younger adopters.

Depending on the type of child you are trying to adopt, you may or may not need proof of infertility. However, if you are attempting to adopt a healthy Caucasian infant, you will be asked about your infertility and may need a letter from your physician confirming this. (Most couples must have a complete fertility work-up before approaching an agency because many fertility problems are easily corrected.)

Fees at nondenominational agencies tend to be higher than those at denominational agencies. When your fee covers housing, maternity clothes, medical services, legal services, counseling, and transportation to medical appointments for the birth mother, fees may be as high as $15,000 or $20,000.

"Our range of costs are between $9,000 and $18,000," says Lillie Petit Gallager of the St. Elizabeth Foundation, "which includes our placement fee and the direct cost of caring for the birth mother." (The agency places infants in Louisiana.)

After randomly interviewing fifty nondenominational agencies, I found the average fee for adopting a healthy Caucasian infant, for example, to be around $9,500. Special-needs adoptions, as previously discussed, usually have lower fees no matter the type of agency, and sometimes fees are waived completely. The average fee for adopting an infant with special needs appears to be around $1,600 when adopting through a nondenominational agency.

There are a few private agencies that do not charge a fee for the placement of children from infants to teens. One such agency, the Nebraska Children's Home Society, is a statewide denominational childcare agency that was established in 1893. According to Harris Van Oort, executive director, the agency is a nonprofit corporation and is not affiliated with a state government agency. "The work of the Society is dependent upon the voluntary gifts and contributions of people who believe in the work that we do and want to support us in our commitment to children," says Van Oort. "Adopting parents are asked to make the Nebraska Children's Home Society their favorite charity." The agency serves the state of Nebraska and although there is no religious requirement, "We do believe a meaningful faith is a positive in building a family. Many birth mothers prefer couples who share and practice their faith."

HOW FEES ARE FIGURED

Some agencies have set fees. Other agencies may base their fees on your income. Suppose you earn $50,000 a year and you approach an agency that has a sliding scale fee. Your fee may be ten percent of your income. Therefore your fee would be approximately $5,000, based on the ten percent, or $2,500, based on 5 percent. The lower your income, the lower the fee. However, some agencies require that you have a certain minimum income because they do not want to place a child with a family who would have difficulty providing for him.

What if you make $200,000 a year? Does that mean your fee will be $20,000? Probably not. Agencies using a sliding scale usually cap the upper fee limit. Families with incomes of $75,000 and over, for instance, would pay the same set fee. At ten percent, the fee would be $7,500 whether you earned $75,000 or $200,000 a year.

Some agencies may have a base fee, say $6,000 plus ten percent of a couple's combined gross income. The Missouri Baptist Children's Home quotes a fee of ten percent of the applicants' income, plus a percentage of the birth mother's hospital bill if it is over $2,000.

OTHER AGENCY REQUIREMENTS FOR U.S. INFANT ADOPTION

If you want to adopt a healthy Caucasian infant from the United States, many agencies require that you be infertile. But if no medical reason has been found for your inability to conceive or if you have a history of miscarriage or stillbirth you should still be able to adopt an American infant through an agency. (You may have to search a little harder to find an agency to place a baby with you, so be assertive or consider independent adoption.)

What if you have a medical condition that would seriously jeopardize your health if you were to become pregnant? You would be considered for a baby at most agencies, as long as you are capable of parenting a child and your life span is considered to be within the normal range.

What if you already have given birth to one child and are unable to conceive a second time? Will you be able to adopt an infant? Maxine G. Chalker, executive director of The Adoption Agency in Ardmore, Pennsylvania, says, "Couples with secondary infertility are welcome to apply for our infant program. Birth parents select the adoptive families, and they often choose families with one child." Often a birth parent asks for her child to be placed in a home with another child because she wants him to have a sibling to grow up with. As a result, many agencies that give birth parents an active role, accept applications from parents who are unable to conceive a second child, or who are seeking to adopt a second child.

If your first child was adopted, generally the agency that placed her will place a second child once your first child has reached a certain age (usually eighteen months or two years). You do have other options if the agency restricts infant adoptions. For one, most agencies will welcome you as parents for an infant with special needs. If you are unable to adopt an infant with special needs, do not give up. Many families with one child have successfully adopted one or more children internationally, independently, or through an agency other than the first ones they contacted.

The number of years you have been married is important to many agencies. If you haven't been married at least three years, you will find that some agencies believe couples need more time together to develop their marital relationship before assuming the responsibilities of parenting. If you run into this requirement, use the time to learn more about adoption and child care. Then, when you meet the marriage requirement you will be ready to proceed.

If you have been formally married a short time, but have been living together for several years, ask the agencies that interest you whether their length-of-marriage requirement can be waived. With social mores changing rapidly, there are many couples in this situation.

There are also more women working outside the home, so many agencies no longer expect the adoptive mother to leave her job when the baby arrives. But some agencies still require one parent to be home with the baby for a specified period of time. Mary is an adoptive mother whose career was affected. "Our agency required me to stay at home with our daughter for one year or until the adoption was finalized," she says. Mary is an attorney who could work at home and, fortunately, whose agency was flexible. "I had a baby-sitter in my home three days a week while I worked. My secretary dropped off my mail and paperwork every evening. On Saturdays when Ken was home, I went into the office. If I had to be in court, Ken used a vacation day. There was no way I could just drop out for a year. I had clients who were depending on me.

Previously divorced couples in a second marriage are usually accepted for both intercountry and U.S. adoption programs, as long as they can demonstrate stability in their present marriage. Some agencies require that a previously divorced couple be married at least three to five years before they apply to adopt a healthy American infant. At agencies that allow birth mothers to choose the adoptive families, you may find that the length of your marriage is not important. Independent adoption is also an option if you are in this situation.

What if one or both applicants have had more than one divorce? Unfortunately, if you are seeking to adopt a healthy Caucasian infant, you will have difficulty finding an agency to work with you. Independent adoption may be your only option, if it is legal in your state. There are also infants available through intercountry adoption programs, and many U.S.-based intercountry adoption agencies will work with you.

MOTIVATION FOR WANTING TO ADOPT

Prospective adoptive parents begin the adoption process for many reasons. The most common is a strong desire to have children, coupled with the inability to achieve a pregnancy or carry a baby to term. Some parents who have biological children may want to add another child to their family through adoption, because there are so many children waiting for permanent homes in the United States and abroad. Some singles, who do not know whether they will marry, nevertheless want the opportunity to become parents before they get any older.

These are all valid reasons for wanting to adopt. But when faced with an application form that asks questions about motivation for adoption, most people wonder exactly what the agency will consider an appropriate response. Here are some examples of what you might say:

> My husband and I are infertile, and desperately want a child to love and raise. We feel we have so much to offer, especially love. We would cherish a child placed with us and would do our very best to meet his or her emotional, physical, spiritual, and educational needs.

> We both come from large families and are very close to our families. We cannot imagine life without children to love, take care of, and raise. Since we are unable to conceive a child, and because we both work with exceptional children, we are hoping to adopt an older child in need of a family. Our families and friends are very supportive of our decision to adopt.

> My wife and I want to share our love and life with more children. We have two children and are interested in adopting two children from South America, preferably a sibling group under the age of ten. We have room in our hearts and in our home. Our children are also looking forward to having more siblings in the house.

> I so much want a child to love. I always thought I would marry someday, but that day has not arrived. When I look ahead and see a future without a child, I feel sad because I truly want one to raise and love forever.

On the other hand, here are some responses that agencies might consider inappropriate:

> My husband and I have tried to have children, but to no avail. We have a large home and a sailboat and belong to a country club. We have much to offer a child. Since I am not employed, my days are filled with leisure time. My husband and I feel a child would give me something worthwhile to do.

> We have one child of our own and would like to have another one. Unfortunately, we are unable to conceive again. We would like our

child to have a brother or sister—someone he can play with. We live in the country and there are no children nearby. We would treat an adopted child like he was our own.

Social workers want to help parents; they don't focus on finding reasons to reject them. If you want to adopt a child for all the right reasons, a response straight from the heart will be very acceptable.

AGENCIES WITH INTERCOUNTRY PROGRAMS

Many agencies that place children from the United States also provide services that lead to an intercountry adoption. Bethany Christian Services (the main office is located in Grand Rapids, Michigan) works in approximately twenty-five states and places a significant number of children through its intercountry program. In a recent year, 611 children were placed through its United States program and 392 children through the intercountry program.

World Association of Children and Parents (WACAP), located in Seattle, serves the entire United States and Canada. In early 1993 the agency was placing children from the United States, Colombia, India, the Philippines, Thailand, The Peoples Republic of China, Romania, Korea, and Hong Kong.

Illien Adoptions International, Ltd. is located in Atlanta. Illien places children born in the United States and other countries with families in the U. S. and in any other country that permits intercountry adoption (such as Italy, England, Scotland, New Zealand, Australia, and Canada.) In early 1993, the agency was placing children from Bolivia, Peru, India, El Salvador, Chile, Brazil, Costa Rica, Honduras, and Paraguay. (Illien prefers that clients initially contact them by mail.)

There are dozens of other agencies that place children from abroad. See the chapter on intercountry adoption for more information.

SMALL LOCAL AGENCIES' SERVICES

Besides placing agencies—agencies that have their own adoption programs—there are other licensed adoption agencies, called local service agencies, which routinely network with referral or placing agencies that are generally located out of state. Local service agencies usually network because they have more prospective parents than children to place. They provide the required home studies and post-placement services most often for local prospective parents pursuing intercountry adoptions, by coordinating their efforts with referral agencies that place children from overseas throughout most of the United States. Placing agencies also benefit from this arrangement because they often have more children available than they can place with their own clients.

Why would someone want to use a local service agency when they can work with a full-service placing agency? Often, prospective adoptive parents do not have a choice. They may be unable to find an agency in their state that places children from a specific country that interests them, or they may prefer to do a parent-initiated (direct) adoption with a foreign source without using a placing agency in the United States.

How do prospective parents locate a source? "Using a local service agency enables you to find your own source from among the dozens available," says Deborah McCurdy, M.S.W., adoption supervisor for Beacon Adoption Center in Great Barrington, Massachusetts. "We encourage our clients to send for the *Report on Foreign Adoption,* which is available from the International Concerns Committee for Children," says McCurdy. "The book identifies dozens of placing agencies that place children throughout the United States and the prospective parents can choose the agency they would like to work with based on its eligibility requirements, its fees, and the age and nationality of the child they wish to adopt."

As explained by McCurdy, out-of-state placing agencies rely on local service agencies in other states to provide the initial and final steps in the adoption process. "Local agencies take responsibility for coordinating with the placing agency, preparing the home study, instructing the family on immigration procedures and state requirements, providing postplacement services, and reporting back to the placing agency in writing as is required. Generally the local agency signs an interagency working agreement with the placing agency so that everyone understands what their responsibilities are." After a child is placed, a local service agency will assist clients with adjustment problems and make the normal postplacement visits required for finalization or re-adoption in the client's state.

Local service agencies can be used for U.S., intercountry, and interstate adoptions. The process of using two agencies to facilitate an adoption is very common and entirely legal.

WHAT TYPES OF CHILDREN COULD YOU CONSIDER?

Most applications provide space for you to describe the type of child you are seeking to adopt. It is helpful to be accepting of as many possibilities as are appropriate for your family. For example, most prospective adoptive parents want their first child to be a girl, but most families expecting a baby by birth want a boy. Your primary goal is to become a parent. Does it really matter if the first baby is a boy or a girl? It is helpful to be flexible regarding the child's sex. You will wait longer if you *must* have a girl. (Most families eventually adopt a second child. You will find the wait easier if you are specific about the sex of the next child since you will have your first child to love and care for.)

A Virginia couple, Marie and Joe, adopted a healthy, Caucasian male infant through an agency within weeks because every other family on the waiting list wanted a female child. This perfectly healthy, beautiful baby was actually rejected by the first five couples waiting.

"We learned that the sex of the child really was not important," says an adoptive mom from Brookfield, Wisconsin. "Our agency would not allow a sex choice if it was to be your first child. We would have asked for a girl. The most beautiful little boy was placed with us and we bonded right away. He has been a wonderful big brother to his little sister."

Must you have a newborn? Sometimes young mothers decide to parent their child, only to discover months later they are unable or unwilling to handle the responsibility. Would you consider an infant six to twelve months old or a toddler, born here or abroad?

Can you accept a child born as a result of rape? Can you accept a child when there is no background information available on the birth father? Would you consider a baby born to a mother who had little or no prenatal care? A premature infant? A baby whose mother used drugs, alcohol, or smoked during pregnancy?

Some adopters feel they must have a healthy infant with complete background information and whose birth mother had full prenatal care and was not a substance abuser. If you feel this way, tell the agency but be prepared for a long wait. Some birth mothers refuse to give any information about the birth father. No one can force a birth mother to share this information. If you are willing to consider some unknowns in your baby's history, be sure to let the agency know. It may mean the difference between waiting months or years for a child.

Remember, many thousands of families in the United States have adopted children from other countries. Many of these children were born under less than ideal circumstances, but they have brought tremendous joy to their new families. "Most of these children are essentially healthy and normal but social forces and extreme poverty have made it impossible for their birth parents to provide for them," says McCurdy. "These youngsters sometimes come into care with untreated infections or other problems, which may be corrected or ameliorated by the time of placement if the foreign orphanage or foster home has had the time and resources to build up the child's health and security."

Says one mother from Wyoming, who has a three-year-old from Korea, "We adopted a special-needs child, but what a special child she is. She is a delight! People need to be encouraged to open their homes and hearts to these children because they are so special."

Medical Problems You May Be Asked
to Consider

	Yes	No	Will Consider
Cerebral palsy			
mild	☐	☐	☐
severe	☐	☐	☐
Hyperactivity			
mild	☐	☐	☐
severe	☐	☐	☐
Rickets	☐	☐	☐
Premature baby (low birth weight)	☐	☐	☐
Cystic fibrosis	☐	☐	☐
Learning disability			
mild	☐	☐	☐
severe	☐	☐	☐
Known physical abuse	☐	☐	☐
Down syndrome	☐	☐	☐
Diabetes			
mild	☐	☐	☐
severe	☐	☐	☐
Seizure disorder, convulsions or epilepsy			
mild	☐	☐	☐
severe	☐	☐	☐
Heart defect			
major (requires open heart surgery)	☐	☐	☐
minor	☐	☐	☐
Muscular dystrophy	☐	☐	☐
Spina bifida	☐	☐	☐
Post-polio			
mild	☐	☐	☐
severe	☐	☐	☐
Clubfoot	☐	☐	☐
Multiple sclerosis	☐	☐	☐
Blindness or serious trouble seeing	☐	☐	☐
Deafness or serious trouble hearing	☐	☐	☐
Eczema	☐	☐	☐
Emotional problems:			
mild	☐	☐	☐
severe	☐	☐	☐
Severe malnutrition	☐	☐	☐
Developmental delays	☐	☐	☐
Child requires wheelchair	☐	☐	☐
Cleft palate	☐	☐	☐
Cleft lip and palate	☐	☐	☐

Many agencies will ask whether you will consider a child with particular medical problems. You are expected to complete this part of the application by indicating yes, no, or that you will consider specified medical conditions. Read your application checklist carefully and discuss the various health problems listed. Talk with your doctor about those you do not understand so you can make an educated decision.

OPEN VERSUS CONFIDENTIAL ADOPTION

If you are trying to adopt an infant born in the States, you must do plenty of reading on open adoption because more birth mothers know they can have a say in choosing a family for their baby. Many agencies, despite their past commitment to traditional policies, are now letting birth mothers choose the adoptive family if they so desire. (Most birth mothers are still choosing confidential adoption whether they select the adoptive family or not.)

Open adoption is not a new concept. In the beginning of this century, confidential adoption was almost unknown. But open adoption did not become common again until about ten years ago.

Some agencies ask applicants to indicate the types of adoption they are willing to participate in. Will you consider an open adoption? A semiopen adoption where no identifying information is exchanged? Are you willing to meet with the birth parents at least once? To share identifying information? Or do you wish to have a traditional confidential adoption? The choice is yours.

Some adoptive parents prefer some contact with the birth parents, at least initially. They may want to meet the birth parents and exchange letters, pictures, or both. These parents feel this will enable them to answer their children's questions in the future. They may also wish to obtain complete medical and social histories of the birth families. Other prospective parents may simply want the opportunity to thank the person who made their dream of having a child a reality.

Think how you might answer a question regarding the type of adoption you are willing to consider. Consider the type of letter you would write to a prospective birth mother because, in all likelihood, you will need one. Start gathering photographs because you may be asked to share pictures with a birth mother. It is never too early to start preparing yourself for an exchange of information with a birth mother. See the chapter on independent adoption for a discussion of various ways you can acquaint a birth mother with your family.

OTHER ALTERNATIVES FOR ADOPTING AMERICAN INFANTS

Identified Adoption

Some agencies that have handled only confidential, traditional adoptions in the past are now implementing identified adoption (also known as designated adoption, agency-assisted adoption, targeted adoption, or fast-track adoption).

In an identified adoption, the birth mother is brought to the agency through the efforts of prospective adoptive parents. The birth mother, who may or may not know the identity of the adoptive parents, identifies the family with whom she wants her baby placed. Identified adoption is a relatively new form of adoption for agencies, but is not new in independent adoption. Identified adoption is especially helpful in states that do not permit private adoptions.

Kristina A. Backhaus, L.I.C.S.W., the program manager of Adoption Services for Lutheran Social Services of New England, explains how an identified adoption works: "A pregnant woman considering making an adoption plan for her expected baby becomes known to a couple through an intermediary who knows of the couple's desire to adopt. The intermediary then puts the parties directly in touch with one another or with our agency for further exploration of a possible adoption. This type of adoption is not to be confused with 'private' adoption, which is illegal in Connecticut."

"Identified adoption is an agency adoption with all the services and protection of an agency. But, as in an independent adoption, the birth and adoptive parents select each other," says Raymond E. Cheroske, director of Adoption Services of Children's Home Society of California. "All prospective parents, even in an identified adoption, must have an approved home study completed before the baby can be placed with them."

Counseling is usually available to all parties at agencies supportive of identified adoption services. (A few agencies only offer counseling to birth parents.) Says Ed Petry, director of the Family Services Department at Lutheran Social Services of the Miami Valley in Dayton, Ohio, "Birth parents receive counseling and support from a professional social worker who fully explains their rights and represents them throughout the adoption process. Surrender of the birth parents' parental rights is handled by the agency."

What about the prospective adoptive parents? Do they receive counseling? "Each family has an adoption worker who provides counseling and support," adds Petry. "The home study process focuses on preparation for adoptive parenting and includes opportunities for prospective parents to meet with birth parents, adoptive parents, and adult adoptees during group meetings. After placement, the agency maintains contact with the adoptive family until the adoption is finalized. Postadoption services are always available through the agency."

If you identify a prospective birth mother and send her to an agency, are you guaranteed to receive her baby if she decides to place the child? Not necessarily. Some agencies insist that they make that final decision after interviewing the birth parents and the prospective parents. Petry says, "The agency respects the birth parents' rights to place their child with a specific family as long as that family is approved for an adoptive placement, either by Lutheran Social Services

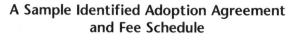

A Sample Identified Adoption Agreement and Fee Schedule

Dear Full-service Client:

In order to assist you in your deliberations regarding the possible provisions by Friends in Adoption, Inc. of adoption placement services, we believe that you should be aware of certain specific policies of this agency.

No placement will be made unless it is determined to be in the best interests of the child and that the prospective adoptive parents are able, capable, fit and ready to assume parental responsibility.

You should be aware that you are financially responsible for all direct costs of the pregnant woman/couple and child. Direct costs include the usual and customary costs of the birth mother's prenatal and hospital care, cost of counseling services to the birthparents, transportation expenditures for the birth mother, the birthparent's legal fees related to the surrender of the child, and medical and hospital costs for the child. Counseling costs are your financial responsibility whether the birthparent surrenders the child or not. Postplacement counseling will be provided up until the adopted child turns eighteen, upon the request of the birthparent, and will not exceed one thousand dollars ($1,000.00). In addition, any other costs actually incurred by the agency on your behalf, prior to the birth of the child (ie. legal, medical, transportation and prenatal care) are your financial responsibility whether the birth mother surrenders the child or not.

The agency is available *without additional fee* to answer your "baby line" from *9–5 on Monday–Friday.* Due to the legalities involved, the agency cannot, depending upon jurisdiction, act on your behalf but can be there to act as a human link between pregnant women and those wishing to adopt. The agency will, for *no additional fee,* make itself available on a *24-hour basis* through a trained answering service to answer the phones of those wishing the agency to do so.

It is contrary to agency policy for any payments to be made to the surrendering parents or other persons either during or after pregnancy. If the agency, prior to accepting surrender, determines that payments in excess of direct costs have been made, the agency may decline to accept such surrender and/or to provide adoption placement services, unless said payments are for legally valid reasonable birth mother expenses and have been previously approved by the agency.

Because of the complexity of the legal considerations involving any identified adoption, the validation of the surrender process, the termination of the birth parents' parental rights, the satisfaction of the Interstate Adoption Compact requirements and the final legalization of the adoption, it is the policy of this agency that all legal services be handled by the agency's legal counsel, Susan Fowler Esq., or other experienced counsel approved by the agency. While the agency's attorney represents the agency's interests at all times and provides legal services initiated at your request, you may wish, in addition, to engage an attorney to represent your own interests.

After you have reviewed the above information and perhaps discussed it with an attorney, Friends in Adoption Inc. will be available to meet with you.

I/We, the undersigned, have read this agreement and agree to abide by its terms and conditions. I/We also understand that fees paid to Friends in Adoption are non-refundable.

Dated at _____ in the state of _____ this _____ day of _____, 19_____.

_____

_____

I.	Informational Meeting	$ 150
II.	Application Fee	$ 500
III.	Application Approval	
IV.	Choice of FIA Services	
	A. Full Service Agency Fee (Due with completed application and Intake Information Form one week before consultation date)	$ 4,500*
	B. Full Service (second time) (Due when Application and Intake Information forms are returned)	$ 3,500*

V. Home study Information
A home study is required prior to an adoptive placement (but not prior to attendance at our Get Acquainted Workshop). Friends in Adoption will accept the home study performed by an agency or individual qualified to conduct home studies in your state of residence.

* payment plan available

F.I.A.'s Adoption Fees Are Non-Refundable

Courtesy of Friends in Adoption, Inc. Fees effective 1/1/93. All fees subject to change.

or by another adoption agency." Before referring a birth mother to an agency, always check the agency's policy on this.

Some agencies that provide services for prospective adoptive parents through the traditional waiting list are also assisting with identified adoptions. So if you are not content to sit and wait on your agency's waiting list, the agency may be able to help you locate a birth mother for an identified adoption by using methods common in locating a birth mother for an independent adoption (such as newspaper advertising).

Other agencies have discontinued their traditional infant program entirely because of a lack of birth parents coming directly to them. One such agency is Adoption Services Associates in San Antonio, Texas, which asserts "The shortage of birth parents coming directly to agencies is a national trend."

Adoption Services Associates was the first agency in Texas to begin an identified adoption program. As with all agencies, applicants are screened carefully before they are approved for an adoptive placement. Once approval is granted, prospective parents are given instructions on how to find a potential birth mother through classified ads. When prospective parents identify an interested birth mother the agency confirms the pregnancy and provides all of the services the birth mother needs.

Identified adoption, like independent adoption, can be quite costly. Adoptive parents' expenses may include the agency's fee, the birth mother's medical costs, her rent, maternity clothing, and transportation to and from doctor appointments during the pregnancy. Always discuss with the agency what expenses you are liable for and what the cost of the adoption will be. Be sure your agreement with the agency is in writing. As in an independent adoption, the risks in an identified adoption are both emotional and financial.

The adoptive parents run the risk that, after paying for the birth mother's expenses, she may decide to parent the baby. An estimated 10 percent of birth mothers change their minds about adoption after the baby is born. Pre-adopters working with Adoption Services Associates in Texas may purchase adoption risk insurance to protect them financially from unexpected circumstances. But even if your agency offers insurance, you may not be fully protected. You may also lose two or three babies before you find a birth mother who decides to make an adoption plan in your favor.

Identified adoption may be the solution for those prospective parents who locate a birth mother on their own but do not want to be involved in a private adoption. Although there are risks, an identified adoption protects you from the greatest danger—having to return the baby to the birth mother after placement because parental rights were not terminated. With an agency involved, the termination of parental rights almost always comes before a baby is placed in your home. The exceptions to this are legal risk adoptions and foster parent adoptions.

LEGAL RISK ADOPTION

There are times when agencies will place a child in an adoptive home before birth parents have terminated their legal rights. An agency will place a child when it is expected that a surrender or court termination will soon follow. But sometimes those papers are never signed and the child is returned to its birth family.

Losing a child for any reason is always very traumatic for a family. Even if you eventually adopt other children, you will never forget the child you once called your son or daughter. This is something you must be prepared for if you are willing to consider a legal risk placement.

Jim and Leah completed their home study with their local county agency in 1989. Ten months later, they were chosen for the legal risk placement of a healthy, Caucasian newborn. "The birth mother had not informed anyone of her pregnancy," says Leah, "and she had no prenatal care. She made the decision to carry the baby, and then place the baby for adoption, without the support of her family and that concerned us."

The birth mother, declining to see the baby, contacted the county agency on the day her daughter was born. Sara Cole was the adoption caseworker who was given the assignment of choosing a family. Sara gave the birth mother basic information about the couple and the birth mother said she wanted Jim and Leah to be her daughter's parents. But she was not ready to sign the papers transferring her parental rights.

"The day we received the call from the agency," says Leah, "we were asked if we were interested in a legal risk placement of a newborn. We said yes, and were able to pick up Celeste at the hospital the next morning. The first ten days were the scariest for us. Every day brought fears that the phone would ring asking us to release Celeste to her birth mother. But ten days after the birth of our daughter, the birth parents appeared simultaneously at the Family Court Center with Sara to sign the permanent surrender papers. We had to wait thirty days for the journal entry before we could sign an adoptive parenting agreement with the county agency. Eight months later, we finalized the adoption." Would they do it again? Jim and Leah are sure they would.

If you will consider a legal risk placement, discuss it with your social worker. Before accepting the placement of a child, ask questions. Find out as much information as you can about the circumstances that led to the tentative adoption plan. Ask questions about the child's extended family. Most important, try to assess the risk that the birth parents will change their minds.

FOSTER PARENT ADOPTION

Some families who are trying to adopt explore the possibility of foster parent adoption. After being screened and licensed as foster parents, the family is eligible to temporarily care for children in their home.

Sometimes the children entering foster care have been forcibly removed from their birth family, but a parent or parents may voluntarily release a child to foster care because of difficult life circumstances.

A foster family cares for a child until he can be returned to his birth family, or until he is freed for adoption. If the child becomes available for adoption, the foster family is often the first choice for adoptive placement, especially if the child has resided with the foster family for a considerable length of time. For more information on foster parent adoption, request a free copy of "Foster Parent Adoption: What Parents Should Know" from the National Adoption Information Clearinghouse.

Pursuing Agency Adoption

The day will arrive when you are ready to apply for a home study. By then you will know the type of child you want to adopt and the type of adoption program you are interested in pursuing. Your next step is to choose an appropriate agency.

Since you have devoted many hours of your time and energy to arrive where you are now, it is important to choose an agency you feel comfortable with. Begin by reviewing the philosophy statement of the agency. How do you feel after reading it? Positive? Negative? Indifferent? Next, attend the free information meeting and ask questions. After attending the meeting, how did you feel? Did the staff answer your questions? Do you feel good about the answers? Do you feel hopeful?

It is extremely significant if you walk out of an orientation meeting feeling discouraged. If you have decided to try and adopt a healthy infant and agency personnel mentioned only the thousands of older children waiting for homes and the lack of available infants, you may feel very discouraged when you leave the meeting. The negative feeling that you have means it is time to consider another agency, an agency that regularly places the type of child you want to adopt.

If you are unable to attend an orientation meeting because of the distance, talk with agency personnel by phone. Be sure you have reviewed agency information beforehand so you can understand exactly what is being said about policies and programs. Ask if this is a good time for the social worker to answer your questions. Again, you should have a positive feeling when you conclude your conversation and feel comfortable with the answers you receive. If you are not satisfied, trust your instincts and find another agency to work with.

Consider the style of the agency. If your goal is to adopt an infant through a confidential adoption, how happy will you be working with an agency specializing in open adoption? On the other hand, if openness is what you desire, will you be pleased working with an agency that encourages confidential adoption? Hoping to adopt a school-age child? A child from another country? If so, do not apply to an agency that primarily places infants born in the United States.

Here are some questions to think about as you review your choices. (It is not necessary to ask the social worker all the questions directly. If you do, you may appear overly anxious.)

Is your age a factor? Consider the length of the waiting list. If you are approaching forty, and it appears you might not adopt before the cut-off age, do you want to take the chance of being disqualified two years later? It's better to find an agency where the maximum age is higher so you can feel confident that you will eventually receive a child.

Consider the agency's attitude toward birth parents. Does it allow the birth parents to choose the adoptive family? Does a social worker select the couple? Does the agency offer a birth parent the choice of a confidential, semiopen, or open adoption? Or does the agency encourage the birth parent to choose the type of adoption it feels is best?

Are other services available to the birth parents? Some agencies have support groups for the birth parents they work with. Do they offer prenatal and postpartum counseling and a support network? These are all helpful in forestalling future problems.

What is the attitude of the agency toward the adoptive parents? Asking the following questions will help you determine an agency's position on these important issues:

- Does it offer parenting classes for prospective parents?
- Does it encourage you to network with other pre-adoptive and adoptive families?
- Are you able to choose the type of adoption you would like to participate in?
- How much information about the birth parents does the agency share with the adoptive parents and vice versa?
- Can you talk with other adoptive families who have adopted through the agency?
- If you are adopting from another country, what type of support is available to you before, during, and after the adoption?
- Can you meet other families who have adopted from the country you are applying to adopt from?
- Can you meet children from that country?

Check the agency's suggested reading list. Does the list include books recently published? What does the reading list tell you about its practices? An agency that claims to assist with an open adoption, but does not include books on that subject on its reading list, may be saying one thing and practicing another.

Find out what future commitment you can expect from the agency. Is the agency willing to keep birth parents and adoptive parents updated on medical issues and social histories? What is the agency's policy on opening a confidential or semiopen adoption in the future, if all parties are willing? Are birth parents, adoptive parents, and adoptees encouraged to come back to the agency as needs develop through the years?

"Always be sure an agency gives you a clear list of all the expenses before you commit any fees to that agency," says Deborah McCurdy, M.S.W., adoption supervisor at Beacon Adoption Center in Massachusetts. "That way you know exactly what your adoption is going to

Other Questions You May Want to Ask

- What were the characteristics of the children placed in recent years? Healthy? Special needs? Infants? Older children? The actual number of children placed is not important, because there are excellent small agencies that work with a few adoptive families but serve them well.
- How soon after you apply will the agency begin your home study?
- If you are not approved for a placement, is there a grievance process?
- Can you learn the reasons why you were not approved?
- If you are not approved, will the agency help you work through the problem areas it identifies so that you might be able to adopt through the same agency at a later date?
- Will the agency provide you with a copy of your home study whether or not you are approved?
- If a local service agency is completing your home study, is it willing to forward copies to several agencies? (If you have your own copy, it will be unnecessary to contact the agency every time you want to mail your home study to another agency.)
- Once your home study is completed, how long will you wait for the referral for a child?
- What happens if you turn down a referral? Will the agency offer another child to you in the future? Or will you be taken off the waiting list?
- After receiving a child referral for an intercountry adoption, how long will it be before your child arrives home?
- For an infant born in the United States, when can you bring your baby home?
- Is it possible to bring the baby home straight from the hospital? Or must the baby remain in foster care until the papers terminating parental rights are signed?
- Does the agency ever place children through legal risk adoption?
- What will the total costs of adopting through the agency be?
- Are there any additional fees that might be incurred?
- Will all fees be in writing?

cost. Most agencies have a fee schedule that you can request at the beginning of the process if it is not included with your application. And most agencies, but not all, will have you sign a contract at the onset."

BEWARE OF BABY BROKER AGENCIES

There are baby broker agencies operating in the United States for immense profits, and as prospective parents you must be cautious. These agencies do manage to get licensed, so they may appear on a listing of agencies from a state social service department. How will you, as a pre-adopter and consumer, spot a baby broker agency?

"I remember the first time I received information from a baby broker agency," says an adoptive mom from Pennsylvania. "I had mailed requests for information to about twenty-five agencies and had received responses to most of my inquires when this one came in the mail. By that time, I had some idea how much an infant adoption in the U.S. would cost. You can imagine my shock when I read their materials. The application fee was $1,500 and the total fee was over $18,000 payable in advance. This was in 1989. I called the agency several times and asked to speak with the director. He was never in, nor was his assistant. The receptionist said if we mailed in our application with the $1,500 fee, someone would call me back."

This adoptive mom decided to pursue her investigation a little further. "First, I called the attorney general's office in the state where the agency was located. I was interested in knowing if anyone had ever filed a complaint against the agency. Several people had. I then called the local county social service agency and talked with a supervisor who gave me enough information to know that we would not want to work with that agency. Later, I discovered that the agency had affiliates in other states under different names," she adds.

Licensed agencies can be baby brokers in disguise. Just because an agency is licensed does not mean its practices are above reproach. Some agencies charge excessive fees or have practices that are not professional. Always compare the fees of several agencies so you will know if an agency is charging too much. Then thoroughly check out the agency before sending any money, even the application fee.

When dealing with all agencies, services should be paid for as they are rendered. The largest sum is usually paid when the child is placed with you, or shortly beforehand. A legitimate agency does not ask for its entire fee up front. Consider what would happen to your money if the agency filed bankruptcy before a baby was placed with you. (In an identified or intercountry adoption, where many expenses are payable to entities other than the agency, you should expect to pay at least several thousand dollars early in the process. This is an acceptable procedure. However, you should ask your agency what its refund policy is in case you become pregnant and need to withdraw your application.)

Sample Local Service Agency Contract
and Financial Agreement for
Intercountry Adoption

 # Beacon Adoption Center, Inc.

66 LAKE BUEL ROAD, GREAT BARRINGTON, MA 01230

Telephone (413) 528-2749   (413) 528-5036

_____ Agency copy
_____ Applicants' copy

RIGHTS AND RESPONSIBILITIES OF ADOPTIVE APPLICANTS
AND ADOPTIVE PARENTS
A Description of Their Cooperative Relationship With Their Agencies

1. Adoptive parents and adoptive applicants (hereinafter called parents) have the right and responsibility to work cooperatively with the staff of Beacon Adoption Center, Inc. (hereinafter called Beacon) during the home study and post-placement period, in order that they and any child placed with them may be served in the best possible way. They have the right to Beacon's assistance in determining whether adoption is right for them at this time. Whenever possible, that decision will be mutually determined. (Although Beacon reserves the right to decline to approve a home study if it does not feel adoption is in the best interest of the child or family, in practice this rarely happens.)

2. Parents are responsible for informing Beacon of any new developments or circumstances in their lives which may affect their readiness to adopt, or to finalize an adoption. These include changes in household membership, changes in employment, illnesses, deaths, etc. In some cases, such as an unexpected pregnancy prior to placement, it may be necessary to postpone plans to adopt, if cooperating agencies insist on this.

3. Beacon is a "local service agency" providing home study and post-placement services. It does not locate children for adoption. The parents have the responsibility of selecting a licensed placing agency that will locate a child for them from among those US-based placing agencies described in the current Report on Foreign Adoption. Beacon is not in a position to endorse or recommend specific placing agencies, but this annual is helpful in describing most US-based licensed placing agencies that place foreign-born children throughout the country. If the parents are adopting an infant or toddler, they may also select an agency or orphanage or approved licensed facilitator in a foreign country for a direct (parent-initiated) adoption, in which they work directly with foreign nationals to locate a child and complete procedures. Parents need to understand that there will be various documents that they must prepare for governments and courts here and abroad, no matter which type of adoption they choose. Beacon will supply general guidelines on documents and procedures, and the parents should direct specific

questions to the placing agency/foreign source, which is responsible for explaining the requirements of the child's country of birth. Some countries require one or both parents to travel to complete the process and pick up the child.

4. Beacon does not participate in designated (identified) adoptions, in which a birth mother chooses the adoptive parents, often with the assistance of unlicensed facilitators. If the parents become aware of a designated adoption opportunity they'd like to pursue and their home study is already completed, they have the right to furnish their home study report to another licensed Massachusetts agency which will explore possibilities and accept transfer of their case.

5. If a US based placement agency is chosen, Beacon will need to exchange copies of licenses with that agency, and both must sign an interagency working agreement—as required by state regulations—before a placement is arranged. This is intended to protect families and clarify each agency's role in the process.

6. Beacon is separate from other agencies and all sources of children. Beacon cannot be held responsible if the parents are disappointed in their chosen placing agency or other source. However, it will work cooperatively with their second choice of source at no additional cost if the parents choose to withdraw from the first source.

7. Beacon can only serve parents who are legal residents of Massachusetts, where it is licensed. In case of an unexpected move out of state before their adoption takes place, they will need to locate an adoption agency in the new state which will agree to update their home study and provide post-placement services. Beacon cannot make refunds on that portion of services already rendered.

8. Parents are responsible for contacting their social worker at least once a month during the post-placement period until the adoption is finalized. They need to be available for daytime interviews with their adoption worker during this period. They have the right to the agency's assistance with normal adjustment problems within the family in the months following placement. After an adoption is finalized in a Massachusetts court, any services that are requested will be provided on a fee-for-service basis, either by Beacon or through referral to another agency.

9. The parents are responsible for the physical care of the child from the time of placement. They are also responsible for the child's expenses from the date of placement (and sometimes sooner). This includes the cost of any medical treatment which is not covered by their insurance or by Shriners Hospital services. Legal custody of the child is granted to the parents by court action at the time of finalization if they have not already been granted custody by a foreign court. Even if the parents have legally adopted the child overseas, it is their responsibility to adopt in a Massachusetts probate court in order to fully protect their parental rights and the child's inheritance rights. The parents are advised to prepare a will naming testamentary guardians and alternative testamentary guardians, which they should sign immediately after completing the legal adoption process.

10. Parents have the right and responsibility to choose a physician for their child prior to placement and to follow medical advice regarding any tests or treatment. Parents may authorize medical treatment for the child, but they should discuss non-urgent surgery and procedures (such as circumcision) with their Beacon

adoption worker in advance since these can be traumatic. If the family's well water has been determined to be unsafe, the child must be given bottled water until the problem can be cleared up, as required by the state Office for Children.

11. In any medical emergency, it is most important that the child be taken to a hospital emergency room immediately, by ambulance if necessary, before the parents take the time to contact Beacon or the placing agency or even their own pediatrician. They should tell the hospital staff that they are the child's parents and that they give their consent to any urgent medical treatment or surgery. In a true emergency of any kind, parents have the right to call Beacon 24 hours a day, seven days a week. The number available on a 24-hour basis is _____. Emergency assistance will be provided as soon as the message is received. (For non-emergency situations, the staff may be contacted 9:00–4:00, Monday through Friday.)

12. Until legal adoption occurs, Beacon must know the child's whereabouts. During the pre-legalization period, parents are responsible for notifying Beacon of their destination if the child is to be away from home for more than 72 hours. Parents are required by law to use an approved child safety seat or seat belt for their child whenever the child is transported by car.

13. Some children settle in rather easily but others continue to have separation problems or other difficulties. If the second parent plans to return to work, the parents should discuss day care plans with their Beacon adoption worker, and the best way to ease the transition (to avoid causing or aggravating separation problems). If, following placement, parents find that they or the child are experiencing minor or major problems in adjusting to their new relationship, they are responsible for notifying Beacon immediately. They have the right to counseling or other services to resolve problems. While the agency cannot absorb the cost of ongoing or intensive psychotherapy that the child and/or family might require, Beacon will make a referral if appropriate and will work cooperatively with the family's chosen therapist. If the parents so request, or if Beacon and the referral agency determine that it is in the best interest of the child or family that the placement not continue, Beacon or the referral agency will ordinarily assume responsibility for removing the child if he has not already been legally adopted overseas. (It is very rare that a child is removed against the parents' wishes. In fact, this has never happened in the 16-year personal experience of Beacon's Adoption Supervisor.)

14. Parents are responsible for submitting a petition for adoption to their county's probate court as soon as possible after the Beacon adoption worker completes a report to the court recommending finalization. (This court process usually occurs seven to ten months after placement, but sometimes there is a delay.) The parents are responsible for hiring an attorney experienced in intercountry adoption to prepare the petition and to represent them in court. They have the right to the agency's assistance in choosing an attorney and obtaining any documents or information required by the court. Parents are hereby advised that there exists a very slight risk that an adoption might not be finalized despite an agency's favorable recommendation, although this has never happened in the 16-year experience of Beacon's Adoption Supervisor.

15. The parents are ordinarily responsible for obtaining U.S. citizenship for any foreign-born child following finalization. Beacon will provide written instructions describing the procedure.

16. Parents have the right to update information in their records at any time by writing a letter to Beacon. Non-identifying information on the child can be given out to any birth parent who may seek such information. Any child adopted in Massachusetts has the legal right to obtain certain information concerning his or her birth family upon reaching the age of majority. Like other Massachusetts agencies, Beacon is not allowed to give out identifying information to adult adoptees or birth parents unless it has written permission from both parties on file. (In practice, foreign-born adopted adults wishing to search for their birth parents often obtain identifying information from their adoptive parents.)

17. Any parent with a complaint concerning Beacon or its policies has the right to present the complaint, verbally or in writing, to his or her adoption worker. If the client is still dissatisfied following a discussion with the worker, a written complaint may be sent to the worker's supervisor. A written reply will be sent within 30 days. The supervisor's decision may be appealed in writing if the client is still dissatisfied. The appeal letter should be sent within 30 days to the Director, who will reply within 30 days of receiving it.

18. Parents are hereby advised that Beacon's organizational structure allows for discussion of cases among staff members and consultants. Also, the Office for Children may choose any parents' records to read and discuss during its regular licensing studies and monitoring visits. In general, parents have the right to confidentiality. Exceptions to confidential communication and privileged communication may occur when Beacon personnel convey information about parents to a foreign or domestic court or agency. The parents, in signing this document, agree to the written or verbal exchange of any information concerning them and their proposed adoption between Beacon and any agency or court that is also involved with their proposed adoption of a child, or with any matter concerning their adoption.

19. Beacon does not participate in domestic legal risk placements, which are technically foster home placements since the child is placed with prospective adoptive parents before he is legally free for adoption. (This is not an issue in intercountry adoptions, since the child's U.S. visa cannot be approved until he is legally free for adoption and emigration.) Parents are free to transfer to another agency if the opportunity for a domestic legal risk adoption should arise.

20. Like all agencies, Beacon provides a service and cannot guarantee a specific outcome. Although all available information on the child is generally presented at referral, any child that is referred to parents may be delayed or prevented from being adopted because of a previously undiagnosed serious medical problem, inadequate documents, governmental changes, or some other factor beyond Beacon's control. If this happens, Beacon will seek to help the parents during this difficult time and will assist them in their efforts to resolve the difficulty. Undiagnosed and/or untreated problems may be present in any child who is placed for adoption, just as they may be present in any child born to its parents.

Adoptive parents have the right to decline to proceed with an adoption if a previously undetected problem becomes apparent in a child that has been referred to them or placed with them. If problems are diagnosed following a child's arrival, the parents should notify their adoption worker as soon as possible. They should also let Beacon know if other stressful family circumstances occur. If they feel that timely legalization of the adoption may not be in their best interest or the child's, Beacon will work with them toward a planned delay or another alternative.

21. Finally, parents have the right to sympathetic counseling on any problem, delay or frustration they may encounter. The Beacon staff consider themselves helpful partners to those wishing to adopt. They hope that parents will look upon the agency as a gate through the wall of paper work and procedures which may appear to separate them from their child, rather than as part of the wall! The staff of Beacon takes great pleasure in helping to unite those who want a child with a child who needs them.

In signing below, the parents acknowledge that they have read, understand and agree to the above, and that they have received a copy of this document for their records. They also agree that they will not hold Beacon Adoption Center, Inc. (or its personnel) responsible if they encounter difficulties in seeking to adopt a child, or difficulties with the child that they adopt.

Signature _____ Date _____
First Parent

Signature _____ Date _____
Second Parent

Financial Agreement with
Beacon Adoption Center, Inc.

Adoptive applicants are responsible for the following fees and other expenses, payable as follows:

a) a non-refundable application fee of $75, payable at the time the completed application is submitted

b) a home study fee of $1,500, payable in three $500 installments—at the time of the first post-application interview, the first individual interview, and the home visit. (Due to the high cost of billing, we ask applicants to provide a check at these interviews.) The home study fee reimburses Beacon Adoption Center for the expenses of overhead, interviews, the home study report, other paperwork, coordination with the source, and all support and direction that the applicants may require in the period prior to placement of a child. If the applicants do not complete the home study process or do not proceed to placement, a portion of the home study fee will be refunded. The amount to be refunded will be the balance remaining after the agency deducts the cost of hours of service already provided to the applicants.

c) an additional fee of $375 for those undertaking a parent-initiated adoption, payable at the time Beacon approves their choice of source.

d) a post-placement fee of $900, payable in two $450 installments at the time of the second and third post-placement visits. (This fee covers all post-placement interviews, paperwork, and overhead costs, but does not include the amount to be paid to the parents' local attorney, who will finalize the adoption in their county's probate court.) If the parents move out of the agency's area of service prior to finalization, any unexpended portion of the post-placement fee will be refunded according to the formula provided above.

e) fees and expenses which are payable to entities other than the agency, such as foreign agencies and orphanages, out-of-state agencies providing placement services, foreign attorneys and caretakers, doctors and medical facilities, hotels and airlines, consulates and immigration service offices, and anyone else providing services in connection with the adoption. These fees and expenses differ in each case and cannot be estimated by Beacon Adoption Center, Inc. It is the responsibility of the adoptive parents to estimate their own fees and expenses, calculating the sums in advance to insure they do not exceed the sum they have budgeted for adoption. They have the right to know in advance the exact fees to be charged by foreign or out-of-state placement sources and to have these amounts in writing before they contract with their chosen placement source, for their own protection.

f) the full cost of the child's support following placement, including the cost of any medical care which is not covered by their insurance.

I/We, the adoptive applicant(s), understand the foregoing information on fees and expenses. I/We agree to be responsible for paying all fees and expenses charged to me/us by Beacon Adoption Center, Inc. and other entities in connection with my/our adoption of a child or children. In the event I/we do not finalize the adoption following placement of the child, I/we will pay the child's expenses, such as foster care and medical expenses, until responsibility for these expenses is assumed by other entities.

(Signed) _____

(Signed) _____

Date _____

SHOULD YOU APPLY OR WORK WITH MORE THAN ONE AGENCY?

You may find two or three agencies with programs you are interested in. Do you apply to all of them? Most adoptive parents will tell you to apply to as many agencies as you can afford (application fees are almost always nonrefundable). But there are times when this is not appropriate.

Planning to adopt internationally? You should definitely apply to only one agency. In intercountry adoption, it is considered highly unethical to pursue more than one possibility at a time. Many foreign countries have laws against simultaneous adoptions of unrelated children. Future adoptions are jeopardized if a family withdraws from an adoption after foreign nationals have put a lot of effort into its successful completion and have begun legal proceedings to make the child theirs.

Applying to adopt a healthy Caucasian infant? You may want to apply to several agencies if the outcome is uncertain, especially if you are applying to traditional agencies with waiting lists. Be sure to find out if the agency has a policy against this.

If the agency does not have a waiting list, but instead lets the birth parent choose a family from personal profiles and if it appears to be placing babies in a time frame that is acceptable, you may want to apply only to that agency. If your application is not accepted at one agency, continue looking until you find another agency that welcomes your application.

There is nothing wrong with being on more than one waiting list initially. The time to decide comes when an agency wants to begin your home study. This means the agency is serious about placing a child with you in a reasonable time frame. Home studies are expensive and it's not fair to ask agencies to duplicate services. Many adoptive parents will suggest that you work with the agency you feel will place a child in the shortest amount of time.

Let us assume you have a local service agency conduct your home study, and you then explore two possible out-of-state sources for an American baby. Both agencies will charge you a fee to review your home study, and two review fees can total $1,000 or more. The longer you work with two agencies, the more money you may pay in fees, since agencies expect payment as services are rendered. Be honest with both placing agencies, and also with your local service agency about what you are doing and why.

THE PROCESS

Adopting an Infant Born in the U.S.

The process of adopting a child born in the United States differs only slightly from one agency to the next. The first step involves completing an application form or a pre-application form. All agencies ask for an application fee. This fee may be as low as $25 or as high as $500. This is the first fee you will pay and it is almost always nonrefundable. (Be cautious with any agency that requires an application fee that is extremely high compared to those of other agencies.)

If your pre-application or application is accepted, you may be asked to attend an orientation meeting if you have not already done so. Attendance is usually required for applicants living within the state and often it is compulsory for out-of-state residents as well.

At the orientation meeting you will learn more about the agency, its procedures, requirements for parents, its waiting list, and the type of children it places. This is your chance to ask questions about the agency. If you have not received a formal application, you may receive one at this meeting.

You will often be asked to attend a smaller group meeting, usually a month or two after the orientation session. Again, attendance may be required. You may meet first with six to ten couples. Then, after this meeting, each couple will be individually assessed by a staff member, and their application will be reviewed. After your assessment, and assuming all went well, you may be given a date when your home study will begin.

The home study process varies from one agency to the next but it usually consists of three or more interviews or groups sessions at the agency and one interview in your home. The evaluation is usually initiated when a placement is expected within one year. The process normally takes two to six months to complete and the fee is almost always due at the beginning.

During the waiting period you may be encouraged to take a CPR course, attend parenting classes, or both. While you are waiting for a referral, carry a beeper or use an answering machine so your social worker can contact you at any time. (If you plan to be out of town during this time, be sure to leave an itinerary with the agency.)

Finally, the day will arrive when the agency calls to tell you there is a child for you to consider. If you feel positive about the child's information, you will travel to the agency or hospital to meet your child. You will sign papers agreeing to clothe, feed, and provide shelter and medical care for the child even though the agency has legal custody. A copy of the background information on the birth parents and the child's medical records will be given to you. Your final fees are due now, unless you have made other arrangements with the agency.

If your child is born in another state, the agency will prepare copies of the child's medical and legal papers for the Interstate Compact on the Placement of Children (ICPC). Those papers will then be sent to the Interstate Compact office in the sending state which will transmit them to the corresponding office in your state, where they will be examined. Once they are approved, the Interstate Compact official will forward the papers to your local service agency. Your social worker will share the information in these papers with you if she hasn't already. If

Sample Private Agency Application

FRIENDS IN ADOPTION, INC.
44 South Street, P.O. Box 1228
Middleton Springs, VT   05757-1228

Date: _____

    We desire to adopt a child and knowing that the state of _____ has laws which govern the writing of procedure and the setting up of standards for adoptions, we request that Friends in Adoption, Inc., make such an investigation as is necessary in accordance with the state laws, rules, and regulations to determine that we are eligible to become adoptive parents.

    To facilitate the making of the investigation, we give the following information:

(1)   How long have you been involved in the adoption process? Please explain.

_____

_____

_____

_____

_____

(2)   Name: _____

Address: _____

City: _____ State: _____ Zip: _____

Home phone: _____

H's work phone: _____

W's work phone: _____

Fax # _____

Additional phone: _____ who? _____

HUSBAND'S INFORMATION
(Questions 3, 4, 5, 6 and 7)

(3)   Full name _____

Birthdate & birthplace _____

Nationality & race _____

Education (Name & # of years)

    High School _____

    College _____

    Graduate School _____

(4)   **Employment**

Occupation _____

Present Employer _____

# of years employed in present position _____

Annual wage _____

Previous employment (list work place[s] & # of years employed):

_____

_____

_____

Social Security # _____

(5) Marital Status

Married (date & place) _____

Date & Place of any previous marriages _____

_____

How & when terminated _____

_____

Names and ages of children from previous marriages _____

_____

_____

(6) Relatives

	Name	*Birthdate*	*Birthplace*	*Address*	*Occupation*
Father:					
Mother:					
Siblings:					

(7) Religious affiliation

Denomination	Name & Address	Participation

WIFE'S INFORMATION
(Questions 8, 9, 10, 11 and 12)

(8) Full name _____

Birthdate & birthplace _____

Nationality & race _____

Education (Name & # of years)
High School _____
College _____
Graduate School _____

(9) Employment

Occupation _____
Present Employer _____
# of years employed in present position _____
Annual wage _____
Previous employment (list work place[s] & # of years employed):

_____
_____
_____
_____

Social Security # _____

(10) Marital Status

Married (date & place) _____
Date & Place of any previous marriages _____

_____

How & when terminated _____

_____

Names and ages of children from previous marriages _____

_____
_____

(11) Relatives

	Name	Birthdate	Birthplace	Address	Occupation
Father:					
Mother:					
Siblings:					

(12) Religious affiliation

Denomination	Name & Address	Participation

(13) Children in immediate family:

Name	Birthdate	Birthplace	School/grade/occupation

(14) Others in home:

Name	Birthdate	Relationship

(15) Description of home: (type, # of rooms, # of bedrooms, type of heat, water supply, property size, proximity to schools, etc.)

_____

_____

_____

_____

_____

(16) References (not related):

	Full Name	Address	Telephone
A.			
B.			
C.			

(17) Prior application relative to adoption made to:

	Agency Name	Address	Year
A.			
B.			

(18) Have you ever been convicted of any charge other than minor traffic violation? If so, please explain:

_____

_____

_____

(19) Insurance Coverage Details:

Name of Insurance Company _____

Address _____

City _____ State _____ Zip _____

Phone _____ Policy # _____

At what point does your insurance coverage include an adopted child?

_____

_____

Feel free to call if you have questions

Vermont regulatory oversight pertains only to cases when FIA takes custody of a child relinquished in Vermont and places that child for adoption. Regulatory oversight ends with the finalization of the adoption.

Please be advised that FIA practices a "no refund" policy.

Courtesy of Friends in Adoption, Inc.

you accept the child, based on her medical report and the birth parents' medical and social histories, you will be asked to sign certain documents. In three to fourteen days, if there are no delays, you will be able to travel and bring your child home. It is against the law to bring the child into her new home state before ICPC's approval is received. However, some parents travel to the child's state so that they can spend time with her while they are waiting for ICPC clearance.

After you bring your child home, your local agency will supervise the placement for six months or more. The number of times your social worker visits your home will depend on state law and agency requirements. The last step of the adoption process is the finalization of the adoption in court, at which time the child becomes yours legally. In most states, this happens three to twelve months after he is placed in your home.

If you adopt from another state, you may not be required to attend orientation and group assessment meetings. However, if the sessions are mandatory you should plan a minimum of two or three trips to the agency, including the trip to bring your child home. If the finalization is to be in the state where the placing agency is located, you may need to appear there in court.

Agency-Initiated Intercountry Adoption

As prospective parents you may have to work with two agencies to adopt a child from another country—a local service agency in your home state, which will complete a home study for you, and a placing agency (often in another state) that will locate and place the child. The second agency will be needed if you cannot find an agency in your state that places children from the country you wish to adopt from. Even if you find that you only need to work with one agency in your state for both a home study and the child's placement, you have the option of choosing a different placing agency if you prefer its programs or fees.

If you work with two agencies, you will need an agency in your state to complete your home study. After your application has been accepted by a placing agency, you will then send it your approved home study and other necessary documents. (See the chapter on intercountry adoption for more information and a list of the documents that are needed for an intercountry adoption.)

Once the placing agency accepts your home study and dossier, it will locate a child for you. Once the child is located, the agency will share the medical information (and usually a picture) of the child with you. If you accept the referral, the birth certificate and proof of relinquishment or orphanhood may eventually be mailed to you. Then you can file a petition with INS for the child's visa. (In some cases you will obtain these documents later, such as when you travel to get the child. In this case you would file the orphan petition with the U.S. consulate or embassy in the foreign country.)

With the help of your source's representative in the other country, the placing agency will arrange for your documents to be submitted to the foreign court. After the paperwork has been approved, a visa granted, and (if necessary) the adoption finalized in the foreign country, your child will be allowed to enter the United States.

You should re-adopt the child under your state's laws, even if the adoption was finalized in the foreign country. In fact, some agencies require this to ensure that the adoption is secure. If the birth mother or another relative came to the United States to reclaim the child, a sympathetic judge could overturn the foreign adoption if the child had not been re-adopted in the United States. Also, a cousin or uncle could challenge your child's right to inherit from his adoptive grandparents on the grounds that the foreign decree failed to make him their true grandchild. (You will need an agency's postplacement services in order to adopt or re-adopt in your state.)

The final steps are to obtain American citizenship and a social security card for your child. You can file for citizenship as soon as your adoption is finalized. There are two ways to accomplish this. One is to file Form N-402, the Application to File Petition for Naturalization on Behalf of a Child. This requires an INS hearing six months later. The second way is to file Form N-643, the Application for a Certificate of Citizenship on Behalf of an Adopted Child, with your local INS office. The second way is usually much faster and is the choice of most adoptive parents, because it enables a child to become a citizen by virtue of being a United States citizen's child instead of through naturalization.

PRESERVING A PRIVILEGE

Through the years, there have been many rumors about Americans' motivations for wanting to adopt children from other countries. Although it's hard to believe, we have been falsely accused of such atrocities as using the children for medical experiments and organ donors and raising them to be servants in our homes. It is very difficult for people in some countries to understand why we would want to adopt their children, especially when they are past infancy or have special needs.

It is a privilege, not a right, for Americans to be allowed to adopt children from other countries. As adoptive parents of a child born in another country, you can show your appreciation by sending letters and photographs to your adoption source. Some foreign sources and many U.S. agencies make this a requirement for a specified period of time. Why not send a letter and picture each year until your child reaches adulthood? Let them see how well your son or daughter is doing. Help pave the way for all of the other prospective parents that will follow in your footsteps. Help preserve the privilege to adopt internationally.

The Home Study Process

A home study is an evaluation written by a licensed social worker (sometimes referred to as a caseworker) regarding the suitability of single people or married couples to become adoptive parents. The term also refers to the process leading up to the report—a series of interviews with the prospective adoptive parents. The interviews may be conducted in a group setting with other pre-adoptive families, or they may be held individually with each family.

In many cases, the entire home study is written by a social worker. However, it is becoming more common for families involved in an agency adoption to be asked to contribute an autobiographical statement to the home study documents. Detailed guidelines for writing an autobiographical statement are usually provided by the agency.

WHEN DO YOU NEED A HOME STUDY?

When you are pursuing an adoption through a public or private agency, you must have an adoptive home study before a child can be placed in your home. In a few states a home study may not be required before placement in an independent adoption, but must be completed within a specific time frame, after placement and always before the adoption is finalized.

According to the Interstate Compact for the Placement of Children, the home study must be completed for an interstate adoption before the child can be placed in the home of the adopting parents. In the case of an intercountry adoption, the INS requires a home study (completed by a licensed agency) before a child can enter the United States for the purpose of adoption.

Beacon Adoption Center, Inc.

66 LAKE BUEL ROAD, GREAT BARRINGTON, MA 01230

Telephone (413) 528-2749   (413) 528-5036

APPLICATION FOR A HOME STUDY FOR INTERCOUNTRY ADOPTION

Names(s) _____

Address _____

Home phone _____ Nearest relative's phone _____

	MALE APPLICANT	FEMALE APPLICANT
Age:		
Birthdate:		
Birthplace:		
Marriage date:		
Where married:		
Citizenship:		
General health:		
Occupation:		
Employer:		
Date employed:		
Education:		
Religion, if any:		
Annual salary:		
Other income:		
Source:		
Life insurance:		
Savings:		
Other assets:		
Type:		
Daytime phone:		
Hours to call:		

OTHER HOUSEHOLD MEMBERS	RELATIONSHIP	BIRTHDATE	ADOPTION DATE

List names and birthdates of children who do not live with you _____

How did you hear about Beacon Adoption Center? _____

Does your home have smoke detectors on each floor? _____ (If not, please arrange to have them installed before the home visit; this is a state requirement for adoption.)

Does your home use well water? _____ (If so, please have it tested for both coliform bacteria and fecal coliform bacteria soon after sending in your application and give us the test results for your file.) See "Physical Requirements for Adoptive Homes."

Has either of you ever been arrested? _____ (Routine, thorough police checks are required by law and will reveal even an expunged or sealed police record. Minor offenses committed many years ago are usually not a deterrent to home study approval, but to avoid future problems, <u>please</u> share this information with us openly at this time. Please discuss any arrests fully in your personal statement.)

Does either of you have a have a medical problem? _____ Have you ever had mental or emotional disturbances? _____ or marital problems in the current marriage? _____ or any alcohol or drug dependency? _____ (Explain "yes" answers in your personal statement.)

<u>Child desired</u>: Do you have a strong preference as to boy or girl? _____

Preferred age range _____ Acceptable age range _____

Are you open to siblings? _____ Sex and age range _____

Is a known minor, correctible medical problem acceptable? _____

Could you consider a child with a known handicap? _____

Which racial backgrounds could you comfortably accept in your son or daughter?

_____ Asian _____ Black _____ Caucasian _____ East Indian _____ Latin American Indian

_____ mestizo (Latin American Indian/Caucasian) _____ moreno (black/Caucasian)

<u>Note</u>: It may be difficult to obtain full Caucasian children overseas. It will give you more options if you can also consider at least one other racial background.

If you and your spouse have different last names, please indicate a file name for your family which corresponds to the surname that you plan to give the child. (We recommend a single, non-hyphenated surname for any foreign-born child.)_____

I/we, the applicant(s), believe that I/we meet the requirements for a home study as described in the agency's introductory material. I/we are are enclosing a non-refundable application fee of $75, personal statement(s), a signed financial agreement, and a Rights and Responsibilities Form. I/we understand that doctors' letters, reference letters and other documents are to be submitted later. Before the home study begins, I/we will try to make a tentative choice of at least one or two prospective referral agencies and/or a promising source of a parent-initiated adoption.

(signed) _____   (signed) _____
        Male applicant   Female applicant

(date) _____   (date) _____

Courtesy of Beacon Adoption Center, Inc. Other local service agencies are welcome to modify Beacon's forms and agreements for their own use. However, written permission to do so must be obtained from Beacon in advance, by writing the agency at 66 Lake Buel Road, Great Barrington, MA 01230.

HOW LONG DOES IT TAKE?

The entire home study process can take a few days, a couple of weeks, or several months. It is hard to predict how long it will take because every agency has its own approach. In some independent adoptions the court may appoint a social worker to conduct the home study, and if the baby is already born or due very soon, the evaluation will be completed in a day or two. The number of social workers employed to conduct home studies, and the number of applicants the agency is currently working with, will affect the timetable.

Since agencies differ in their approaches, and since the type of adoption can also influence the timing, it is hard to estimate how long an agency home study will take. Ordinarily, it requires two to six months to complete and is valid for at least one year.

When the home study expires, it can be updated easily. The update is generally based on one visit to your home. The social worker will want to know about any changes that have occurred since the original study was done. Maybe your mother-in-law lives with you now, or you have moved across town. The social worker must know about these changes so that your home study will be current. Your caseworker will also talk with you to confirm that both of you still want to adopt, and if Mom has moved in, he will want to talk with her also.

As clients you can speed up the home study process by providing your social worker with the required references, visiting your doctor as soon as possible for physical exams, and submitting all the paperwork on time.

WHAT WILL IT COST?

Home study fees may vary considerably among agencies as endowments and overhead vary. Even agencies' prices in the same city can be hundreds of dollars apart. Most private agencies have a set fee for a home study, but there are some agencies that base the fee on your income. One couple contacted three private agencies in their hometown. The first agency quoted a flat fee of $500. The second cited a fee of $2,500 based on their income, and the third said its fee was $750.

After learning about another agency from a support group member, the couple explored that possibility. Although the agency was almost 100 miles from their home, it agreed to conduct the home study for $360! It pays to shop around, especially if other considerations are roughly equal.

When you are considering a particular agency, be sure it has experience in writing the type of home study you need. A home study for an intercountry adoption will read much differently than one for a U.S. adoption. A home study for an intercountry adoption must contain the information needed by the foreign source and must be simply and clearly written so it will translate well. Otherwise, it might be rejected and delay your adoption for several months to a year or more.

Tom and Barbara, a couple in their early thirties, decided to pursue an independent adoption in El Salvador. A local religious agency conducted their home study after assuring Barbara and Tom they were qualified and experienced in writing a study for a foreign adoption. "We had no reason to doubt them," recalls Barbara. "After the study was completed we had it translated and prepared for the foreign source. We then mailed the document to El Salvador, in care of a judge who was a contact person for adoptions to the United States." According to Tom, the judge kept a file of prospective parents in his desk drawer, and when he had a child to place he would choose a family and notify them. One year later, Barbara and Tom were notified by their contact person in the United States that their home study had not translated well and they would need to complete another one if they still wished to proceed with an adoption from El Salvador.

"I was so upset, so angry!" says Barbara. "We literally wasted one full year because our home study had not been prepared properly. I always tell people it isn't enough to ask if an agency is experienced in writing a study for an international adoption, you should talk with others who have adopted successfully using that agency." Nine months later, after submitting another home study, Barbara and Tom finally received a referral for an infant who became their son Daniel.

If you are comfortable with the agency fee and feel confident that you will receive the type of home study you need, contact the agency for an application form. Some agencies require a written request for a home study. The application often satisfies this requirement, but some agencies insist you write a personal letter asking for this service.

Whether the waiting list is long or short, try to get your name added to it. Should you find an adoption possibility and need a home study quickly, your application will be on file. Usually agencies respond promptly and will complete your home study quickly if you have located a child to adopt.

A home study prepared by a local agency for an out-of-state agency will be subject to review fees by the placing agency. In other words, once your home study is completed locally it will be forwarded to the placing agency, which will charge a fee to examine it. Agencies usually list review fees in their information packets. Review fees are common and often cost around $500.

Expenses add up quickly, so spend your money wisely. Consider the mistake Matt and Lynn, a couple in their mid-thirties, made. They decided to have their home study completed before they really knew the type of adoption they were interested in.

"Since we planned to pursue an infant adoption privately, we wanted our home study completed just in case it was needed quickly," says Lynn. "So we requested a study from a local agency." After the home study was completed, Matt and Lynn decided to pursue an infant adoption through another agency in their state. "At the orientation meeting we learned our home study would not be accepted by the agency," says Matt. "State law required the agency to conduct its own study."

Matt and Lynn's original study cost them $750. The second study totaled $825. "The agency did refer to our original study," says Lynn, "but only for basic information which we could have given verbally. In reality, we threw away $750." The best approach: Do your homework before beginning a study on your own.

DOCUMENTS YOU WILL NEED

Once you receive word that your application for a home study has been accepted, you will be expected to provide the agency or a licensed social worker with certain pertinent documents by the time of the first meeting, or at a later date.

These documents usually include:

- Marriage certificate
- Birth certificates
- Divorce decrees, if applicable
- Death certificate for former spouse, if applicable
- Insurance policies
- Letter from employer(s)
- Financial statements or bank letters
- Medical reports
- A copy of your federal income tax return form from the previous year

You will also be asked to provide the names of personal references. Three to six references appear to be the average. The application form may ask for three references from friends that know you well and two relatives. Or you may need one reference from your employer, one from your church, one from a relative, and four from friends. It is never too soon to start thinking about who you will ask for a personal reference.

Usually, references are contacted by the agency and asked to write a letter in support of your application. Excerpts from these letters are often incorporated into your home study document. If you are fortunate, your social worker will let you see these reference letters. Reading these glowing reports can be a great ego booster.

Choose your references carefully. The social worker must hear from people who really know you well—people who can vouch that you have a stable marriage, are of good moral character, and would parent a child with love, maturity, and understanding.

SUCCESSFULLY COMPLETING THE HOME STUDY

If you are a first-time adopter, the thought of a home study may send chills down your spine. You are not alone. First-time adopters all have the same fear: What if we are not approved for an adoptive placement?

The truth is that nearly all families "pass" the home study. If you want to be a parent because you genuinely enjoy children, you are already halfway there. If you are of good character, manage your money well, are emotionally and physically able to care for a child, and have no criminal record within the last fifteen years, you will pass the home study.

It is important to remember a social worker is not out to get you. One of the reasons she is there is to help you build a family. As she assesses you, she also hopes that she can approve you for an adoptive placement.

Your caseworker should also help prepare you for adoptive parenthood. Because adoption is a lifelong commitment, not an event that happens on one particular day, your social worker should help you prepare for issues unique to adoptive families. You may be encouraged to meet with other adoptive parents and to read books on adoption and child care. You may be required to attend child-care classes with other prospective adoptive parents. Such activities are designed to prepare you for the road ahead.

The home study process is an ideal opportunity for you to ask specific questions or address concerns regarding the child's medical condition, behavior, schooling, or adoption in general. Do not be afraid to ask questions, no matter how insignificant they may seem.

If you like your social worker and she appears to like you, you will probably enjoy meeting with her and will sense if you'll be approved for a placement. What a great feeling that is. But what if your worker makes you feel terribly ill at ease; disagrees with your views on specific parenting issues, such as which discipline techniques are best; and seems extremely judgmental? (This is rarely the case, but a few families have encountered problems like this.)

Make the best of the relationship by trying to improve communication with the social worker. Stay calm and work through the first interview as best as you can. Later you can approach members of your support group. It may be that someone in the group has worked with your social worker and can advise you as to the best way to proceed.

Then discuss your concerns with your social worker. If the situation does not improve and you fear that you may not be approved, talk with the supervisor at the agency and ask to be evaluated by another social worker. Be prepared to explain your reasons for this request and be aware that changing social workers will complicate and delay the home study process.

Once a home study is successfully completed, you will receive a letter from the agency approving you for an adoptive placement. Depending on the agency's policy, you may also receive a copy of the home study report including the agency's recommendation for placement signed by your social worker. You are now one step closer to adopting a child.

WHAT IF YOU ARE NOT APPROVED?

What if, despite all your efforts to improve your communication with agency personnel, you are not recommended for an adoptive placement? First, find out the exact reason or reasons you were not approved. Ask that this information be put in writing if it has not been done already. It is possible that some casual comments of yours may have been misinterpreted. One couple, the Howards, had remarked several times during the home study it would have been much easier if they could have "had a baby of their own." The social worker took offense at this phrasing, which is actually a common, though unfortunate, distinction in our society between children by birth and adopted children. Because her main responsibility was to find the best possible homes for the children the agency placed, the social worker assumed adoption was "second best" for the Howards and did not recommend them for a placement. The Howards appealed the decision to the worker's supervisor and eventually they were approved for a placement.

In another case, a husband made racial slurs during the home study process. The worker was justifiably concerned, especially because the couple wanted to pursue the international adoption of a minority child. Consequently, the application to adopt was denied. The couple went before a review board, but it was decided that the husband needed to work through his prejudices before adopting.

Bear in mind that the vast majority of licensed social workers are mature, intelligent, and warm human beings who have been well trained. It is rare for a social worker to misread casual remarks, so do not hesitate to freely share your thoughts and feelings with her. If you are paralyzed by fear and give partial, stilted, or unauthentic answers, your social worker may feel that he cannot approve you because he does not *know* you. Try to relax and be yourselves so that the social worker can be fully effective in his goal of helping you prepare emotionally for adoption.

If you are asked questions you do not understand, ask for clarification. Do not give an answer and hope it is correct. Above all, do not lie. It is extremely important to be truthful during the home study process. If you lie and are caught, you may lose the opportunity to adopt. No one is perfect. If you have made mistakes and learned from them, talk about them before someone else does. Agencies are looking for sincere, honest, loving people to place children with. They are not looking for perfect parents—perfect parents do not exist.

In specific areas of questioning such as infertility, decide who will answer the questions. Let the spouse who can speak about the infertility, without becoming emotional, do the talking. It is assumed, if you are trying to adopt, that you have come to terms with your infertility. In fact, at one time, there were agencies that insisted prospective adoptive parents practice birth control during the adoption process.

Before you ask someone to serve as a reference, ask how he or she would feel about recommending you for adoption. We would all like to believe that our friends and family would support us no matter what the endeavor, but that is not always the case. Always request permission before supplying references' names. If a person hesitates, do not pressure him or her. Find someone who is pleased to be a part of your efforts to add to your family. Be sure your references know the age and the type of child you want to adopt and how important adopting a child is to you.

Sue and Don, both forty years old, were the subject of a rather negative reference letter written by friends in their forties who had grown children. The couple wrote they were pleased to learn that Sue and Don wanted to adopt because they felt the couple would be excellent parents. However, they were shocked to learn the couple was trying to adopt a baby. The letter said, "We hope Sue and Don have given much thought to adopting an infant and hope they realize they will have to give up nearly all of their outside activities. This greatly worries us since we do not feel they understand the magnitude of this decision. We hope you will discuss this with Sue and Don and convince them that they are much better suited to adopt an older child because they are really too old to parent an infant."

Don and Sue admitted that they had not asked this couple if they were willing to give a reference in their behalf. They assumed, because they had known the couple for many years, that their friends would give them a positive reference whatever the circumstances. The rule here is never assume anything. Clarify the details with your references, and move on to others if you detect a lack of support.

Is a negative reference enough to halt the entire process for the prospective parents? No! Rarely would one negative response deny you approval for a placement. It is rare for any couple to receive even one.

If your application to adopt a child is not approved, try to find out the reason. Not all agencies will share this information with the applicants. In fact, a few agencies clearly state on their application forms that they have the right to discontinue the home study at any time, for any reason, and will not disclose their reasons. If such a statement disturbs you, then look for another agency to work with. Most agencies will discuss the problems they see. Some will help you work through what they perceive to be problem areas so you can eventually adopt.

Most adoptive parents will tell you their home study went smoothly. Some will even say they were glad they were given the opportunity to examine their motives for wanting to parent.

THE TYPE OF QUESTIONS TO EXPECT

What kinds of questions can you expect during the home study? "All sorts," laughs one adoptive father. "The questions ranged from very personal, emotional issues and financial and goal-oriented questions to our views on child rearing. We discussed why we wanted a child, what we felt we had to offer a child, and what we expected from a child."

A home study report will usually be about four to six pages long, typed single spaced, although some are much longer. One couple's report was more than forty-five pages long, most of it consisting of their autobiographical statements. But keep in mind that although most agencies require applicants to write personal statements, few incorporate them into their home studies and most prefer that they be limited to a few pages.

QUESTIONS YOU MAY BE ASKED

While each home study will vary depending on the particular agency and circumstances, here are some general questions that you may be asked to respond to:

Background Information

- What schools did you attend? What diplomas or degrees did you earn?
- Where have you worked and in what capacity? What are the dates of employment?
- How old are your parents, or what were their ages when they died?
- What are your parents' occupations or former occupations if retired or deceased?
- What was your relationship like with your parents as a child? How has it changed now that you are an adult?
- What values were you taught as a child? Would you raise your child with the same values?
- How were you disciplined as a child? Would you discipline your children the same way?
- What types of activities did you participate in as a child with your family? With other children?
- What types of outside activities did you participate in during grade school, high school, and college?
- What is the number and sex of your siblings along with their ages, occupations, health, and family size? What is your relationship with each?

Marriage Stability

- How did you meet each other and when?
- How long did you date before you married?

Sample Guidelines for
Personal Statements

Each adoptive parent should write a paragraph or two on each of the following subjects. (Please write clearly or type.) This will serve the purpose of acquainting us with you and your family and will enable us to make better use of our interview time. *Please use the subject headings we have provided.* We hope this exercise will be as helpful to you as it will be to us!

Description: Please describe yourself in terms of physical appearance, personality traits, skills, interests, and strengths.

Type of child desired: Discuss your preferences as to the sex, age, skin color, and nationality of your child. What do you see as the reasons for these preferences? Indicate whether you can be flexible in any of these areas. What type of known medical problems, if any, could you consider in your child?

Reasons for applying: Why do you want to adopt? And what are your reasons for choosing a foreign-born child? Discuss your hopes and expectations for the child as he or she grows to adolescence and adulthood. How do your family, friends, and community feel about intercountry adoption?

Reflections on marriage: We would like each married applicant to describe his or her partner and the relationship. Include what you see as your strengths as a couple. How do you handle decisions and conflict? In what respects would you like your marriage to change and grow? Briefly mention shared interests and family activities, and how you divide up responsibilities. What have been your feelings about infertility, if applicable, and how have you dealt with the problem? Please mention any previous marriages, including their dates.

If you're not married at present, please discuss your close relationships and any past marriages. Include your thoughts and feelings about marrying in the future. As a single parent, how would you deal with a crisis in your life or the child's? Who in your support system of friends and relatives can be counted on to help with the day-to-day stress and responsibilities of parenthood?

Your early life: Give a complete and concise description of your childhood, adolescence and family relationships. (We realize that no one has ever had perfect parents or a trouble-free life. But we also recognize that coping with difficult experiences can help people become stronger individuals. The more honest you can be with us about your feelings and relationships, the more helpful we can be when the adoption process becomes stressful.)

Children: Briefly describe any children that you already have, including their personalities, interests, strengths, and challenges. What is your relationship with each of them? How will they be affected by the proposed adoption?

Employment: Briefly discuss your present work, any earlier long-term employment, and future vocational goals. How do you feel about your work? Do you plan to continue in your job? If so, estimate the leave of absence you would obtain when the child comes and discuss proposed child care arrangements after it ends. (Note: There is no set requirement, but we hope that one parent can take at least a few months following placement, and the other a minimum of two weeks. This will greatly facilitate the child's adjustment.)

Home, community, and school: Describe your house or apartment, the type of neighborhood you live in, and community resources for children. What are the local schools like? How are children and adolescents of other races accepted in your town or city?

Religion and values: In what religious tradition were you raised? Comment briefly on your thoughts about God and religion. In what faith, if any, would the child be raised? Discuss the moral and spiritual values that you would seek to impart to your child, whether or not organized religion is important to you, especially as those relate to the larger community and people of other races and nationalities.

Finances: Will you feel comfortable with the financial responsibility of another family member? Do you have a reserve fund or a generous relative to help out in the event of an emergency? Do you plan to take out a loan to cover your adoption expenses? (Many people exercise this option.) If you are a homeowner, try to estimate the market value of your house and land.

Health: Do you have any disabling condition or any chronic medical problems? If so, mention how these are being controlled or managed. Is there a known cause of infertility? Comment on your general health and emotional well-being. If you have had emotional difficulties, or problems with alcohol or drugs, please discuss these and provide the name of a therapist or doctor who will recommend you for adoption.

Parenting skills: What experience have you had with children of various ages? How do you tend to guide and discipline children in your care? Mention what you think would be your strengths as a parent, and any tendencies you'd need to watch in yourself. Discuss what you see as the special rewards and problems of parenthood.

Courtesy of Beacon Adoption Center, Inc. Other local service agencies are welcome to modify Beacon's forms and agreements for their own use. However, written permission to do so must be obtained from Beacon in advance, by writing the agency at 66 Lake Buel Road, Great Barrington, MA   01230.

- Describe your marriage and your partner.
- What are the strengths and weaknesses you see in your marriage?
- How do you handle disagreements?
- How do you make decisions?
- What goals are you working toward in your marriage?
- Have you given thought to how a child will change your lifestyle? Are you prepared to make the required changes?
- Do you think a child will change your relationship with your spouse? In what ways?
- How will you handle child-care responsibilities?
- Explain your views on disciplining a child. Are you in agreement?
- If you both work, what type of child-care arrangements will be made?

Infertility

- How long have you been trying to have a baby?
- Have you consulted an infertility specialist?
- What were the results of your medical workup?
- Have you come to terms with your infertility? Have you let yourselves grieve for the child that may not be born to you?
- Have you fully changed your focus from pregnancy to adoptive parenthood?

Experience with Children

- Do you baby-sit for friends or siblings?
- Did you baby-sit while you were in school?
- Did you care for siblings as you were growing up?
- Are you, or have you been, involved in any children's organizations?
- Have you worked with children or been involved in volunteer work with children?

Religion

Religious views are a strong focus if you are working with a denominational agency and may involve many more in-depth questions than you might expect. The questions outlined here are more basic and may be asked by a social worker at any agency.

- What is your religious affiliation, if any?
- Are you a member of a church or synagogue?
- How often do you attend services?
- How often do you do volunteer work for your church or synagogue? In what capacity?
- What are your plans for your child's religious education?

Health

Most of the necessary information will be taken from the medical forms your physician has completed, but you may be asked to further explain some aspect of your health. Your worker may want to know more about the medication you take and how it affects you. She may request more facts from you or your doctor if you have a medical problem or a physical disability. Unless your condition is life threatening or would prevent you from functioning as a parent, it should not be a problem.

Hobbies and Life-style

- What types of activities do you and your spouse enjoy together or with friends?
- What types of activities do you enjoy separately?

Financial Status

- What is your combined monthly or yearly income?
- What are your assets and liabilities?
- Do you own your own home? What is its market value, your equity, and your mortgage payment?
- Do you have a pension plan?
- Do you carry medical insurance? Will coverage include your adopted child from birth, at placement, or after the adoption is finalized?
- What is the name of your insurance company?
- Do you carry disability insurance?
- How much life insurance do you carry?

Previous Marriage

- Date of your first marriage?
- Date of your divorce?
- What types of problems did you encounter during your first marriage?
- Did you seek marriage counseling?
- Who filed for divorce and why?
- If you have children from a previous marriage, do you have custody?
- If not, do you pay child support? How much? How often do you see your children?
- What types of activities do you engage in when you are with your children?
- What is your relationship with your spouse's children?

Foreign and Minority Adoption

- Can you love a child as your son or daughter who is different from you?
- Can you accept a child with an unknown family background, and little-known medical history?
- How do you plan to introduce your child to his heritage?
- Will you seek out children and adults of the same race or culture for your child to identify with?
- Have you given thought to whom your child will date?
- Have you given thought to whom your child will marry?
- Can both of your families accept a child of another race? Do you realize your family will be interracial for generations? Are you comfortable with this?
- How will your neighbors feel about a child whose skin is lighter or darker and whose facial features are different from yours?
- How will you handle remarks and questions about your family from strangers?
- How will you handle a grandparent (or another relative) who will not accept your child as a family member?

Feelings about Birth Parents

- How do you feel about a woman who becomes pregnant when unmarried?
- What are your feelings about a mother who makes an adoption plan for her baby?
- Do you believe a birth mother does not love her baby and will eventually forget the child she gave birth to?
- How will you feel if your child eventually wants to search for her birth parents, or wants to travel to her country of birth?
- Will you be able to relay positive feelings about the birth parents to your child, no matter what the circumstances may have been?

Miscellaneous Questions

- Why do you want to adopt?
- What type of child do you want to adopt and why?
- How flexible can you be about the child's age, race, and health?
- What qualities do you have that you feel will make you a good parent?
- What goals would you like to see your child achieve?

Now that you have an idea about the types of questions that may be asked during the home study, think about how you will respond.

Ask other adoptive parents about the questions they were asked. One prospective mother, Patti, from Fremont, Indiana, says, "I was asked what thoughts came to mind when I heard certain words like 'anger,' 'noise,' and 'loud.' For a few seconds it threw me off track. I hope I answered appropriately." She did, and she and her husband now have a beautiful baby boy.

WHEN THE SOCIAL WORKER COMES TO VISIT

At least one session with your social worker will take place in your home. This visit serves two purposes: it allows the caseworker to meet with you in your familiar surroundings, where he hopes to acquire a more accurate impression of you as a family; and it gives your worker the opportunity to see your house, including the bedroom where your child will sleep. Your social worker only wants to know that you have thought about which room will belong to your child. He does not expect to find this room already furnished and decorated. Your social worker does expect to find a clean, safe house. "Clean" does not mean immaculate (although most people needlessly clean for days).

If you have children, the social worker will not expect them to be on their best behavior. Most young children act up at the home visit, in response to the subtle tension they sense in their parents, and it's important not to overreact to normally naughty behavior.

Safety is a major consideration and as your social worker tours your house, he will check to see whether it is safe. So you'll be prepared, you may need to take a few hours to install simple handrails on all stairways; put up photo-electric, battery-powered smoke detectors on each floor; or move flammable materials away from woodstoves and furnaces. Are there fire extinguishers in the house, especially in the kitchen? Do you have cabinets above floor level in which you can secure cleaning materials, bug sprays, and other hazardous items? Are your smoke detectors in working order? What is your plan of evacuation in case of a fire?

The social worker will notice if there is no fence around your in-ground pool or, if your property runs along a freeway, that you don't have a backyard fence. Take a walk around your house before the worker visits to see if you need to improve areas to guarantee a child's safety. Even if you are unable to work on the trouble spots before your home visit, at least mention that you are aware of the hazards and comment on what you plan to do to correct the situation.

Offer your social worker a cup of coffee or a soft drink along with a snack. This simple act shows you are nuturing people. Have pictures of your families displayed in the house. One couple had a collage of family pictures in their foyer. It was the first thing their social worker noticed and commented on. Use this opportunity to show your love for family and family life.

Parents who have already been through the adoption process will tell you not to worry about the home visit. Usually, no one will look through your cabinets or closets or give your house the white glove test. But if this possibility worries you, follow the example of one prospective mother. Directly addressing the concern, she asked, "I have heard some social workers look through closets and check under the beds. Will you be doing that in our home?" Their social worker assured them he would not. Another woman remembers, "The house

Physical Requirements for Adoptive Homes

(excerpted from current regulations of the Department of Social Services of the Commonwealth of Massachusetts)

1. The adoptive family home shall be clean, safe, free of obvious fire and other hazards, and of sufficient size to accommodate comfortably all members of the household.
2. The adoptive family home shall have adequate lighting and ventilation, hot and cold water supply, plumbing, electricity, and heat.
3. The adoptive family home shall have sufficient furniture to allow each child to sleep in a separate bed and to have adequate storage space for the child's personal belongings.
4. The adoptive family home shall be equipped with smoke detectors in working order.
5. If the adoptive family uses well water, it shall be tested and determined safe, and a report of the test furnished to the licensee.

NOTE FROM BEACON: It is not necessary to own your own home. Your house or apartment does not need to be large. If you are in the process of building, you are not required to wait until the house is complete. By the time of the home visit, please try to have your house or apartment child-safe indoors and outside—or plans to make it so soon if carpentry work is involved. (If you have questions about this, ask us.) We don't expect a major cleaning effort, and we don't look in closets or under beds!

If you do not yet have smoke detectors, we recommend that you install the photo-electric battery-powered type.

If you have well water and it does not pass the required tests for coliform bacteria and fecal coliform bacteria, there are solutions to this problem which we can discuss with you.

Courtesy of Beacon Adoption Center, Inc. Other local service agencies are welcome to modify Beacon's forms and agreements for their own use. However, written permission to do so must be obtained from Beacon in advance, by writing the agency at 66 Lake Buel Road, Great Barrington, MA   01230.

looked great but it took her about two minutes to look around. She never looked in the bathroom or in our bedroom. I was disappointed and relieved at the same time."

COPIES OF YOUR HOME STUDY REPORT

After the time, energy, and worry you have put into your home study, you should ask for a copy of the report. Many agencies routinely provide a copy, but not all do. There are agencies that will tell you they cannot give you a copy, that it is against their policy. If you cannot obtain a copy of your study, ask if you can read it at the agency.

If your agency won't allow you to read the written report, you can protest. "Agencies cannot withhold this information," says Debra Smith, director of the National Adoption Information Clearinghouse in Rockville, Maryland. "The Freedom of Information Act states you have the right to see what has been written about you. Parties who are being denied access should ask their attorney to write a letter to the agency. If this letter does not get results, there are, of course, further legal steps that can be taken." These steps include appealing to your local court by filing a federal Freedom of Information Act request, in addition to filing a complaint with your state's adoption agency licensing department. However, if your home study has been approved and you are awaiting a child through the same agency that is withholding the report, it is usually counterproductive to pressure the agency to accommodate your wish to see the report.

Your home study report can be very valuable to you as prospective adoptive parents, particularly if you are adopting through a second agency. Be sure the agency knows you want a copy before your home study begins.

Your home study can open doors that were previously locked. For instance, assume you find a picture of a child available for adoption and you call the child's placing agency for more information. Because you have a current study, the worker may be willing to give you some information over the telephone and send an application immediately. Or you may hear that a social worker at another agency is looking for parents for a biracial baby that you are interested in. You might also hear that an adoption attorney is looking for a couple who meets a birth mother's requirements, one of which is very unusual but one that you meet. In any one of these situations you can send your home study to the adoption source immediately without having to depend on your local agency's social worker to act promptly.

AN EXAMPLE OF A HOME STUDY REPORT

Having the opportunity to review someone's home study report can help alleviate the fears that surround this evaluation. You, no doubt,

Adoption Home Study

SOURCE OF REFERRAL:

Mr. and Mrs. Wells contacted this agency to inquire about having the agency prepare an adoptive home study for the purpose of an interstate adoption. The Wellses were self-referred.

CONTACTS:

The home study was conducted to achieve the goals of: evaluating the physical, mental, moral, and financial capabilities of the prospective adoptive parents; assessing their ability to rear and educate a child properly; and determining if their home is an acceptable living accommodation for a child and themselves.

The couple was seen three times at the agency and once in their home between December 18, 1991 and January 11, 1992.

HISTORY OF ADOPTIVE PARENTS:

Paternal:

Mr. Robert Wells is six feet four inches in height and weighs 181 pounds. Mr. Wells is of English and German ancestry with a light complexion and brown hair, and brown eyes.

Born on July 18, 1952, Mr. Wells has lived all of his life in Anytown, U.S.A. Mr. Wells' parents are still living and in good health. His father has been retired for one year from managing a hardware store and is 65 years old. His mother worked from 1964 to 1985 as a third grade school teacher at an Anytown parochial school. She is 64 years old.

Mr. Wells described his childhood as happy and full of many activities. He feels he was taught a strong work ethic, as evidenced by his keeping a paper route during grade school, working at a country club during high school, and working at J.C. Penney during his senior year of high school and first year of college.

After graduating from high school in 1970, Mr. Wells attended the University of Anytown in the School of Business. He was also in ROTC. After college, he went to work for a television station selling advertising. Three years later, Mr. Wells took a position as regional sales manager at Anytown Advertising Agency. Two years ago, Mr. Wells was promoted to his present position as vice president.

Mr. Wells is an outgoing, people-oriented man. He is very ambitious and has already achieved many goals in his life. He thoroughly enjoys his work and present employment. In his leisure time, Mr. Wells enjoys golf, landscaping, sailing, and horses.

Maternal:

Mrs. Leanne Courtney Wells (née Crowell) is five feet seven inches tall and weighs one hundred twenty-five pounds. She is of Anglo-Saxon ancestry with a light complexion, brown hair, and blue eyes. She was born on January 30, 1956 in Anytown and grew up there.

Mrs. Wells is the oldest of three children. She has two brothers. Both are married and each has one child. Mr. and Mrs. Wells are godparents to her fifteen-month-old niece. Her nephew is seven months old. Mrs. Wells' father has recently retired from sales; he is sixty-one years old. Her mother is fifty-eight and sells real estate, which she has been doing for the past twenty-two years.

Mrs. Wells describes her family as fun. They had a lot of good times together and did many things as a family. Her mother was strict when Mrs. Wells was growing up; she was the major disciplinarian in the family. Her father was less serious than her mother and they complemented each other well. The couple enjoys spending time with her parents and considers them contemporary in their life-style.

Mrs. Wells was an active A student in high school. For two years, while she was in high school, she had a permanent baby-sitting job caring for three small children. She also sang in the church choir and took dance lessons for twelve years. She received her bachelor's degree in social work, cum laude, in 1979 from the University of Anytown. She worked for the Anytown YMCA as associate director for seven years before becoming a homemaker.

Mrs. Wells was married between 1979 and 1981 to her first husband. Her divorce was final on April 11, 1981. There were no children born to this marriage.

Mrs. Wells is an attractive, outgoing, and artistic woman. Her interests are reading, art work, writing, sailing, and gardening. She is a people-oriented person like Mr. Wells.

DESCRIPTION OF COUPLE:

Bob and Leanne have casually known each other for thirteen years. They dated two years before they were married. They began dating in 1982 and were married on August 22, 1984.

Mr. and Mrs. Wells have good communication in their open, loving, and mature relationship. As a couple, they provide excellent emotional support for each other. Together they share many interests: shopping, photography, boating, traveling, gardening, and reading.

RELIGION:

Mr. and Mrs. Wells belong to St. Agnes Catholic Church in Anytown. They were both raised as Catholics and plan to bring up their children in this faith.

HOME:

Mr. and Mrs. Wells own a lovely two-story, four-bedroom home located on twenty acres of land. The home has a three-car, two-story garage connected to the house by a breezeway. The home also has a patio deck as well as a washer, dryer, and freezer. The first floor contains a living/dining room, den, kitchen with breakfast bar, utility room, hobby room, family room, screened-in porch, and two half-baths. Located on the second floor are three bedrooms and a master suite. The master suite has a bedroom, dressing room, walk-in closet, and full bath. Another full bath is located on the second floor next to a bedroom prepared to serve as a nursery.

FINANCIAL:

Mr. and Mrs. Wells are in a good financial state to raise a child. Mr. Wells' income is $80,600 at present and his potential for future employment and advancement with his company is excellent. He has $250,000 in whole life insurance on himself and Mrs. Wells. The couple owns their house, which has a market value of $225,000, and they have about $15,000 in their savings account. They manage their money very well.

HEALTH:

Mr. Wells was examined on December 14, 1991 by Dr. John Jones and found to be in excellent health.

Mrs. Wells was also examined on December 14, 1991 by Dr. Jane Smith and found to be in very good health. The couple is unable to conceive a child but the cause of infertility has not been determined.

FEELINGS ABOUT ADOPTION:

Mr. and Mrs. Wells have been considering adoption since they married. Their goal is to share their lives and home with a child, regardless of that child's origin, because they have a great amount of love to give a child.

The Wellses have a positive attitude toward the birth parents and are understanding about the difficulty the birth mother must have had making the decision to surrender her child for adoption. The couple's friends and family are supportive of their adoption plans.

REFERENCES:

This agency has received reference letters about Mr. and Mrs. Wells from four couples.

Mr. and Mrs. Mark Crowell, Leanne's brother and his wife state, "Leanne and Bob are open, warm, and affectionate with children and would provide a stable, loving home environment with consistency in discipline and common sense."

Paul and Cindy Stein, who have known the Wellses for several years, have written: "As a couple they are warm and loving and are truly devoted to each other. Please consider our highest recommendations."

Mr. and Mrs. William Steward, who have known Leanne for twenty-two years and Bob since they began dating, wrote: "I know they would make excellent parents as they both demonstrate such love and affection toward children that are around them."

Mr. and Mrs. George Fender, who have know the Wellses both professionally and socially since they married, have written: "They have given this decision much thought; they have shared it with each other and with us. We feel they are committed enough to each other as a married couple to have an excellent potential for parenthood."

RECOMMENDATIONS:

Mr. and Mrs. Robert Wells are both warm, loving people who I feel will make wonderful parents. They possess the qualities essential to providing a loving, stable home for children. There is no question that they are ideally suited to be parents. I highly recommend that the Wellses be approved for adoptive planning and placement of the type of child they desire, a healthy Caucasian infant of either sex under ten months of age.

Erin Baker, M.S.W.

will be surprised to see that, despite all of the questions asked, a home study report is actually very brief and broad in content.

The preceding is an actual home study report, which is slightly modified. Only identifying information was changed to protect the privacy of the adoptive parents. This home study was prepared by a denominational agency for the adoption of an American infant.

FOR MORE INFORMATION ON
THE HOME STUDY

Check the reading list for prospective adopters at the end of chapter one. Some of these books have chapters on the home study process. Also, send for a copy of the article "The Adoption Home Study Process," by Debra Smith, available at no charge, from the National Adoption Information Clearinghouse.

Intercountry Adoption

Each year thousands of families from the United States adopt children from abroad. In the years after World War II and until 1991, the largest number of children entering the United States for the purpose of adoption came from South Korea. Since 1991, the number of Korean children has declined in relation to the total number of children placed from Latin America, Africa, and Eastern Europe. Today children from all parts of the world are being placed, largely in the United States, Canada, Europe, and Australia.

As people are waiting three to eight years to adopt in the United States, thousands of couples and singles from the United States and other nations are preparing to adopt internationally. The available children they are adopting from other countries also number in the thousands, and their chief delay is the court process and governmental procedures that are necessary to ensure that the adoptions are handled properly. Even with these time-consuming procedures, most foreign adoptions take only a year or two from start to finish. Many children arrive as infants, although they are usually at least five months old at placement.

Children of all races and many nationalities are now waiting for homes. Countries where children are available for adoption at present include: Korea, India, the Philippines, Thailand, Taiwan, China (including Hong Kong), Vietnam, Colombia, Peru, Chile, Paraguay, Costa Rica, Haiti, El Salvador, Mexico, Honduras, Guatemala, the Dominican Republic, Ecuador, Japan, Samoa, Bolivia, Brazil, Panama, Belize, some eastern European countries, Portugal, Ethiopia, Uganda, Mali, and Greece. From year to year other countries may be added—for example, adoptions from Somalia just began in the spring of 1993. And sometimes a country may put a temporary hold on adoption while it rewrites its regulations. (For this reason, it is helpful to

107

choose a placing agency that has a back-up program for another country that you're interested in.)

REQUIREMENTS FOR PARENTS

As you explore intercountry adoption, you will learn that the requirements prospective parents must meet are more relaxed than they are for pre-adopters pursuing adoption in the United States. While only a handful of agencies in the U.S. would consider placing an infant with a couple in their mid-forties, many foreign countries welcome couples of this age or older. This flexibility also applies to such requirements as length of marriage, number of children already in the family, and previous divorces.

According to Betty Laning of the International Concerns Committee for Children and the Open Door Society of Massachusetts, "Some Asian countries (Korea, Philippines and India) have a top age limit of 43 to 45 years to adopt infants. China requires adopters of healthy infants to be 35 years or older and childless, but also has infants with correctable physical problems (clubfoot, birthmarks, crossed eyes) available for those 30 years of age and older who already have children. Currently, China and Africa have no upper age limits. Eastern European countries, with the exception of Romania, tend to welcome older parents at the present time. Countries can change their requirements at any time, however, and applicants need to check with adoptive parent support groups or licensed agencies for possible revisions."

Most countries require at least one parent to travel there and stay for at least a few days. Some countries require a stay of a few weeks, or two separate trips. At this time, the countries which *do not* necessarily require travel include: Korea, India, El Salvador, Guatemala, Hong Kong, Jamaica, Thailand, Taiwan, the Philippines, Ethiopia, Mali, Niger, Russia, and Bulgaria. Some programs in these countries may require at least one parent to travel to pick up the child.

ABOUT THE CHILDREN

In most cases, the children available for adoption range in age from infancy to fifteen years old. A U.S. agency placing children from Honduras, for instance, may have only infants and toddlers to place, whereas another U.S. agency may place only school-age children from Honduras. So if you have your heart set on adopting a child of a specific age from a particular country, say age two or younger from Guatemala, and the agency you contact only has children older than four, continue to contact agencies until you find one that can help you.

Are the children coming from abroad healthy? "I guess that depends on your definition of healthy," says Jackie, who has adopted four children from South America. "Our nine-month-old was considered healthy by South American standards, but by American standards he was small and underweight for his age. Within two months though, he gained several pounds and actually grew almost two inches. By fourteen months, he was right on target. Our second child was not walking at sixteen months, but he caught up eventually. The third child came home with an upper respiratory infection and scabies, nothing that couldn't be taken care of. The fourth child was older. He was five years old, but healthy."

What about medical history? "What's that?" laughs Jackie. "I have nothing to speak of on one of my children and a little information on the other three. But we've been okay. Our pediatrician has just been great to work with. That's important, finding a pediatrician who accepts the fact that these kids don't have much medical history."

Not only will there be little, if any, medical history available for parents who adopt a child from overseas, but social background information is rarely available as well. Of course, there are always exceptions, and you must remember that children born in the United States do not always arrive with a full medical and social history either. Parents can usually expect to get a recently written medical report; you should ask the agency you are considering whether you can review the written report with your pediatrician before committing funds to a particular child's adoption. Most countries will test for AIDS and Hepatitis B if the parents request it.

Deborah McCurdy, M.S.W., adoption supervisor at Beacon Adoption Center in Great Barrington, Massachusetts, developed a Spanish-English medical form for use in Spanish speaking countries. This is a simplified version of the American Academy of Pediatrics' form. The form is especially helpful in parent-initiated adoptions if pre-adopters are working with foreign placing agencies or attorneys who are receptive. Parents can point out that the form is clear, comprehensive, easy to fill out, and is essentially self-translating.

WHAT TYPE OF CHILD IS ELIGIBLE TO BE ADOPTED?

For a child born in another country to be eligible for adoption by a U.S. citizen, and to receive a visa for the child, the child must be classified as an "orphan," as defined by the Immigration and Naturalization Service law. This law states that the child must (1) be certified as "abandoned" by the foreign country or (2) have only one parent who irrevocably releases, in writing, the orphan for emigration and adoption outside the country of birth. Children with two living parents are *not* eligible for an orphan visa, unless one or both of the parents have disappeared or abandoned the child. The placing agency's lawyer overseas is responsible for making sure the children she selects for adoption meet these requirements.

Reporte Clínico

POR FAVOR DESCRIBA ENFERMADADES QUE HA TENIDO LA FAMILIA DEL NIÑO O PROBLEMAS CON EL EMBARAZO O EL NACIMIENTO, SI LO SABE (Please describe any illnesses in the child's family or problems with the pregnancy or birth, if known):_____

_____

_____LA TRADUCCIÓN

(translation):_____

_____

ESTATURA Y PESO AL NACIMIENTO, SI LO SABE (Height and weight at birth, if known):_____cm. _____gm. POR FAVOR DESCRIBA ENFERMADADES QUE HA TENIDO EL NIÑO Y DROGAS QUE HA TENIDO, SI LO SABE (Please describe illnesses and drugs child has had, if known):_____

_____

_____LA TRADUCCIÓN (Translation):_____

_____

POR FAVOR ENUMERE LAS INMUNIZACIONES CON LAS FECHAS QUE HA TENIDO EL NIÑO (Please specify immunizations child has had, with dates):_____

_____

_____LA TRADUCCIÓN (Translation):_____

_____

SI EL NIÑO HA TENIDO EXAMENES DE LABORATORIO, POR FAVOR ESCRIBA LAS FECHAS Y LOS RE- SULTADOS (If the child has had laboratory tests, please give dates and results):_____

_____

_____LA TRADUCCIÓN (Translation):_____

_____

SI EL NIÑO TIENE UNA CONDICIÓN QUE NECESITA UN TRATAMIENTO CONTINUADO, POR FAVOR DESCRÍBALO (If the child has a condition that requires continuing medical treatment, please describe):

_____

_____LA TRADUCCIÓN (Translation):_____

_____

NOMBRE Y APELLIDO DEL MÉDICO:_____
(Doctor's name)
DIRECCIÓN DEL MÉDICO (Doctor's address):_____

_____

_____

REPORTE CLÍNICO (ESPAÑOL-INGLÉS) DEL NIÑO QUE SERÁ ADOPTADO
(Spanish-English Medical Report on Child to be Adopted)

NOMBRE Y APELLIDO DEL NIÑO (Name of child):_____

FECHA DE NACIMIENTO (Date of birth):_____ SEXO: _____M _____F

EXAMEN FÍSICO (Physical examination).   FECHA (Date):_____

ESTATURA (Height):_____cm. PESO (Weight):_____Kg. O (or) _____gm.

CIRCUNFERENCIA DE LA CABEZA, SI LA EDAD DEL NIÑO ES APROPIADA (Head circumference, as age

appropriate):_____cm.
¿SON LAS MEDIDAS DE ARRIBA NORMALES PARA LA EDAD DEL NIÑO? (Are the above measurements

normal for the child's age?) _____SÍ (yes) _____NO
EN LOS PUNTOS DE ABAJO, PONGA LA Q SI ES NORMAL O LA X SI ES ANORMAL (For the following, put Q
if normal or X if abnormal):

___PIEL (skin)   ___DIENTES (teeth)   ___ESPALDA (back)

___VISIÓN   ___CUELLO (neck)   ___ABDOMEN

___OJOS (eyes)   ___PULMONES (lungs)   ___GENITALES (genitals)

___OÍDO (hearing)   ___CORAZÓN (heart)   ___EXTREMIDADES (extremities)

___OREJAS (ears)   ___NARIZ (nose)   ___GARGANTA (throat)

___NEUROLÓGICA (neurological)

POR FAVOR DESCRIBA LAS ANORMALIDADES (Please describe any abnormalities):_____
_____
_____
_____
_____

_____LA TRADUCCIÓN EN INGLÉS (English translation):_____
_____
_____
_____
_____

¿ES EL CRECIMIENTO DEL NIÑO AL NIVEL ESPERADO PARA SU EDAD? (Is the child at the expected level

of development for his age?) _____SÍ (yes) _____NO

SI NO, POR FAVOR EXPLÍQUELO (If not, please explain):_____
_____

_____LA TRADUCCIÓN EN INGLÉS (Translation):
_____

¿SI EL CRECIMIENTO NO ES AL NIVEL ESPERADO PARA SU EDAD, PUEDE EL NIÑO EN SU OPINIÓN
CRECER NORMALMENTE SI RECIBE BUENA NUTRICIÓN Y BUEN CUIDADO EN UNA CASA ADOPTIVA Y
CARIÑOSA? (If the child is not at the expected level of development for his age, can he, in your, opinion grow

normally if he receives good nutrition and good care in a loving adoptive home?) _____SÍ (yes) _____NO

Reprinted from the *Report on Foreign Adoptions* (1993), courtesy of Deborah McCurdy and
the International Concerns Committee for Children. Agencies are welcome to use this form
as it is, or to modify it for their own purposes.

WHO ADOPTS INTERNATIONALLY AND WHY

One Iowa couple decided to adopt from Brazil. For them, the decision came easily. The adoptive father traveled to Brazil frequently on business and they were already aware of the number of children available for adoption. "Although we have friends in Brazil who could have helped us arrange a private adoption, we decided we needed the guidance and support of an agency since we had no other children," says the adoptive mother. "We then checked with Adoptive Families of America for help in locating an adoptive parent support group and an agency that worked with Brazil. We adopted our children with the help of Holt International Children's Services."

Another couple, Lara and Matt from Scotch Plains, New Jersey, joined their local adoptive parent support organization after Lara learned of the group from a co-worker who had adopted from Korea. "At first, I couldn't understand how the group could help us," says Lara, "but through the group we met others who had adopted or were trying to adopt internationally. They were a tremendous help."

Lara and Matt first pursued a Colombian adoption after meeting members from their group who urged them to contact an attorney who was placing children from there. A few days before they were to mail their documents to Colombia, they learned that the attorney could no longer place children from there because of a change in the Colombian adoption laws.

"We were devastated," says Laura. "We called our home study agency and they suggested we call an attorney in New Jersey who had a foreign adoption program. In February, we met with the attorney and decided to adopt from Peru. In mid-July, we brought our Peruvian daughter home with a finalized adoption."

WHERE TO BEGIN

If you are considering intercountry adoption, you undoubtedly have many questions. How does one choose a country? What do the children look like? Will the child fit into our family? Can we handle the complexity of adopting internationally? Thinking about these questions, and many others, is just the beginning of the intercountry adoption process.

Lori and Chuck knew they wanted a baby and were comfortable with the idea of adopting internationally. Although initially they had no idea what country they would adopt from, many of their fellow support group members had adopted from El Salvador so they made the same decision. "We felt a child from El Salvador would fit easily into our family and our community," says Chuck, "so we used the same agency everyone else had."

If you are considering intercountry adoption, you may have some idea where you would like to adopt from. Possibly a child from an Asian nation would be right for you. Or maybe you envision a child from Central or South America becoming a member of your family. Although the programs are new, maybe you see yourself adopting from Eastern Europe. The choice is yours and only you can make that final decision.

Once you have decided to adopt from abroad, begin by locating others who have adopted internationally and talk with them about any concerns or questions you may have. Talk with people in your support group. Attend free information meetings at local agencies. "You may not be able to resolve all your concerns before beginning the adoption process," says Deborah McCurdy, M.S.W., "but the home study is designed to help you think through your decisions as you move ahead. There is less emphasis these days on screening clients, and more interest in instructing them and helping them make their own decisions."

Choose a country that accommodates your age, length of marriage, and other characteristics. Visit the library and look through the many books available on different countries. Specifically, learn about the physical characteristics and culture of the people from the country you're interested in adopting from. Once you have made a decision, decide what age child you want to adopt and then organize yourself as quickly as possible.

PAPERWORK FOR THE IMMIGRATION AND NATURALIZATION SERVICE

You can begin your paperwork for an intercountry adoption after you have checked with your state's department of social services to make sure intercountry adoption is permitted in your state. You may even begin your paperwork before you have identified a specific country and before your home study has been completed.

First, write a letter to the United States Department of Immigration and Naturalization Service office that serves your area. Your letter should be short, like this example:

To Whom It May Concern:

We are writing to request the international adoption packet. Thank you in advance for your help.

Sincerely,

Mr. and Mrs. John Doe
1111 Main Street
Anywhere, USA
(222) 555-9876

In this adoption packet you will receive:

- Form I-600A (Application for Advance Processing of Orphan Petition)

- Form I-600 (Petition to Classify Orphan as an Immediate Relative)
- Four fingerprint cards (Form F D-258)

For Form I-600A to be processed, it must be accompanied by (1) proof of citizenship of the prospective petitioner(s)—only one spouse needs to be a United States citizen, but both must submit birth certificates; (2) proof of marriage of petitioner and spouse; (3) divorce or death certificates for prior marriages, if applicable; (4) your four completed fingerprint cards, and (5) the required fee ($140 as of 1993). Remember this form can be filed as soon as you have gathered these documents. If the home study is not finished, file form I-600A *now* and send the home study report later to save time.

Once your child has been identified, you (or your foreign representative) will file Form I-600, together with the appropriate documentation concerning your child, with INS or a U.S. consulate in your child's country. With this form you are requesting approval of your "visa petition" for the child. (Your child must have an immigrant visa to enter the United States.) If the child's documents are not in English, you must have them translated before submitting them. Once the child's visa is received, your child may enter the U.S.

With Form I-600 you must provide the following, which your orphanage or foreign attorney will obtain:

- Proof of the orphan's age
- If the orphans' parents are deceased, death certificate(s) of the parent(s)
- Evidence that the sole or surviving parent is incapable of providing for the orphan's care and has in writing irrevocably released the orphan for emigration and adoption.
- Evidence that the orphan has been unconditionally abandoned to an orphanage, if the child has been placed in an orphanage.
- Certified copy of a final decree of adoption, if the orphan has been legally adopted abroad.
- Proof that the pre-adoption requirements, if any, of the state of the orphan's proposed residence have been met, if the child will be adopted in the United States. (Your agency will explain this.)

Petitioners do not need to re-submit documents filed with Form I-600A. However, if those documents were not previously submitted, they must be submitted with Form I-600.

DOCUMENTS NEEDED FOR AN INTERCOUNTRY ADOPTION

The following documents are often required for an intercountry adoption. *Not all are required for each adoption. Your source will provide a list.*

- Bank letter showing total savings in your account(s) and when they were opened
- Letters of reference (usually three or four)
- Financial reference letter from your employer(s) showing your current salary, job security, and date of employment
- IRS returns for the last year or two
- Police statement for each petitioner, in letter form, indicating no criminal record
- Certified copy of marriage certificate (if applicable)
- Certified copy of divorce decree for prior marriage (if applicable)
- Certified copy of death certificate of former spouse (if applicable)
- Notarized home study report
- Certified copy of birth certificate for each adoptive parent
- Family pictures
- Pictures of the outside of your house (some countries also want pictures of the inside)
- Physician's letter indicating generally good health for each of you and/or explaining all serious conditions as not life-threatening

Some of these additional documents may be needed, depending on the country you are adopting from:

- Copies of the first page of the passport for each petitioner
- Notarized copy of the agency license
- Notarized copy of license of social worker who wrote the home study report
- Psychological evaluation of adoptive parents.

THE HOME STUDY

You must have a home study to adopt from overseas. This is a federal requirement for intercountry adoptions. (United States citizens living abroad can have the local U.S. embassy or consulate conduct a home study instead of an agency, or a licensed social worker.)

There are good reasons for using an agency instead of a licensed social worker for a home study, even if your state allows both. First, an agency home study will be accepted by the Interstate Compact on the Placement of Children and if you are using an out-of-state U.S.-based international agency which is networking in your state, and your child arrives without a final adoption decree, the ICPC may play a role in your adoption. Second, if you have the home study completed before you have identified your source, a favorable agency home study will generally be accepted by your placing agency if it is located out of state. It should also be fully acceptable to your adoption source overseas. Third, you have certain protections through an agency that you do not have with an individual. Using a licensed social worker may be fine for some types of adoption, like independent U.S. infant adoption, but for international purposes a home study by a licensed agency is often required by the foreign court or government.

THE CHOICES

You can choose the type of intercountry adoption you want to pursue, but keep in mind that, no matter what your choice, intercountry adoption is a challenge. There is no simple way to adopt from a foreign country. Adopting internationally is a complicated, time-consuming, and expensive process. (Expenses will be similar to the costs of adopting a U.S. infant through a nondenominational agency.) You will have a large amount of paperwork to complete, papers that need to be notarized, verified, translated, and authenticated. And, again, you may need to travel to the foreign country.

Just as there are delays and uncertainties in U.S. adoptions, there can be setbacks in intercountry adoptions too. Envision completing all of the paperwork and actually receiving a picture of your child. Imagine carrying that picture around for weeks or months, showing it to your family and friends. Think of falling in love with the child in that picture. Now consider how you would feel if that two-month-old baby was unable to come home for many months. Or worse yet, became seriously ill while you were waiting. In rare cases, that assigned child never makes it to you because of changes in government regulations or court procedures. These are the uncertainties you will be unable to control. Fortunately, these things happen only occasionally. But when they do, your placement agency should be prepared to promptly help with another child or program—if you have chosen your agency with a back-up program in mind.

On the bright side, many thousands of families have adopted successfully from foreign countries over the years with minimal frustration and delays, and other families have experienced no problems.

There are basically three avenues you can follow to adopt internationally. The first route involves using an adoption agency to locate a child for you. This is often called an "agency-initiated adoption." The second option is a "parent-initiated adoption," in which the parents deal directly with a contact overseas to find a child. (Sometimes a parent-initiated adoption is called a "direct international adoption," or simply, a "direct adoption.") The third avenue is called an independent adoption.

Before pursuing any avenue, check with your agency state government and learn which requirements must be satisfied at that level. Some states only require pre-adopters to complete a home study, which is also a requirement of all adoption agencies and of the Immigration and Naturalization Service. However, in a few states you may have to approach your local probate court first, or bond must be posted in your state before your child can be placed with you. In some states you may not be allowed to bring your child home until she has been adopted by you in her country of birth.

AGENCY-INITIATED ADOPTIONS

Agency-initiated adoptions are those that use a U.S.-based adoption agency with its own programs and sources. In an agency-initiated adoption, the agency will help you prepare your paperwork, communicate with your local service agency and the foreign source, and refer a child to you. Once a child is assigned, your agency will either arrange for him to be escorted to the United States or for you to appear in the foreign country to meet him and then escort him home. The agency generally has a representative overseas—an attorney, a licensed facilitator, or an orphanage director—that will assist you with procedures.

Using a reliable U.S.-based agency to expedite an intercountry adoption is still considered the safest route by many. The agency will have worked in the foreign country and have all of the necessary contacts to ensure the legality of the adoption. As prospective parents, you will also receive the support and assistance you need from your agency before, during, and after placement.

Finding an agency to work with should not be difficult. Check the annual *Report on Foreign Adoption* (available from the International Concerns Committee for Children). The importance of this directory for those considering intercountry adoption cannot be stressed enough. This report is filled with all sorts of helpful information that cannot be found elsewhere in one publication. You will find frank discussions on medical considerations in adopting children born in another country; questions to ask yourself about adopting a child from another culture, race, or both; articles on intercountry adoption issues; a list of documents you will need for INS; a description of agencies that place children from abroad, including the requirements for parents, costs, children available, waiting times; a listing of local services agencies by state; and a reading list.

PARENT-INITIATED ADOPTIONS

In a parent-initiated adoption (also called direct adoption) you will be responsible for the entire adoption process. This includes finding your own foreign adoption source, handling the paperwork, communicating with the foreign source, traveling to the foreign country to adopt your child or arranging for the child to be escorted to the United States, and completing a home study to meet state and INS requirements. (A local agency can provide the home study.)

In a parent-initiated adoption you deal directly with a foreign source throughout the adoption process. Usually the source is an agency or orphanage in another country, but sometimes it is an attorney. If you use an attorney, you should be extremely careful and use only an attorney that you, or someone fairly close to you, knows personally. One way that a placing agency protects you is by carefully reviewing the background and reputation of any attorney it uses.

The U.S. consulates and embassies in each country have lists of lawyers authorized to do adoptions, but they are often restricted from giving an opinion of an attorney's competence or efficiency in handling adoptions.

"In a parent-initiated adoption, especially if you go to an out-of-the-way orphanage where children are not regularly adopted, one that is away from the major cities, it may be that you will spend less money," says Deborah McCurdy. "We are working with a single parent who cannot spend more than $8,000, so she's going to do a parent-initiated adoption in a remote area because she knows she can do it for that amount there. Most foreign orphanages have their own attorneys and they can do a legal adoption for a fee that is reasonable by local standards."

It is extremely important to know your source in a parent-initiated adoption. Prospective adopters can learn about adoption sources from local adoption agencies, parent support groups, and adoptive parents who have accomplished a parent-initiated adoption. An excellent resource is the Latin American Parents Association (LAPA), which has chapters in the following locations:

LAPA New York
P.O. Box 339
Brooklyn, NY 11234

LAPA National Capital Region, Inc.
P.O. Box 4403
Silver Spring, MD 20904

LAPA Northern New Jersey, Inc.
P.O. Box 77
Emerson, NJ 07630

LAPA Connecticut
P.O. Box 523
Unionville, CT 06085

LAPA New Jersey State
  Chapter, Inc.
P.O. Box 2013
Brick, NJ 08723

There is also an outstanding book by Jean Nelson-Erichsen and Heino Erichsen, which is especially helpful to those doing a parent-initiated adoption. It gives an overview of the adoption process, along with specific information on laws, orphanages and central government adoption authorities in each country permitting foreigners to adopt. You can order the book, *How to Adopt Internationally*, for $20 from Los Niños International Adoption Center, The United Way Building, 1600 Lake Front Circle, Suite 130, The Woodlands, TX   77380-3600.

You should contact the Bureau of Consular Affairs, Department of State, in Washington, DC, before you choose a source for a parent-initiated adoption. The bureau issues warnings about adoption scams and provides travel advisories that alert you to the problems you might encounter.

Travel advisories fall into two categories: warnings and cautions. Warnings are issued for violence which may be occurring in specific areas within a country. Cautions may be given for health hazards, political unrest, or high-crime areas. Call or write the Citizens' Emergency Center, Bureau of Consular Affairs, Room 4811, United States Department of State, Washington, DC 20520, (202) 647-5225, to obtain a recorded advisory on the country you plan to travel to.

Next, contact the foreign country's government office that concerns itself with the welfare of children. This office can give you a complete up-to-date copy of the adoption laws and explain the current procedure for adopting through a government agency or orphanage. *How to Adopt Internationally* lists the phone numbers and addresses of every country's central adoption authority.

Before contacting a source overseas, prepare a one- or two-page letter describing yourself and your family. In the letter, include your ages, marital status, health, financial status, other children (if you have any), and your attitudes and your families' attitudes about intercountry adoption. Explain your reasons for wanting to adopt and describe the type of child you are interested in (the sex, age, and race of the child). Do not specify skin color; this could offend the readers of your letter. Give the name you have chosen for a child. Or if you have decided to keep the original name or part of the original name, write about this in your letter. Some adopters give infants a new first name and use the original name as a middle name, but you should plan to keep an older child's name or nickname. Explain how you will meet the child's needs and how he will be granted full rights as your child.

Let the foreign source know that you are required by INS to have a home study completed in the United States for an intercountry adoption. Indicate when your home study will be completed. Summarize your state's pre- and postadoption requirements and the requirements of the INS. Comment on your willingness to meet their government's adoption requirements. (See the sample letter to a foreign source in this chapter.)

If it is an agency or orphanage that you are contacting, ask about fees and what those fees cover. Find out how long it will take before a child is assigned once they have received your home study report. Will you need to travel? If yes, for how long? Re-read the first half of chapter five and ask any other questions you have.

Is your source an attorney? Ask how many adoptions he has completed. Ask if your source will locate a child for you. Some attorneys only handle the legal work involved. **Ask for references and check those references.** (Presumably you will have already spoken with someone who used the attorney and can recommend him.) Find out what the fee is and what that fee includes. Ask for a written fee schedule. **Do not send large amounts of money to any attorney in**

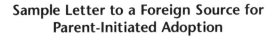

Sample Letter to a Foreign Source for Parent-Initiated Adoption

Dear _____,

My husband (or wife) and I are writing to you because we very much want to adopt a child. We have been married for 8 years and during that time we have unsuccessfully tried to conceive. The pastor at our church suggested we try to adopt internationally. He told us there are children in need of families and we know we can open our arms and our hearts to a child from a different nationality and culture.

We have talked about this and want very much to adopt a child from your country—a child we can raise and love as our own. We hope that you can help us find a child to make our family complete.

Please permit us to introduce ourselves. My husband's name is Richard Hunter and my name is Michele Hunter. Richard is 35 years old and is in excellent health. He is an engineer and he has worked at _____ for 10 years now. I am 32 years old and also in excellent health. I work as a secretary at _____ and have worked there for 5 years. As mentioned, we have been married for 8 years and have no children. We are financially secure, own our house, have adequate life and medical insurance (our medical insurance will cover an adopted child from the time he or she is placed with us), and have money saved in the bank.

We are writing to you with the full encouragement of both of our families. Our families know what a privilege it would be for us to adopt a child from your country and our parents are eagerly awaiting their first grandchild. When a child is placed with us, we will have our attorney draw up a will that states the child will share in our family inheritance. In other words, the child will become the legal heir to our estate. Should we adopt other children, all the children will then share our estate equally. We tell you this because we want to emphasize that the child we adopt will be a full member of our family and will be accepted as our child by our families.

We are specifically interested in adopting a child from the age of infancy to approximately two years old and hope that you can place a child with us. It does not matter if the child is a boy or girl. We are open to a child that is Latin American Indian or mestizo (Latin American Indian/Caucasian), and we would consider a child with a minor correctable medical condition. If the child is a boy, we will name him Andrew and if the child is a girl, we will name her Christina. In either case, the child's present name will become the child's middle name. Both of the names we have chosen, are very special to us. Andrew is my father-in-law's name and Christina is my mother's first name.

We have read many books and magazine articles about adopting a child from another country. We belong to an adoptive parent group made up of many families who have adopted internationally and they have shared their stories and experiences with us. We have also chosen a good pediatrician who will provide medical care to our child.

We have been approved for adoptive placement by an adoption agency in _____ (name the city, and your state). Our home study is currently up to date. It meets the pre-adoption requirement of the state government of _____ (name of your state), as well as the requirements of the Immigration and Naturalization Service (INS). Both _____ (name your state) and the INS state that we must have a home study to adopt internationally. INS also requires that we be cleared by the Federal Bureau of Investigation (FBI) before it will issue an orphan visa. Without FBI clearance, we cannot adopt and bring home a child, so you can be confident we have no criminal record. As soon as we hear from you, we will send a copy of our home study in your language. Once you receive our home study, providing it is acceptable, how long will it take for you to choose a child for us?

In the meantime, we have been studying your laws and procedures for adoption. We will be sure that we comply with all of the necessary laws and requirements of your country and the United States.

We will also need information on the fees involved in adopting from your orphanage and what those fees will cover. We know we must travel to your country. Can you give us an idea of how long we need to stay and if we need to come back a second time?

After placement, the adoption agency in _____ (name of your state) will send supervisory reports to you for several months. These reports will be written after our adoption caseworker visits our home to see how our child is adapting to our family and home. The state law in _____ (name of your state) says that our caseworker must visit our home _____ times after placement.

Again, we very much want to adopt a child from your country and hope that you can assist us in our efforts. We have a room prepared for our new son or daughter and are very eager for the day when our child comes home. We look forward to hearing from you. Thank you so much for your kindness and help.

Yours truly,

Richard and Michele Hunter

advance of placement. You may be asked to send some money for child care and other expenses. This is to be expected, but be sure those fees are in line with what other attorneys charge. According to the *Adoption Factbook,* published by the National Council For Adoption in 1989, the initial payment should not exceed $2,000. Talk with other adoptive parents so you know what fees are normal.

Lastly, attach a photo of your family. Send your letter to the one source you have carefully chosen. Later, you may need to send a picture of your house and, possibly, pictures of the inside rooms.

Prepare to wait for a reply because sometimes it takes two or more months to receive an answer. If, after two months, you have not received a response, have someone who speaks the language contact the source you have written to. (The current *Report on Foreign Adoption* includes a list of translators who may be able to help you.)

You should put a lot of thought into choosing your source, being sure to consult others who have successfully used the source you are considering. Do not write to two sources at the same time, because they may invest much time and effort in working with you toward an adoption, only to have you withdraw in favor of another possibility. **Pursuing two foreign sources at the same time is considered highly unethical.** When you do this, you run the risk of alienating both sources and may cause them to withdraw their children from consideration for adoption.

If this all sounds overwhelming, remember U.S.-based international agencies deal with these matters every day, and using a placing agency is an option for you. Do not forget about the many adoption attorneys in the United States who place U.S.-born children and those born abroad. These attorneys may have contacts in several countries and can also assist you in adopting a child internationally.

INDEPENDENT ADOPTIONS

In the United States, as more birth mothers began choosing independent adoption, we saw a rise in the number of attorneys specializing in adoption. Prospective parents had been waiting on adoption agencies' lists for years, but in the 1980s adoption attorneys saw an increase in the numbers of pre-adopters approaching them to adopt American infants. Because of this, adoption attorneys looked to other sources for infants; some began intercountry adoption programs, networking with colleagues in foreign countries. Today, in the states that permit independent adoption, these attorneys are helping couples and singles adopt infants and toddlers through independent intercountry adoption. (Remember: Some states allow only licensed adoption agencies to assist with adoptions.)

As of spring 1993, independent intercountry adoption in certain states is an alternative to agency-initiated or parent-initiated adoption. Contact adoption attorneys in your area if your state's department of social services tells you independent adoptions are legal in your state. If these attorneys do not have an intercountry program, they may be aware of other attorneys who do. Check with parent support groups and adoption agencies. Local service agencies may be particularly helpful, because they network with many different adoption sources, including attorneys.

THE FEES

Fees for intercountry adoption vary greatly. It is difficult to compute an average fee because of the many variables involved, such as different fees for different countries; the different fee schedules, even for the same country; travel, hotel, air fare, and length-of-stay expenses; and other miscellaneous costs. You have some control over what you spend, because sources generally present their fee schedules upfront—there is a wide range of options in programs, hotel accommodations, and airfares. Remember: When you choose your source, you are also choosing what you will pay for your adoption.

A survey of agencies, indicates that $11,000 to $12,000, with travel, is close to an average fee. There are, however, families whose adoptions ran from $4,000 to $5,000 when the child was escorted to the United States. But there are also the families whose adoptions totaled between $18,000 and $29,000. Most, but not all, of these families worked with child-finding attorneys. One family adopted a baby from Central America through an agency that did not require them to travel. Their fees were excessive—over $22,000—totaling about $8,000 more than the figure they had been quoted at the beginning. Unfortunately, this couple did not check the agency's record. Had they telephoned the attorney general's office, they would have saved several thousand dollars because the agency had previously lost its license to operate in other states. (Understand that the attorney general's office may not be completely up to date on an agency's reputation.)

Your fees need not be excessive if you choose your adoption source carefully. Many reputable placement agencies are listed in the *Report on Foreign Adoption,* and you can choose an agency with two or more programs that fit your budget. You'll be signing a contract which should list fixed fees for legal, medical, and agency costs. Avoid using any adoption source that does not cap its fees, or that states in its contract that your medical or legal costs may exceed the stated sum in unusual circumstances. Not all foreign fees should be payable before placement. However, some expenses are payable to entities other than your placement agency, so you may be expected to pay several thousand dollars early in the process. This is an acceptable procedure, but, again, be sure you understand the refund policy.

If the cost seems overwhelming, consider taking out a loan before you proceed with your adoption. Perhaps a home equity loan, or a gift or loan from a relative will make your dream of a child feasible. Most agencies do not mind if you borrow to cover the cost of your adoption, as long as at least one of you is employed and can count on a regular income.

ENSURING A LEGAL INTERCOUNTRY ADOPTION

Do your homework. Research intercountry adoption and learn as much as you possibly can *before* signing a contract with an agency, attorney, or other facilitator in the United States or abroad. Read! There are excellent books on intercountry adoption written by adoption professionals. Some books clearly summarize our government's pertinent regulations. Know the laws in your state and INS' requirements.

The *Adoption Factbook* recommends you keep the following in mind as you consider an adoption source:

- Check references. Be wary of any agency, attorney, or facilitator that promises a "quick and easy way to adopt internationally" because there is no simple method. There is only one legal way and, unfortunately, the right way is time-consuming.
- Insist that all fees be in writing. Do not pay a fee to an individual simply to locate a child for you. For example, an attorney may tell you he does not have sources for children but if you send him money to locate a child he could probably find one for you. If you are told this, do not send money. Find another source.
- All reputable agencies and attorneys will share their source's name with you once you become their client. This information should never be confidential, nor should any information about the child be confidential, including where the child is presently living. If an agency or individual is unwilling to provide this information, you may be getting involved in a black-market adoption, in which case you may never be able to legally adopt a child placed with you.
- Thousands of children from abroad are legally adopted by parents in the United States every year. Do not let any agency or individual pressure you into working with them or adopting a specific child. You should never feel pressured into making a decision. Again, be a smart consumer.

FINAL THOUGHTS

An adoptive mother of a one-year-old from Chile, who lives in Pocasset, Massachusetts, offers this advice to prospective parents planning to adopt internationally:

> In addition to learning what documents and procedures are necessary for an international adoption, clients must also learn who is responsible for what. Be clear about what the agency believes its

obligations are, and be sure the agency understands what you expect of it. Sometimes these sets of expectations do not match up.

Try to establish a time frame for each step of the process and follow through. Keep accurate records. Document the date and time of a phone call or a conversation with someone. If you leave a message, check to see if it was received. When you mail or deliver a document, ask when it should arrive. Once received, find out when it will be acted on and when it will be returned. Call to confirm each step. For example [ask], 'Did you receive my dossier?' or 'When can I expect to hear from you?,' or 'Is there a problem? What can I do to help you resolve it?' Be calm and pleasant. Stay on top of things. Don't expect that someone else will be taking care of business. Follow through.

Keep in touch with your agency and others who have been through the same process or are adopting at the same time as you. Documents and travel requirements in foreign adoption change and sometimes no one tells you. You can spend money and time seeking papers that are no longer needed or not have a complete dossier because you were not told about a new requirement.

Expect delays, confusion, misunderstandings, disappointment, anger, frustration, anxiety, stress, and a wonderful child. Laugh when you can; cry when you must. Hang in there because it will happen.

A LOOK AHEAD

Most agencies placing children from abroad have several programs open at the same time and occasionally may have one or two programs on hold. Sometimes programs are on hold because the courts are overloaded with adoption petitions, or because the policies have changed and, until the details are worked out, the courts will not accept more petitions. At other times a program may be closed temporarily by an agency when it has a backup of prospective parents waiting.

Still, despite the problems, red tape, and expense, waiting times are relatively short in intercountry adoption, compared to waiting times for infants at most agencies in the United States. So if the idea of adopting a child from another country appeals to you, you are ready for considerable paperwork, and traveling sounds exciting (even if you are a little apprehensive), then start checking out the programs you are interested in.

Some changes in intercountry adoptions are expected to take place in the mid-nineties. According to Betty Laning, an adoption educator on intercountry adoptions who is affiliated with the International Concerns Committee for Children in Colorado and the Open Door Society of Massachusetts, member countries of The Hague Convention will meet in 1993 to sign a treaty covering intercountry adoptions. This is because some countries have reported problems with intercountry adoptions that are not covered by existing pacts. If the United States signs the treaty—as it probably will—

and if the U.S. Senate ratifies it, foreign-adoption procedures may undergo some revisions over the next few years.

So many new countries are now permitting foreign adoptions that it is sometimes difficult to keep current on the rules and regulations as they are established in these countries. Many of these countries have had no experience with intercountry adoption and are gradually learning which types of regulations are needed. As a result, new policies are frequently emerging.

Many of the available adoption publications, as well as national adoption organizations, like the International Concerns Committee for Children and Adoptive Families of America, will keep you updated on any changes in intercountry adoption. In addition, adoption agencies in the United States with intercountry programs will advise you of changes if new policies go into effect.

RECOMMENDED READING LIST

Erichsen, Jean Nelson and Heino R. Erichsen. *How to Adopt Internationally,* 1992. Available from Los Niños International Adoption Center, The United Way Building, 100 Lake Front Circle, Suite 130, The Woodlands, TX   77380 for $20.

Register, Cheri. *Are Those Kids Yours? American Families with Children Adopted from Other Countries.* New York: The Free Press, 1991.

International Concerns Committee for Children. *Report on Foreign Adoption.* Boulder, CO: ICCC, 1993. Available from ICCC, 911 Cypress Drive, Boulder, CO   80303. Send check for $20 to ICCC.

Sheehy, Gail. *Spirit of Survival.* New York: William Morrow, 1986. Also covers adoption of older children.

Wirth, Eileen M. and Joan Worden. *How to Adopt a Child from Another Country.* Nashville: Abingdon Press, 1993.

Single Parent Adoptions

Shelly is thirty-eight years old and has two little girls: Becky, age six, and Sherrie, age three. Both children were born in India and adopted by Shelly a few months after their births. Shelly is a single adoptive parent.

Tracy is thirty-five years old and a teacher. She has a son who is two years old. Tracy and a friend traveled to Paraguay and met David when he was only three weeks old. They arrived back in the United States when David was six weeks old. Tracy is a single adoptive parent with a very supportive friend.

Rick is forty-two years old and the single father of one son, Kevin, who is fourteen. Rick and Kevin enjoy playing baseball, basketball, and football together. They also enjoy just hanging out with each other, but that was not always the case. Kevin became Rick's son when he was eleven years old.

Shelly says "I never gave adoption a thought until one Sunday morning when I awoke early and turned the television on." The local talk show that caught her attention was about three single moms who had adopted internationally. "As I sat there and listened to their stories I knew I wanted to learn more. At the end of the show, they gave the name and phone number of the agency that the three women had used," says Shelly. "Monday morning I was on the phone and within a year and a half Becky arrived. When Becky was two, I applied for a second child. Sherrie arrived fifteen months later. Friends thought I was crazy to take on a second child, but I had the best support system anyone could ask for—my family."

Tracy had always wanted children but had never met the right man. Because she enjoyed teaching children with learning disabilities, and felt love for children in general, she knew she would make an excellent parent. Tracy heard of an attorney placing infants from Paraguay, and it was not long before she found herself on a plane for South America. Tracy also had a wonderful support system behind her.

Rick's wife died when he was thirty-two years old. "We had tried to start a family but Ellen was unable to get pregnant. After a few tests we found out why. She died a year later," says Rick. "I never met anyone else I wanted to spend the rest of my life with, but I always wanted to be a father." Rick eventually connected with Big Brothers and found the experience so rewarding that he decided to pursue adoption. "It's not easy for a single man to adopt. I found that out right at the start, but I was determined and I've never been one to take no for an answer. I had to convince people that a single man could take care of a child. It took two years and five months from the time I started searching until Kevin was placed. My parents and Ellen's parents were behind me one hundred percent. They all accepted him without question and love him. He is their grandson."

Shelly, Tracy, Rick, and countless other singles have adopted children because they wanted a family. "I came from a large family, went to college and studied law," begins SueAnn, the adoptive mom of a little girl named Janie. "After passing the bar I was accepted into a law firm and was kept busy from day one. I dated, but never met the right man. I had this beautiful house, two little dogs, and lots of friends. I traveled whenever I could take the time. One day I thought to myself, 'Is this it? Is this how I'll spend the next thirty or forty years?' and I found that very distressing."

It did not take SueAnn long to realize that what she really wanted to add to her life was a child. "Some of my friends thought I was nuts. One fellow even offered to help me out," she laughs. "I knew that wasn't what I had in mind, but I still wasn't sure how to make it all happen."

SueAnn figured out how to make it happen one day when she picked up the newspaper and read an article about Dave Thomas, the founder of Wendy's fast-food chain, and his involvement in building adoptive awareness across the country. SueAnn thought adoption was a logical choice. Thus, her search for a child began. She eventually located a private agency in another state and adopted her daughter from Panama. "Now, when I reflect back to life before Janie, I realize that she was what I was missing. My life has so much more meaning to it now and I treasure every moment we share together," she says.

GATHERING THE INFORMATION

Shelly, Tracy, Rick, and SueAnn completed their adoptions fairly easily, but, unfortunately, that is not always the case. Some single people, just like some couples, get lost in the process. They seem to hit dead ends no matter which direction they turn, become discouraged, and often change their minds about adopting. This is unfortunate indeed because there are many children available for adoption and there are agencies and attorneys that will work with single applicants. It may be more difficult sometimes for singles to adopt, but it certainly is possible for those who are patient and persistent.

Single people, just like anyone else attempting to adopt, need to begin by learning about the adoption process. An excellent source of information is the Committee for Single Adoptive Parents. Hope Marindin, executive director, says the organization has existed since 1973 as an information source for prospective single adopters and single adoptive parents. According to Marindin, "Many thousands of single women and men in the United States and Canada have adopted children in the last several years. Statistics are nonexistent, but we know that the number grows steadily." More women than men become single parents by adoption, but single men adopters are not uncommon. "One in ten members of this committee is a man," says Marindin.

Membership is open to singles and agencies. Members receive a listing of agencies or direct sources that place children from this country or abroad and will work with single prospective parents. The listing describes programs, costs, waiting times, and the types of children available for adoption. Also available are lists of single adoptive parent support groups, a recommended reading list and, if requested, a list of single parents in your area who are in the process of adopting or who have already adopted. The organization publishes *The Newsletter,* which is $18 for two years and includes updates. As a single person attempting to adopt, subscribing should be one of the first things you do. Contact the Committee for Single Adoptive Parents at P.O. Box 15084, Chevy Chase, MD   20815.

For an additional $15 you can purchase a copy of *The Handbook for Single Adoptive Parents,* which was compiled and edited by Hope Marindin. This handbook covers topics such as the following: adopting from the United States, adopting internationally, the practical aspects of managing single parenthood (including finances), and coping with challenges. *The Handbook* also includes personal experience stories by singles about adopting in middle age, adopting older children, adopting physically challenged children, and managing life as a single parent. The book concludes with two articles written by adoption professionals. This is required reading for anyone considering single parenthood.

Another excellent international publication for singles is *Single Parents With Adopted Kids.* The subscription rate is $20 per year. Contact Dannette Kaslow/SWAK, 4108 Washington Road, #101, Kenosha, WI   53144.

There are several single adoptive parent support groups across the United States. Once you have contacted national adoption organizations for information, find a support group in your area. Some groups may appear to focus on two-parent adoptions, but they often have single parents who are members. Other groups are just for single parents (see the appendices). What is important is that you find other single applicants and single adoptive parents to network with. These people can help you learn more about adoption and guide you through the process of selecting the type of child you want to adopt. They can also help you locate an adoption source. And after adopting, group members can provide support and information on dealing with issues unique to single parents.

Another organization to contact is: Single Parents Adopting Children Everywhere (SPACE), 6 Sunshine Avenue, Natick, MA 01760. Every other year SPACE presents the national Conference on Single Parent Adoption in the greater Boston area. Contact SPACE for single parent adoption information and ask them to add your name to their mailing list so that you'll receive information about this excellent conference.

Adoptive Families of America, Inc. (AFA) will also provide you with information on support groups, and through them you'll meet other singles attempting to adopt and adoptive parents who have good advice to share. Also contact the National Adoption Clearinghouse (see the appendices for addresses) and ask for its factsheet, titled "Single Parent Adoption: What You Need To Know."

OLDER CHILDREN AND CHILDREN WITH SPECIAL NEEDS

As previously discussed, there are many school-age children and children with special needs available for adoption in the United States. These children may be physically, mentally, or emotionally disabled, or they may be part of a sibling group that needs to be placed together. If you are willing to consider adopting one of these special children, then start your search by approaching public or private agencies in your state.

Most public agencies work with single applicants, and some believe that singles may be the best parents for certain children who wait for an adoptive home (primarily those who need undivided attention or a particularly strong one-to-one relationship). However, if you meet resistance with either public or private agencies, be persistent and do not give up. Follow the procedures suggested in chapter four for adopting children who wait. You should also consider intercountry adoption if you find yourself competing with a lot of couples who are trying to adopt the same type of child.

Not all singles are willing or able to parent a child with special needs or one who's school-age. Most people know their own limitations and if you feel that you are incapable of parenting such a child, then be truthful with yourself and agency personnel. As a single parent, you must work (unless you are independently wealthy), and you may not have the time or energy to meet the additional challenges of a child who is disabled in some respect. If you feel you can raise an older child or a child with special needs, there are many children waiting for a special person like you—both in the United States and abroad.

ADOPTING YOUNG CHILDREN

Some single pre-adopters are interested in adopting only a healthy infant or a young child under the age of five. If this is your goal, you may be met with strong resistance when trying to adopt a U.S.-born child. Healthy Caucasian infants and young children are usually reserved for two-parent families, and public and private agencies have dozens of these families waiting in line. However, the good news is that many of the agencies listed in the appendix will work with singles, particularly those who are interested in an African-American child, a child born in another country, or a child with a mental or physical disability.

BABIES THROUGH INDEPENDENT ADOPTION

Another option to consider is independent adoption if it's legal in your state. Many attorneys are willing to place minority infants and infants with special needs with single applicants. Like many agencies, they often have difficulty finding two-parent families for such children, so let them know you are interested in adopting such an infant. Most attorneys know other attorneys in other states. Ask them to network with their colleagues out of state. Tell everyone who might help that you are pursuing the adoption of a healthy minority infant or an infant with special needs.

What do you do if you want to adopt a healthy Caucasian infant? "Find an attorney who is willing to work with you, but realize most birth mothers want a two-parent family," advises a single mom who successfully adopted independently. "I had my résumé on file with several attorneys. It took me three years but finally a birth mother asked to meet me. I was so nervous, but we hit it off and she decided she wanted me. She was impressed with the size of my immediate family and how supportive they were about my adopting. I assured her that if anything ever happened to me, I had plenty of brothers and sisters who would also love and care for her child."

Another single mom suggests newspaper advertising. "Say in your ad that you are single and want to adopt a baby, and be prepared for some crank calls from men offering to help you out." This mom had only three calls over a ten-month period but she was eventually successful. She did not adopt the newborn she originally had hoped for, but instead adopted a five-month-old whose birth mother could not afford to support the child. "I'm twelve years older than the birth mother, own my own house and have a good job. The birth mother thought a single parent was fine as far as providing care and love because she had been doing that, but she felt her daughter deserved more." (Newspaper advertising is illegal in many states. Check state adoption laws.)

Whether you work independently or through an agency, how likely is it a birth parent would choose a single person to adopt her baby?

Dawn Smith-Pliner, owner and director of Friends in Adoption, Inc., in Middletown Spring, Vermont, says some birth mothers do choose singles. Why would a birth mother choose a single parent over a married couple? "Sometimes in a rape situation a birth mother will choose a single woman to raise the child," says Smith-Pliner, "because she is so angry with men. Or maybe the birth mother has had a very positive experience growing up with a single parent and she knows this arrangement can work.

"One woman who was considering a man said she felt less threatened as a birth mother knowing the baby would be parented by a man, that the role of adoptive mother and birth mother would not be in conflict," explains Smith-Pliner. "One birth mom we worked with answered an ad placed by a single man and she did place her baby with him. The little girl is three or four years old now and she's thriving. It is working out very well."

To learn more about independent adoption, talk with others who have adopted privately, consult an adoption attorney, and read the books available on independent adoption. Singles should pursue an independent adoption in the same way married couples would.

CHILDREN FROM OTHER COUNTRIES

Countless numbers of children are homeless and available for adoption from foreign countries because of war, poverty, natural disasters, or social circumstances, and a number of countries are in favor of United States citizens adopting their children. Many people successfully adopt from overseas through U.S.-based agencies, and many foreign countries are willing to work with prospective adoptive parents who are single. Jean Nelson-Erichsen, supervisor of social work at Los Niños International Adoption Center in Texas, says the agency works with several countries whose governments permit adoption by singles.

Nelson-Erichsen says the agency "welcomes singles between the ages of twenty-five and fifty years of age, with or without children, of all races and religions." Los Niños networks with other adoption agencies across the United States and works with Americans living abroad. Many other U.S. agencies also have sources overseas.

Casa del Mundo, Inc., was established in late 1990. According to Carol S. Perlmutter, adoptive parent, attorney, and executive director, "the agency places babies, toddlers, and occasionally older children from Honduras, Guatemala, and El Salvador with both singles and couples living in the United States." The agency will work with citizens living abroad who have home studies that are acceptable to INS. "All programs are open to single women. Single men are considered on a case-by-case basis," says Perlmutter, "and information on international adoption programs is subject to change."

One important advantage for singles adopting from overseas is that children of all races are available to them, and they don't have to compete with couples. Applicants are considered more or less in the order they apply. While there are not enough Caucasian, Asian or Hispanic infants in the United States for all those who want to adopt them, the reverse exists overseas, where there aren't enough parents for the number of young children who need homes.

The current *Report on Foreign Adoption,* which is available through the International Concerns Committee for Children for $20, is an excellent source for singles wishing to adopt from abroad. The report lists those agencies that welcome single applicants.

THE FEES

As explained in chapter four, public agencies usually charge no fee. In fact, if you choose to adopt a child with special needs, you may find that she is eligible for the Federal Title IV-E adoption assistance program under the Social Security Act or a state adoption subsidy program. Before the child is placed in your home, her eligibility for the Title IV-E or state program is determined. Be sure to ask about subsidy programs if you are thinking of adopting a child with special needs.

Private agencies may also place older children, and children classified as having special needs. Private agencies may or may not charge a fee for these adoptions. If they do, it is usually a modest one. They may also offer subsidies. However, should a birth mother choose you to adopt her newborn through a private agency, you may have to assume the responsibility of paying for her medical and legal fees and, possibly, other expenses.

Fees for independent adoptions vary greatly. You will have to pay your attorney's fees and those of the birth mother's. You will also be responsible for the birth mother's medical fees, including prenatal care and delivery, unless the birth mother has medical coverage. Even if the birth mother has medical coverage, you may still be responsible for the doctors' and hospitals' charges for the infant's care.

Depending on the state the birth mother resides in and her financial circumstances, you may also pay for her housing, maternity clothing, transportation to obtain medical care, counseling, and other maternity-related expenses. If you are involved in an interstate adoption, you must follow the requirements of the Interstate Compact and the state laws in both states. Know what expenses you can legally pay for in your state and the baby's birth state.

Using a competent adoption attorney will minimize your risks. However, all independent United States adoptions are risky because the birth mother may change her mind after giving birth and decide to parent her baby. If this happens, you might lose all of the money you have spent up to that point because most birth mothers are not in a position to reimburse you. An independent adoption can be as low as $2,000 or $3,000 (if the birth mother's medical fees are covered) or as high as $15,000 or $20,000. Most, however, run between $10,000 and $15,000.

International adoptions can also be rather expensive. Fees vary considerably; they can range from $4,000 to more than $15,000 ($11,000 to $12,000 appears to be average) depending on whether travel is required, the length of stay in the foreign country, and how much you choose to spend for your hotel and airfare. Sometimes adoptions arranged by private attorneys in the United States, who work with reliable sources in a foreign country, may run $20,000 or even higher.

You will get a much better idea of costs for all types of adoption programs as you receive written information from the sources you have contacted. Check the background of any source you are considering working with and be sure to network with other prospective and adoptive single parents.

RECOMMENDED READING

Adamec, Christine A. *There ARE Babies to Adopt: A Resource Guide for Prospective Parents.* New York: Pinnacle, 1991.

Dougherty, Sharon Ann. "Single Adoptive Mothers and Their Children." *The Philadelphia Inquirer,* June 13, 1990.

Groze, Victor K. and James A. Rosenthal. "Single Parents and Their Adopted Children: A Psychosocial Analysis." *Families in Society* 72, no. 2 (February 1991): 67–77.

Marindin, Hope. *The Handbook for Single Adoptive Parents.* Chevy Chase, MD: Committee for Single Adoptive Parents, 1992.

Michelman, Stanley B. and Meg Schneider with Antonia van der Meer. *The Private Adoption Handbook: A Step-by-Step Guide to Independently Adopting a Baby.* New York: Dell, 1988.

Oliver, Stephanie Stokes. "Single Adoptive Fathers." *Essence* 12 (1988): 114–6, 146.

Sullivan, Marylou. "Perceptions of Single Adoptive Parents: How We View Ourselves, How Others View Us." *OURS* 22, no. 6 (November/ December 1989): 34–35.

Independent Adoption

You may find an agency that can help you adopt a baby in a reasonable amount of time, or you may never connect with an agency. What then? You are going to have to find your baby independently, without the help of an agency, like thousands of families do each year. In fact, it is estimated that more than sixty percent of all infant adoptions in the United States are handled privately today. Only estimates can be given because most states do not require reports on the number of independent adoptive placements that occur each year.

What we do know is most adoption agencies have few healthy Caucasian babies to place because the majority of pregnant women interested in making an adoption plan for their babies are not turning to agencies. These women are choosing independent (private) placement over agency adoption for several reasons that will be discussed later in this chapter.

We also know that prospective parents who want to adopt a baby have a good chance of succeeding if they pursue independent adoption. However, prospective parents should try to get on an agency list while they search for a baby to adopt independently. You can increase your chances of succeeding by not limiting yourself to one approach. "Being on an agency list, while we searched independently for a baby, was like insurance for us," says Bridget, a 32-year-old from Sacramento. "We knew we would eventually get a baby from the agency, but we felt we might adopt sooner if we pursued private adoption also."

INDEPENDENT ADOPTION MYTHS

The average person does not know much about independent adoption. One prospective adoptive parent relayed this story:

> I asked my neighbor if she knew anything about independent adoption. She answered, "I hope you two are not that desperate." So I

135

decided to ask a co-worker. She said, "How can you even think of private adoption? First of all, I know it is very expensive, and secondly if the real mother wants the baby back, you would have to return it." I then asked my best friend. "Why would you even think of a black market adoption?" she replied. "I know how much you want a baby, but how can you think of doing something illegal? You wouldn't even have a birth certificate, unless you could buy one someplace."

I thought about this for a while and decided independent adoption was really black market adoption and only desperate people with money would pursue it. Well, we were neither desperate, nor wealthy, but I decided to check with an attorney anyway.

What this couple found was the opposite of what they had been told. An independent adoption is legal if handled according to state law. If it is legal, it is not a black or gray market adoption. The baby will have a birth certificate. This type of adoption does not have to be outrageously expensive and all kinds of people attempt private adoption, not just wealthy people.

As you explore independent adoption, realize that friends and families will have their own ideas about private adoption and much of the information they have will be inaccurate. Unless, of course, your cousin is an adoption attorney or your friend has just recently completed two independent adoptions in the last two years.

No adoption attorney in your family or among your friends? Then your best source of information will be attorneys who routinely handle independent adoptions, adoptive parents who have successfully completed a private adoption in your state, and books on independent adoption.

Most people are vaguely aware of how an agency adoption works (apply to an agency, accepted by agency, approved home study, wait for child, child is placed), but are confused by independent adoption. Information has been available on agency adoptions for years now. One only needs to view a list of adoption books to see how many of these books have been published over the years. The first books mentioned very little about private adoption. When it was mentioned, it was often with concern and caution. As pregnant women began to choose independent adoption and moved away from agencies, much more was written on the subject. It was not, however, until the late eighties that books with an emphasis on independent adoption were published. If independent adoption is a consideration, make an effort to read these books.

As in agency adoptions, you should spend time learning about private adoption: Find out how it works, how to locate a birth mother, how to find an adoption attorney, the amount of money involved, how to ensure a legal adoption, and how to help your birth mother receive the support services she needs to make the best possible adoption plan for her baby. This is just a partial list of things you will need to consider as you attempt a private adoption.

HOW INDEPENDENT ADOPTION WORKS

Independent adoption is recognized as a legal and ethical method of adoption in almost every state. Private adoption is cleared through the court system and adheres to the same state adoption laws agencies operate under.

Independent placement is an adoption in which the birth mother places her child herself instead of using an adoption agency. Basically, a couple hears about a woman who wants to make an adoption plan for her unborn baby. The woman is usually instructed to contact the couple's attorney directly if she is interested in placing her baby with them. The necessary paperwork is then started. Or the prospective birth mother may ask her family attorney to help place her baby. In this case, the attorney will actively search for a prospective family.

After the baby is born, the birth mother has the right to accept or reject the adopting parents' request to adopt until the papers transferring parental rights have been signed. In some states, once consent has been given, it is irrevocable unless it was obtained through fraud, misrepresentation, or under duress. In other states, birth parents may have a certain number of days, weeks, or months in which they can alter their decision, while still other states allow the court to permit a withdrawal of consent up to the final adoption decree. Some states permit withdrawal of consent for any reason; others allow consent to be revoked only if the court finds that it is in the child's best interest. When, or if, the consent may be withdrawn and for what reasons vary by state. Always check with an attorney for a correct interpretation of your state's laws.

In cases where one or both birth parents have not signed papers terminating parental rights, the baby may still be placed with the prospective adoptive parents. This is a risky situation because the baby is not yet free for adoption. This means the adopting parents could lose the child if one or both parents decides not to sign the papers. Before accepting a baby for placement be sure you know if the signatures have been received, or when the signatures are expected to be obtained.

If the birth parents are married, the rules change. But what if the birth father of the child is not the legal father? Again, laws vary from state to state and a competent attorney will know the answer to this question.

If you live in a state where independent adoption is illegal, you may be able to locate a birth mother on your own and refer her to an adoption agency for placement of her baby with you. Such adoptions are called identified adoptions. (See the chapter on understanding agency information and requirements for more information.)

EXPENSES AND LAWS

Always check your state's adoption laws before pursuing an independent adoption situation. A copy of your state's laws can be obtained at no charge from the National Adoption Information Clearinghouse, 11426 Rockville Pike, Suite 410, Rockville, MD 20852 (301) 231-6512. You can also check with an adoptive parent group in your area, with an adoption attorney, or with your county court. This information is not difficult to find. If private adoption is legal, be sure you know of any restrictions your state may place on these adoptions.

In some states the adopting parents may pay for many pregnancy-related expenses such as medical, legal, counseling, housing, maternity clothes, and transportation to obtain medical services. In other states, only the birth mother's medical fees and legal expenses may be paid by the adoptive parents. No state allows you to pay for a birth parent's education, even if it is only minor vocational training, nor can you send a birth mother on a vacation, buy her a new postpregnancy wardrobe, or do anything else that may suggest you are buying

Questions to Ask about State Laws

1. Are private adoptions allowed in this state?
2. Is a home study required? If yes, before or after the child's placement?
3. Which of the birth mother's expenses can be legally paid for by the adopting parents?
4. Are there limits on the amounts adoptive parents can pay? (For instance, if payment for maternity clothes is permitted, how much exactly can parents spend?)
5. Can anonymity between parties be protected?
6. Must adoptive parents be represented by an attorney? Does the birth mother need separate counsel?
7. In this state, may prospective adoptive parents advertise in the newspaper for a baby to adopt?
8. How soon after delivery can the birth mother sign relinquishment papers transferring her parental rights?
9. Is the birth mother permitted to revoke her consent after signing relinquishment papers?
10. Must the birth father also sign the relinquishment papers?
11. How long after placement is the adoption finalized?

her baby. Generally, courts require that all expenses be documented and reported to them. Find out from your attorney if there is a limit on the amount of money that can be spent on certain expenses, either by state law or by judgment of your local court system.

Other laws, including those that mandate when a home study is conducted, vary from state to state. Some require a home study before placement; others after. In a few states, a home study is conducted only if the judge requires it. Adoptions may be finalized in three months in one state and twelve months in another.

Because the laws vary by state, and state laws can change, you should know that the state laws listed in some adoption resource books may have changed. A current interpretation may save you many headaches.

Call your state's social service department (may also be listed as the Department of Human Services, Department of Public Welfare, or Department of Family and Children's Services), located in your state's capitol, or contact an adoption attorney for verification of state laws regarding independent adoption.

In order to complete an adoption legally when two states are involved (the one you reside in and the state the baby was, or will be, born in), your attorney must adhere to the adoption laws in both states. Your adoption must be cleared through the Interstate Compact on the Placement of Children. The Interstate Compact describes the procedures one must follow before transferring a child across state lines. An adoption attorney can handle the arrangements for you.

There are many variables involved in an independent placement. Because of this, prospective parents should read everything they can on private adoption, talk with other adoptive parents, and consult with a competent attorney before beginning to look for a child.

WHY MANY CHOOSE PRIVATE ADOPTION

Couples choosing private adoption may do so for many reasons. Independent adoption satisfies the needs of the adoptive parents who want a newborn from the hospital without an enormous amount of red tape. It also gives the birth mother the satisfaction of knowing her baby has been placed directly in the adopting parents' home, sometimes with the family she has chosen. Some see it as a faster way to adopt compared to the long waiting lists at most agencies. Others opt for independent adoption because of agency restrictions such as the age of the adopting parents, religion, or length of marriage. Couples near or older than forty, for instance, may be rejected only because of their age, not because they would make unsuitable parents. Additionally, some choose to adopt independently because, even today, some agencies require the adoptive mother to stay at home for a specified length of time after placement. Often that arrangement just is not feasible.

Even couples who meet agencies' requirements often decide to follow through with an independent adoption when given the choice. In fact, one couple who adopted their first child through an agency was on two agency waiting lists for a second child when a private adoption situation became known to them. The baby was born a few weeks later and because the birth parents were in agreement on an adoption plan, this couple opted for the private placement.

One other reason adoptive parents cite for choosing private adoption is getting the chance to have some control over their adoption. "We felt we could make our adoption happen quickly," says an adoptive father from Montana, "based on the amount of time and effort we were willing to put into it. We adopted in less than five months." This is not an unusual time frame. Many people who adopt independently succeed in less than a year.

Birth parents commonly choose private adoption for several reasons also. One reason is the privacy it affords them. Birth parents often do not wish to work with an agency because they fear they will be subjected to close scrutiny and what they perceive as judgmental treatment. Second, in a private adoption, some or nearly all of the birth mother's expenses may be covered by the prospective adoptive parents. This means the prospective birth mother does not need to depend on welfare to pay her medical or living expenses. (Some agencies still insist their birth mothers go on welfare.) Often, a birth mother chooses private adoption because it allows her to have more control over the placement of her child.

In fairness to agencies, many now give more control to the birth parents, enabling them to place their child with the family of their choice, and some agencies provide private medical care, but this is not always the case.

There are risks involved in private adoption, but there are also benefits, the most important being the shorter waiting time for a healthy newborn. Judging by the number of people who adopt privately each year, the benefits appear to outweigh the risks.

MAJOR DIFFERENCE BETWEEN AGENCY AND PRIVATE ADOPTION

Private adoption differs most from agency adoption in that the birth parents place their baby directly with the adopting family (in a confidential, semiopen, or open adoption). The birth parents usually sign the termination of parental rights after the baby is placed with the adopting parents (not before, as with most agency adoptions), unless all are in agreement that the baby be placed in foster care until the birth parents sign the necessary papers for adoption.

Courtwork is usually processed in the adoptive parents' state of residence, but sometimes it can be processed in the state that the baby is born in. In the case of an agency adoption, the adoption may be processed in the state that the agency is located. When adopting an infant born out of state, your attorney must obtain permission from the Interstate Compact for the Placement of Children, for both the placing and receiving states, before the baby may enter your state of residence.

HOW MUCH WILL IT COST?

It is very difficult to estimate expenses in an independent adoption because so many variables are involved. Attorneys charge different fees. Support for a birth mother may be higher if you are working with a birth mother who lives in New York City than if your birth mother resides in the Midwest. Medical costs may differ from one hospital to the next. There are no set fees in private adoption. However, total fees over $20,000 are questionable in most states.

If the state you reside in prohibits paying for anything but the birth mother's medical fees, your adoption will be much less than if you reside in a state where you are permitted to support her for several months, for instance, at $500 a month or $1,500 per month. However, if your prospective birth mother lives at home, has medical insurance, or is on welfare, you may only have to cover legal expenses and the doctor's and hospital's charges for the baby's care.

The Bakers are in their late thirties. Their first adoption was through an agency and the fees totaled $11,000. They decided they could adopt privately for less if they could locate a birth mother who did not need financial support and had medical coverage.

The first birth mother they found fit this description. (They admit they were fortunate because a mother considering adoption usually needs some financial assistance.) Their expenses for this adoption totaled $3,450. Of that amount, $1,200 was a hospital nursery fee not covered by the birth mother's insurance. Fortunately, the Baker's medical insurance paid the full nursery fee. In reality, the Baker's adoption cost them $2,250; $750 for the birth mother's attorney and $1,500 for their attorney. Most independent adoption fees, however, range from $10,000 to $15,000 (including everything).

If you need to keep expenses to a minimum, then you have to focus on finding an arrangement you can afford. Spread the word that not only are you trying to locate a pregnant woman who is considering adoption, but you also must find a woman who has insurance. You could also limit your search to the states that restrict adopting parents from paying for anything other than the birth mother's medical and legal services. For information on the fees that are permitted in each state, refer to *Adoption Laws: Answers to the Most-Asked Questions,* published by the National Adoption Information Clearinghouse. This publication, however, is not meant to serve as a replacement for legal advice. Always seek legal advice from a competent adoption attorney.

ADOPTING THROUGH AN ATTORNEY

Many adoption attorneys in the United States maintain lists of prospective adoptive parents. They keep such lists because several social service agencies, churches, and schools refer pregnant women who are considering adoption to them. Prospective parents present the attorney with a personal résumé (not to be confused with a job résumé), which is then left on file. If the birth mother does not wish to read résumés and choose an adoptive family, the attorney judiciously chooses a suitable couple. Should the birth mother want to choose, and she has specific criteria that she wants in a family (a childless, Lutheran family who lives in the country, for example), then the attorney will present her with several parent résumés that meet her qualifications.

Once the birth mother identifies a couple she is interested in, the attorney may arrange a meeting between the prospective couple and the birth mother (with or without disclosing their identities). Or, the couple may be asked to provide more information about themselves to the birth mother in the form of a letter. (Letters to birth mothers are fully discussed later in this chapter.)

If you find an attorney who maintains a list, by all means try to add your name to it. Then continue to look for a birth mother on your own. In fact, actively search for attorneys with lists and put your name on as many lists as possible. Some attorneys may encourage you to mail in your résumé. If a birth mother selects your family, you may then be asked to place money to cover her expenses in an escrow account. Other attorneys may want to meet you first. They may or may not charge a consultation fee so be sure to ask. Attorneys do not usually charge to keep your résumé on file.

If you must limit the amount of money you can spend, be sure the attorney understands this. (Although, do not overly emphasize your financial constraints or your attorney may wonder whether you can afford to support a child.) Then, you will only be contacted about situations within your budget. Always take the time to compare attorney fees as you would compare agency fees.

Some attorneys will teach you how to locate a birth mother on your own. They may also permit you to use their office phone number in a newspaper ad if you plan to advertise. Often these attorneys provide their clients with a list of newspapers that carry adoption ads. (Newspaper advertising is illegal in many states, so always check state adoption laws.) Once you locate a birth mother, your attorney interviews her and handles many of the arrangements and details, such as confirming the pregnancy.

In some states, an attorney can handle the legal work for an adoption, but is not allowed to place a child for adoption because state law says only the birth parents can do this. Intermediaries are not permitted to handle direct placements in such states.

Before looking for an adoption situation independently, speak with an adoption attorney. You may have one of the best attorneys in town as your legal counsel, but if she does not routinely handle nonrelative adoptions, she is not your best choice. Nonrelative adoptions can be difficult cases depending on the circumstances. Find an experienced attorney who understands state adoption laws, especially if the adoption will involve the Interstate Compact.

Nadine and Bill engaged the services of their family attorney for an independent adoption. Because the attorney was unfamiliar with the adoption laws of their state, he had to research them. The placement was to be an interstate adoption and he knew nothing about the paperwork involved. Again, more research was necessary. Naturally, Nadine and Bill had to pay for the extra legal work, making their fee higher than normal. Although, they appreciated having their attorney handle the adoption and are thrilled everything was completed successfully, they are resentful they had to "pay for all the research" because, as Nadine says, "We paid for it, but every couple who follows us [using this attorney] will not have to pay for the extra work." These parents should have hired an adoption attorney instead. Always be sure you understand the fee schedule before hiring an attorney. Get it in writing!

Always check the attorney's reputation with other adoptive parents and with other attorneys. You can also check with the state

Questions to Ask Your Attorney

- Is there a retainer fee?
- Will he interview the birth mother or birth parents for you?
- Is there a set fee for services or are you billed according to services rendered?
- Are you expected to place money in an escrow account? If so, how much? For what expenses? Will you receive a monthly statement indicating how those fees have been dispersed?
- Who will the attorney represent in court? Some states insist that two attorneys be involved; one representing the birth parent and one representing the adoptive parents.
- Will the attorney handle the medical arrangements for the birth mother?
- How many independent adoptions has she handled?
- How many interstate placements has he handled?
- Will the attorney suggest to the birth mother's attorney that she receive counseling before the birth of the baby?
- How much money could we lose if the arrangement falls through? (Some attorneys erase their fees, others do not. Get this in writing.)

attorney general's office in the appropriate state. How do you find an adoption attorney? Refer to the list in the appendices and talk with adoptive parents in your support group.

BIRTH PARENTS' MEDICAL AND SOCIAL HISTORY

No matter what type of adoption you become involved in, be sure to obtain as much information about the birth parents as you can. All agencies ask questions or have birth parents complete forms concerning their social and medical history. Attorneys also have forms they ask the birth parents to complete.

Ruth Werth, adoption specialist for Lutheran Social Services in Griffith, Indiana, recommends families request that the following information be obtained from the birth parents:

1. Height, weight
2. Hair color, eye color
3. Complexion
4. Race
5. Religion
6. Nationality
7. Last grade completed
8. Grades
9. Favorite subject
10. Special honors, programs and activities in high school and/or college
11. Any additional training
12. Career goals
13. What do you want your child to know about the other birth parent?
14. Are other children being parented?
15. Use of drugs, alcohol during pregnancy
16. What is your favorite leisure time activity?
17. Who is your favorite author?
18. Who is your favorite music group? Type of music?
19. What is your favorite season? Why?
20. If you could tell your baby anything, what would you say?
21. Family medical/health information

"Medical and social history information is extremely vital," says Valerie Miller, director of the Child Welfare Department for Catholic Charities in Toledo, Ohio. "We explain to the birth parents how important it is for the child and the adoptive parents to have access to this information. We ask our birth parents to complete a thirteen-page questionnaire. That information is then compiled and presented to the adoptive parents."

The following is an excerpt from that thirteen-page questionnaire covering the medical history of the birth parents and their biological relatives. Miller recommends that adoptive families obtain information about these medical concerns and the age at onset, if applicable.

Please indicate by checking yes or no if you or any genetic relatives (i.e. your mother, father, sisters, brothers, grandparents, aunts, uncles, or any other children you have had) ever had or now have the medical items listed.

Medical Condition	No	Yes— Self	Yes— Other Relatives (Specify)	Comments
1. Clubfoot				What part of body? Both Sides? How severe?
2. Harelip (cleft lip) or cleft palate				
3. Congenital heart defect				
4. Any other malformations				
5. Muscular dystrophy				Parts of body involved? Age at onset?
6. Multiple sclerosis				
7. Cerebral palsy				
8. Other paralysis or crippling disorder				
9. Seizures, convulsions, or epilepsy				Age at onset? How frequent? What treatment?
10. Blindness or serious trouble seeing				Age at onset? Any suspected cause?
11. Deafness or serious trouble hearing				
12. Speech problem				
13. Learning disability				Special Education?
14. Mental retardation				Any diagnosis or cause? Hospitalized?
15. Diabetes				Age at onset? How treated?
16. Thyroid disorder				

Medical Condition	No	Yes—Self	Yes—Other Relatives (Specify)	Comments
17. Other hormone disorder				
18. Eczema				Any cause known? What treatment? What medication?
19. Asthma or hay fever				
20. Other allergy				
21. Hemophilia				
22. Sickle cell anemia				
23. Other blood disease				
24. Schizophrenia				Age at onset? Treatment? Hospitalization?
25. Manic depressive				
26. Other mental illness				
27. Hypertension				
28. Stroke				
29. Heart attack (coronary)				
30. Other cardiovascular problems				
31. Cancer				What kind? Age at onset? Treatment? What part of body?
32. Cystic fibrosis				
33. Huntington's disease				
34. Any other characteristics or conditions that run in your family?				

Courtesy of Catholic Charities, Diocese of Toledo, Ohio.

DECISIONS TO MAKE

No doubt, you must first decide how much money you can afford to spend on an adoption. Then, how much of that money can you afford to lose? Private adoption is risky! This warning is not meant to discourage you from pursuing an independent placement, but you should be aware of the risks involved before committing yourself to a potential adoption situation since an estimated ten percent of birth parents change their minds about adoption after the baby is born.

Are you willing to have any contact with the birth parents? Are you willing to meet the birth parents? Would you prefer to have someone else, like an intermediary, intervene for you? (Check your state's law to see if you can use an intermediary.) Are you open to an exchange of letters? Will you speak with a birth mother on the telephone? Do you wish to maintain complete anonymity? The state of Virginia, for instance, passed a law in 1989 that requires birth parents and adoptive parents to meet in person and exchange identifying information before a decree of adoption will be granted. In other states, it is possible to complete an independent adoption with complete anonymity.

How much work are you willing to put into finding an adoption situation? Would you prefer to wait on file with one or several attorneys?

Discuss what you will do if the baby is born with a disability. What disabilities could you accept? Can you handle the added expense of a cesarean section? A C-section could push a $5,000 or $6,000 adoption to nearly $10,000 or more.

LOCATING A BIRTH MOTHER

How do you locate a baby to adopt on your own? You begin by telling everyone, even strangers, that you are interested in adopting a baby privately. If you are unable to tell people you may not succeed. Success often depends on the number of people that are looking on your behalf.

A prospective adoption is often put together by intermediaries. Intermediaries are usually doctors, attorneys, clergy members, teachers, social workers, and other professional people. But your family, friends, friends of friends, and acquaintances may also act as informal intermediaries, so it is imperative that you tell these people about your desire to adopt. A friend who does volunteer work may hear of a pregnant woman. Your brother, who's a teacher, may have a colleague who has a pregnant woman in one of her classes. A relative may have friends in another state with a pregnant daughter. Every person is a possible contact for you.

One woman mentioned to a cashier in a grocery store where she regularly shopped that she and her husband were trying to adopt a baby. You can imagine her shock when the cashier said there were two pregnant women working in the store and that one of them was considering adoption. You guessed it. That baby became their daughter. What if this woman had been too shy to mention her desire to adopt?

You must be assertive, and the more assertive you are in your approach the easier it will be to find a potential birth mother. Remember, you are marketing yourself. Use your imagination and try different strategies or a combination of several approaches.

A NETWORKING CAMPAIGN

Notes enclosed in holiday cards expressing your desire to adopt a newborn baby may produce a lead for you. Some people have had success

Sample Cover Letter
to Send with Résumé

Dear Friends and Relatives,

As many of you know, we have been trying to adopt a baby. The adoption agencies we have contacted have not been able to help us, so we have decided to pursue independent adoption (nonagency adoption), which is legal in our state. We have also hired an adoption attorney who helps couples, like us, to locate a baby to adopt.

Our attorney says we can adopt much more quickly if we tell everyone we know that we are trying to adopt a newborn, so we are asking for your assistance. Here's how you can help us. If you know of a pregnant woman or teen who is considering adoption for her baby, please share our résumé with her and encourage her to call our attorney. Should she want to know more about us before contacting our attorney, we would be happy to write her a letter either directly or through a third party, or we could telephone her. If you hear of someone through work, church, or your volunteer work, please give us a call. At that point we can decide how to proceed.

Attached is our résumé. You may share this with your friends and acquaintances. John Smith, our attorney, can be reached at 555-1234. Our telephone number is 555-4321.

Thank you for any help you can give us.

Warmly,

John and Jane Doe

passing out business cards that state their interest in adopting. Cards are printed with your name, address, and phone number. People have tacked up cards in laundromats, grocery and drugstores, health clubs, and on school campuses. Some prospective adopters have also mailed their business cards to high school guidance counselors. Others have enclosed them, along with their checks, when paying monthly bills.

Another approach is to launch a letter-writing campaign. Prepare a short, one-page résumé and attach a photo. Make your résumé personal. Remember, you want to adopt a child, not apply for a job. Initially, mail letters to family, friends, friends of friends. Today physicians, attorneys, health specialists, and other similar professionals are besieged with requests to help locate babies. Contact them, but only after you have tried family and friends first. Other possible sources include churches and synagogues, abortion and health care clinics, colleges, pregnancy crisis centers and Planned Parenthood clinics.

The preceding generic letter is the type of cover letter to use when mailing your résumé to family and friends.

If you opt to do a mass mailing of your résumé, you must decide whether you want to remain anonymous to a birth mother. If you do, then include only your first names on your résumé and use the phone number of your attorney, a close friend, a relative, or a clergy member. It should be someone you trust and can rely on to accept telephone calls in your behalf. Use a cover letter to explain to family and friends what you are doing, how they can help, and what they should do if they locate a possible adoption situation. Do they call you first? Talk with the woman themselves? Have the woman call your attorney? Telephone you? Most people need to be told *exactly* what to do if they locate a possible birth mother. If anonymity is not important, include your name and home telephone number, plus one additional number on your résumé if you cannot always be reached at the first one, unless you plan to use an answering machine when you are not available.

ONE COUPLE'S APPROACH

Pam and Bob pursued agency and independent adoption simultaneously. Hoping for an open, independent adoption, they wrote a résumé complete with a cover letter, and designed a business card. Their mailing was sent to high schools, universities, clinics, doctors, and attorneys. They also passed out their business cards wherever they went. They adopted a beautiful baby girl within six months, a result of their networking, and are now enjoying an open adoption arrangement with their daughter's birth family. Their business card carried a personal appeal message and was tastefully done.

Pam and Bob O'Neill
111 Any St.
Any City, Any State 00000
(555) 555-6729

HAPPY COUPLE WANTS TO ADOPT A BABY!
If you know a pregnant woman who would like
someone to adopt her baby, please contact us
or our attorney, collect.

Harry Freedman (555) 555-3286

This was their cover letter:

We need your help and any assistance you can lend will be greatly appreciated. We are Pam and Bob O'Neill and we have just begun an extensive search to locate a baby to adopt. We'd like to tell you more about us.

Bob is a high school band director, and Pam is a laboratory supervisor in a hospital. We are excited and ready to have a baby join our family. We hope you may know of someone who is pregnant and might be considering adoption as a choice. Please don't hastily throw out our letter because you have no one in mind for us at the moment. We might be exactly the couple a future birth mother will be looking for.

We plan to adopt our child through an open, independent adoption. We feel that birth parents need to know how their child is doing. In our case, we would like to maintain contact with the birth families, if they so wish.

We have a lot of love to share and a good home to offer. Please call collect if you know of a baby available for adoption or if you know of a mother who would like to give her baby a good home.

Phone: 1-555-555-6792
Address: 111 Any Street
         Any City, Any State 12345

With many thanks,

Pam and Bob O'Neill

Pam and Bob O'Neill

This was attached to Pam and Bob's cover letter along with a picture:

Dear Expectant Mother,

We are Pam and Bob O'Neill and we would be honored if you would consider us to be the parents of your baby.

We are two outgoing and giving people. Pam is a laboratory supervisor in a hospital and Bob is a band director for junior high and high school students. We both have qualities important for a good family life. Bob, as a teacher, is very patient and is willing to spend whatever time it takes for someone to learn. He is also a person with a sense of humor and is always smiling and happy. Pam is very affectionate, caring, and loving. She is a responsible person who would take care of all of a child's daily needs. Pam wouldn't hesitate about staying up all night to care for a sick child.

We live in a two-story home in a small, friendly community outside of _____. We enjoy it with our two cocker spaniels, Jake and Scooter. When we designed our home, we envisioned our spare room as a baby's room. We can picture what it will be like with a crib, mobile, and other baby supplies—then later with a small bed, a toy chest, and toys scattered everywhere!

Both of us are close to our families. Bob's folks live in Norwalk, _____ which is about an hour from our new home. We would be able to visit these grandparents frequently. Pam grew up in northern Illinois and tries to visit as much as she can. She has several nieces with babies and small children and looks forward to holiday get-togethers.

Bob is an avid sports fan and particularly likes baseball. We are looking forward to taking our child to an occasional game and supporting our son or daughter in whatever activities he/she might select. Pam and Bob both like to sail and also do a little downhill skiing in the winter. We would like to see our child develop a number of interests that would provide him/her with recreation and happiness in the years to come.

After church on Sundays, we love to take the dogs for walks in the park. It would add so much to be able to take our son or daughter with us to share that peace and beauty.

We know this is a difficult decision for you. We both have much to give and can provide your baby with a safe and loving home to grow up in. And what a lucky baby to have two sets of parents who care! If you would like to talk to us about adopting your child, please call us collect at 1-555-555-6729, or contact our attorney, Harry Freedman, collect at 1-555-555-3286 for more information.

Wishing you well,

Pam and Bob O'Neill

Pam and Bob O'Neill

PREPARING YOUR RÉSUMÉ

A personal résumé (or profile) is a one-page description of you and your spouse that summarizes such things as your length of marriage, reasons for wanting to adopt a child, hobbies and interests, personal characteristics, and any additional information you feel is pertinent. A résumé contains your name, sometimes your address (if you're not concerned with anonymity), and two phone numbers. A personal résumé always includes a picture of you and your spouse and any children you may already have.

You may be asked to submit a personal résumé to an adoption attorney or agency. When an attorney or agency helps a birth mother find an adoptive family, often it is the résumé that is presented to the birth parent, with or without identifying information.

You may also use a personal résumé if you decide to search independently for a baby. Personal résumés are usually what you mail to your friends, family, acquaintances, doctors, and others on your mailing list.

A personal résumé is like a letter in many ways. It is not, however, a letter written to a specific birth mother. A letter written specifically to a birth mother is called a "Birth Mother" letter and it usually follows the résumé. If a birth mother is interested in knowing more about you after reading your résumé, you then send a letter to her or an intermediary who has agreed to give it to her. An agency or attorney may also ask for a birth mother letter to keep on file.

A personal résumé is typed single-spaced on $8 \frac{1}{2}$ x 11 paper. It should be attractive and eye catching. Be sure it is printed with black ink. Black ink copies well and a recipient may want to make a copy of your résumé and send it to someone else.

What do you say in your résumé? Here are some suggestions:

1. In the opening paragraph state how long you have been married and how much you hope to add a child (or another child) to your family through adoption and why.

2. If you mention infertility, do so in one sentence. Your résumé must be positive. When a prospective birth mother reads your résumé, she must see you as a potential solution to her situation.

3. Do not include a physical description of yourself. Your picture will say it all.

4. Describe each other using two short paragraphs. For example: David graduated from the University of Michigan School of Engineering. He has worked in his chosen field for eleven years. He has a wonderful sense of humor, but it was his gentleness that attracted me. David is soft spoken and loves being with family, especially his nieces and nephews. He is also a patient man. He would be such a good father because...

5. Do not give your age. The birth mother may be set on a family in a specific age group of which you do not belong. Even 34 sounds old to a 17-year-old, especially if she was born when her parents were 18. That makes you her parents's age and they, obviously, are old enough to be grandparents. Age can be discussed later, if the birth mother asks.

6. If you work with children professionally or on a volunteer basis, say so. (This includes baby-sitting nieces, nephews, and neighbors' children.) If you are a child's godparent, mention it.

7. Mention your extended family. Write about how much your parents are hoping and waiting for a grandchild, and how your siblings are waiting for a niece or nephew.

8. If you are affluent, do not brag about it. Wealth is often intimidating.

9. Talk about the love and care you can give a child now and in the future.

10. Mention your religion only if it is important to you.

11. Provide two phone numbers and put the numbers at the top or bottom of your résumé so they cannot be missed. Give numbers where someone is usually available. If you plan to use an answering machine, let her know she can leave a message and you will return the call. State that collect calls will be accepted.

12. Sign your résumé (in longhand). It is a wonderful personal touch.

13. Write your résumé in language that enables a birth mother to envision her baby with you. Remember, the clearest sentences create the least complicated images. Watch for words that are often used unnecessarily. (For example, replace phrases like "in order to" with "to.") If you can say it in one sentence, don't elaborate. You might want to have a couple members of your support group read your résumé for terminology, grammar, punctuation, and clarity.

THE RÉSUMÉ PICTURE

Because of the inherent power of photographs, your résumé picture must say exactly what you want it to. Following these guidelines will help you get the right picture:

1. The picture should convey a feeling of warmth and love between the two of you. You want the perfect picture that says everything about your relationship. It may take several tries before you find the ideal photo. Do not settle for anything less than the best.

2. Have the picture taken professionally if possible. An outdoor setting is best; take it sitting under a tree or near a stream, in a relaxed position. It should be a casual picture, one where you are dressed neatly but casually. If you have a child, position the child between you. Be sure the child does not look like an afterthought in the picture.

3.   The picture should be no larger than a 5" × 7" and no smaller than 3" × 4". Your résumé should be tightly written because the picture will take up more space than you may realize.

4.   The picture should be permanently attached to your résumé. Do not use paper clips. If you have children and pets, include them in the picture.

NEWSPAPER ADVERTISING

Newspaper advertising is a controversial issue. At least one prominent national adoption organization openly opposes it, claiming that all parties are at risk for potential abuse, and some adult adoptees find advertising degrading. However, it has worked for some adoptive parents and birth parents.

Sometimes newspapers in states that prohibit adoption ads will accept an ad. Do not assume the law has changed and you were given wrong advice. Often, newspapers are totally unaware that a law against adoption advertisements exists.

In states where such advertising is legal, you may still have difficulty finding a paper that will accept your ad. Such policies are difficult to understand. See Stanley Michelman, Meg Schneider, and Antonia van der Meer's book, *The Private Adoption Handbook* (Dell, 1988), for a state-by-state listing of newspapers that will accept your ad. Keep making phone calls and you will find newspapers that will be pleased to accept your ad. Some papers will not bill you, so be sure to have your credit card handy.

All types of newspapers accept adoption ads, including city papers with large circulations, weekly suburban papers, and papers with national circulation like *USA Today*. Names and numbers of newspapers around the country can be found in the *Gale Directory of Publications* at your local library. There are all sorts of theories about the types of papers that produce the best results. Large city papers and papers with national circulation most certainly reach the largest audiences, which is a major plus, but you will also find that your ad is one of many, giving a prospective birth mother several families to choose from. The cost of running an ad in papers like *USA Today* is expensive. Still, it is a possibility and splitting the cost with another couple is always an option. In this case, both parties must realize that only one couple may actually adopt a baby. But then again, you may get several good leads from one ad. In small weekly papers you may find your ad is the only one running, which is a nice advantage. Plus, these publications' rates are lower, making it affordable.

When is the best time to advertise? Some swear Sunday is by far the best day. Others say the best time to run the ad is from Wednesday through Sunday, and many suggest you run ads in several newspapers at the same time. Obviously, the number of papers and the number of ads you run is based on your budget. Remember, this is just a small portion of the costs of a private adoption. The best times of the year to run ads appear to be in fall after school begins, the end of December, and mid-April to mid-May.

Many people have a separate phone line installed in their home when they decide to use newspaper advertising. Some do this because they want to remain anonymous. Others install the extra line because they will know when that phone rings, it is most likely an adoption call. You can also use an answering machine on that phone line with a special message asking a caller about a possible adoption and to please call back or to leave a phone number so you can call her back. Crank calls are, unfortunately, part of the package, so late at night you can turn that telephone off. Do not be surprised if you receive a few calls from other prospective adoptive parents wanting to know if this method works.

Before placing an ad, check newspapers for other adoption ads and create an ad that is different from the rest. This means altering the wording, the length, and the style. (Do not write "We are a happily married, financially secure couple hoping to adopt a newborn

Sample Classified Adoption Ads

ADOPTION Childless, Caucasian couple seeking to adopt newborn baby. Lots of love from us and grandparents is waiting for your baby. Let us help you. Legal and medical expenses can be paid in compliance with state law. Call Debbie and Mark collect, 555-5555.

ADOPTION Young Christian couple with one adopted child seeking to adopt second baby. Financial help available. Can be agency-assisted adoption or independent through attorney. Your choice. We would cherish your child forever. Call Matt and Ann collect, 555-5512.

ADOPTION Caucasian professional couple with country home, lots of love, large extended family, seeking to adopt newborn. Have approved home study completed by adoption agency. Can pay expenses allowed by state law. Let us provide a nurturing, stable home for your child. Call Mike and Jenny collect at 555-3333, or our attorney John Doe at 555-4444.

ADOPTION Executive father and stay-at-home mother seeking to adopt an infant or child up to 2 yrs. old. Have one adopted 3-year-old and much love left for second child. We have been approved for second adoptive placement. We enjoy horses, picnics, gardening, and children's sports. We can help financially. Call Bonnie and Doug collect, 555-2211.

Questions for Birth Mothers
Answering Ads by Phone

Keep several copies of these questions near your telephone.

1. Have you seen a doctor yet? _____ Yes _____ No
2. When is your due date? _____
3. How are you feeling?
4. Does the father of the baby support a plan for adoption?
   _____ Yes _____ No _____ Doesn't know about pregnancy
5. Is your mother giving you emotional support? _____ Yes _____ No
6. Have you answered other ads? _____ Yes _____ No
7. How old are you? _____ How old is the father? _____
8. Do you have other children?

Before ending your conversation:

9. Are you interested in contacting our attorney?

Date of call _____

Caller's name _____

Phone number _____

Address or city _____

Description of her situation:

Outcome of conversation:

infant...." This type of ad is overused.) Use a border or put the word "adoption" in bold capital letters. Make your ad stand out.

Keep track of the newspapers and dates you have ads running. When speaking with a caller, ask her where she read your ad so you can ascertain which papers are producing leads.

If the birth mother is answering other ads, she is interviewing other families. Try to obtain her name and a number where she can be reached. If you both seem to be working toward the same goal, ask her if she would be interested in talking with your attorney. Your attorney can then ask other pertinent questions. If the woman calls your attorney, you may have an adoption coming together. If she is not ready to talk with an attorney, offer to send her a copy of your résumé. This is a particularly good idea if she is talking with other prospective parents. Summarize the conversation in a cover letter to her.

It is especially important that you ask questions 4, 5, 7, and 8 from the checklist. Birth fathers have specific rights, so it is truly helpful when they are in agreement with an adoption plan, since their rights usually must be terminated or relinquished voluntarily. The ages of the mother and father are important. The younger the birth parents, the more involved their parents may be. The parents usually, but not always, have more control over younger birth parents. In other words, if the grandparents-to-be do not support an adoption plan for the baby, there is a good chance that the birth mother will parent the baby in the end. Does the birth mother have other children? If she does, she will have an idea of what parenting a second child will mean. There's a good chance she will place the baby for adoption in this case. (A word of caution: Never give your complete address or place of employment to strangers.)

Questions regarding financial assistance, health concerns, drug usage and HIV testing, for example, should be asked by your attorney. (Always ask your attorney about questions she would rather you did not ask.)

Do not let this method discourage you. It may take several months of advertising and even more telephone calls before something clicks, but many parents have found children this way and some have found them quickly.

WRITING A BIRTH MOTHER LETTER

The day will come when a birth mother who has read your résumé expresses an interest in you as a possible family for her child. You may be asked to write a letter to her, or present a life book or video, because she wants to learn more about you. This is why you keep the personal resume short. You want to arouse her curiosity so she wants to learn more. Now is the opportunity to convince her that your family would be her best choice.

Before writing your letter, try to find out the age of the birth mother, whether she is married or single, and any other pertinent information that will help you personalize your letter. It is difficult to write to an anonymous person and the result can be a generic-sounding letter. You must take a different approach if you are writing to a 15-year-old instead of a 25-year-old.

A Dear-Birth-Mother letter is an extension of your personal résumé. It can be any length you want it to be. Here are some tips to keep in mind:

1. Your letter should be handwritten. This shows you took the time to make it personal. If your handwriting is not legible, then print and use a ruler to keep your letters straight.

2. Do not start your letter by writing, "This is a difficult letter to write." Far too many people begin this way. Writing this letter should not be difficult. The birth mother is in the difficult position and is the one with a complicated decision to make. This is your chance to tell someone who really wants to listen how much you want a child and what you have to offer. It should be easy for you to write.

3. Begin your letter with something like this: "We were overwhelmed and excited when we learned you wanted to know more about us. We have waited anxiously for this opportunity." Or, "It is with great excitement that we are writing this letter to you."

4. Include her in your letter by referring to her. Do not ramble on about yourself. Try to make her a part of every paragraph. Here are some ways you can include her: "We know you face a difficult decision choosing the adoptive parents for your baby"; "We can provide your child with . . ."; "We want only the best for you"; "We do not know much about your circumstances but because you have chosen life, we know you want to find the best family possible for your baby. We hope we can be that family"; or "May you find peace and comfort with your final decision."

5. Again, do not dwell on your infertility. Never refer to being unable to have a child of your "own." An adopted child will be your own child. Please think of how a birth mother would feel if you express sorrow in not being able to bear a child of your "own." What would her child become to you?

6. Tell her what you can do for her, not what she can do for you. If you are willing to accept a letter, pictures, or both from her, tell her. Let her know you will treasure those items and share them with the child at the appropriate age. If you want to meet her, say so. She may not want to meet with you, but she will know you care about her, not just the baby she is carrying.

7. Tell her you realize an adopted child will have two sets of parents and that you will always speak positively of her. Let her know the child will be aware this was a difficult choice for her to make and why.

8. Mention how you would love and cherish her child.

Sample Birth Mother Letter

This is the type of letter you would write to a woman considering adoption for her unborn child. Your personal letter may be much longer in length.

Dear Expectant Mother,

We are extremely grateful for this opportunity to tell you about ourselves. We know you face an extremely difficult decision and we hope that after reading our letter we can make your decision a little easier.

After years of trying to conceive a child, we have decided to adopt because we want the opportunity to love and parent a child. Both of us love children (we often baby-sit for our nieces and nephews and neighborhood children) and we want the opportunity to share our lives with a child. We have so many things to offer a child: a warm, nurturing environment, the love of our extended families, educational and traveling opportunities, and stability. Without a doubt, we would love and cherish your child forever.

David and I were raised in Florida and met while we were in high school. We married during our senior year in college. We are both 33 years old. David is in sales and I am a teacher. After adopting, I do plan to stop teaching and be a full-time mother. Once our child is in elementary school, I will probably then return to teaching.

David is my best friend. He is an outgoing person who never fails to bring a smile to my face. He also has a marvelous sense of humor and is a sensitive, caring individual. His kindness extends to neighbors, family, friends, and co-workers. David enjoys children so much that he coaches little league baseball at the Catholic school around the corner from our house and many of the neighborhood children stop by our house just to visit with him. I know he would be a marvelous father.

Heather is a beautiful young woman inside and out. She is my best friend; someone that I can share anything with and know that she will always be there for me. She is that way with all the people she knows and loves. I have watched her with children and know she will make a wonderful mother. She often takes our nieces and nephews to the zoo, to movies, and for walks in the park. She enjoys making Halloween costumes and baking cookies for the children she knows.

We both are familiar with adoption. David's best friend of 26 years was adopted and my cousin adopted a little girl 15 years ago. We think adoption is a wonderful way to create a family. We also know many families with adopted children. We met these families through an adoptive parent support group and we can see how happy they all are.

We respect your decision to place your baby for adoption and we will always convey our positive feelings to your child. We believe that all adopted children have the right to know about their backgrounds and we will share information about you with our child at the right time. We would enjoy meeting you, with or without full disclosure of information, and hope that you feel the same. Either way, we would be happy to exchange letters and pictures with you once a year if you desire.

If you feel we might be the right family for your child, please call our attorney Dale Jones, at 555-4328. Dale is a sensitive individual who understands adoption and how it affects all involved. If you would like more information about us or have any questions, please call us directly at 555-4744.

Thank you,

David and Heather Miller

David and Heather Miller

When You Already Have a Child:
One Couple's Birth Mother Letter

Barbara and Tony Hill were trying to adopt a second child. They received a lead from a friend about a woman who was eight months pregnant and planned to place the baby for adoption. Unsure of the type of adoption the birth mother was interested in, Barbara asked their friend if he would try to locate someone, a third party close to the birth mother, who might accept a letter from them and give it to the birth mother. Their friend located an intermediary, and Barbara and Tony mailed the letter to her. This is their birth mother letter.

Dear Birth Mother,

We are adoptive parents who have been searching for a second child to adopt for over two years. Our son is now four years old and was adopted as an infant.

It is hard to put into words the love we feel for him. He is our joy, our treasure, the love of our lives. The best decision we ever made as a couple was to adopt him. He has given us so much, just being the little person he is. We hope to be given the opportunity to adopt another little one so we can fall in love with a child all over again. For this reason, we are so grateful for the opportunity to introduce ourselves to you.

As a family, we enjoy activities with our son such as sailing, swimming, picnics, outings to the zoo, walks in the park, ice cream cones, and taking him fishing. At home, we play games, roast marshmellows in the fireplace, bake cookies, go on treasure hunts, read books, and take him to the library for story and craft time. His dad lets him "help" with our latest project—adding on to the house. He's "helped" with staining and painting and has even pounded in a few nails.

We enjoy being together as a family and also enjoy getting together with our extended families. Both sets of grandparents are eagerly awaiting the arrival of another grandchild to love and, yes, spoil—something grandparents do well, don't you agree?

As a couple, we enjoy many things together. After $7^1/2$ years of marriage we are still each other's best friend. We always make time to be together. We talk things out and both of us are willing to compromise for the sake of each other's happiness. Our marriage is very secure and based on mutual love and respect.

My husband is a gentle man. It is obvious to those around us that our son and I are most important to him. He talks quietly and never raises his voice. He is a patient man and possesses a wonderful sense of humor. He's been employed with the same company for sixteen years and was recently named vice president. He enjoys building projects. In fact, he built our house eight years ago and is always working on something. He also has a talent for gardening and landscaping.

Over the past two summers he has built three decks off the house with connecting wood sidewalks through the woods. All this is beautifully landscaped. I am very proud of him. He is a wonderful husband and father and provides for us very well.

My wife is a full-time mother and loves caring for our son. She spends a lot of quality time with our son, and she's a good mother. Usually when I come home from work, they are cuddled together reading books. She has plenty of room in her arms and love in her heart, as I do, for another child. She also does volunteer work from our home. For over three years, she's been helping others adopt. She enjoys children and at one time taught pre-school. Her hobbies are writing, drawing, photography, bicycling, and needlework.

As a mother of four years now, I STILL find myself staring at our child and thanking God and his birth mother for sending him to us. I still get up once or twice during the night to check on him. I always want him to feel our love. We tell him every day how much we love him and how much he means to us. Having worked so hard to adopt a child, we have never taken him for granted. We want so much to give the same to another child.

We live in the country so there is ample room to play and explore. We enjoy seeing rabbits, raccoons, and deer on our property. Each year we plant a large garden. Our son helps with this and enjoys seeing the vegetables and flowers as they grow. We are teaching him to appreciate the outdoors and the simple pleasures of life.

We often think of our son's birth mother and pray that she somehow knows he is loved and well taken care of. She did not want to communicate with us and we respect her decision. We regret, however, that we were never able to thank her for the child she entrusted to us.

We want you to know that we have utmost respect for a mother who makes an adoption plan. Our son knows he was adopted. He knows his birth mother made a plan out of love so he could have both a Mommy and a Daddy. We can promise you that your child will know of your love also. We will always answer our childrens' questions truthfully based on the information we have.

We realize that material things are not everything, but we are financially secure. We can provide for another child without hesitation. Our children will have the opportunity to reach their highest potential in life if they are willing to work for it. In other words, they will be given the opportunity. The rest, of course, is up to them.

We know little of your situation, but we promise you we would love and cherish your child. We are willing to communicate with you or meet with you if, and only if, you desire.

If we have not answered all of the questions you have about us, we are certainly willing to provide more information. Just let Paula know.

If you feel good about us as prospective parents for your child, please call our attorney, Jim Walker, at 555-5433. Jim has handled adoptions for many years in this area. He is a moral man and non-judgmental. He strives to handle all adoptions with respect and dignity for the birth mother and the child.

Jim can advise you of the legal steps that need to be taken and of your rights. He can offer counseling also. We have spoken to Jim and he knows we are sending this letter to you. You need only tell him we referred you. If he should be unavailable when you telephone, please leave a number where you can be reached and he will return your call.

We would like to tell you again that we would love and cherish, with all of our hearts, the child you carry. We would be honored and humbled if you chose us to be the parents of your baby.

Barbara and Tony Hill
Barbara and Tony Hill

9. Say what you can give a child, not what a child can give to you. Share with her what you have to offer a child: love, grandparents, a sibling, values, appreciation for music or nature, every opportunity to reach her fullest potential, good schools, a nice neighborhood, travel opportunities, etc.

10. Mention religion if it is important to her. If she wants a Catholic family and you are Catholic, confirm this for her. If you plan to send your children to Catholic schools, tell her.

11. Reassure her that her child will become a member of your family in the fullest sense. Avoid saying things like "hopefully, we will develop a family bond." Using expressions like this or talking about having your "own" child only tells everyone, including the birth mother, that you have not resolved the feelings surrounding your infertility and that you see adoption as second best.

12. If you are not sure about something because it does not sound right, leave it out.

13. Be positive throughout your letter.

14. Make it a warm and caring letter.

MAKING A BIRTH MOTHER VIDEO

One of the newest methods of providing a birth mother with more information is through the use of a video. With a video, the birth mother no longer has to form a mental picture of you. She can see and hear you, so it is important that your video conveys a feeling of warmth.

Making a video is not as easy as it sounds. First, you need to decide what you want to emphasize; determine what will present you as wonderful, sensitive, caring people—the type of people that a birth mother would want to raise her child. Dawn Smith-Pliner, director and owner of Friends in Adoption in Middletown Springs, Vermont, says, "Talk about things that are important to you, whether it's the church, holiday times or spending time with your families. Talk about your long term goals, how you see that child being a member of your family for a long time."

"What people should not do, is try to outdo the Joneses. Do not show your vacation home, the Volvo in the driveway, or mention the nanny who is waiting to come to work. This is very intimidating to a birth mother, especially if she does not come from that background and does not want that for her child. Many women say they want a full-time mom because they don't want anyone else taking care of the baby. They don't want a nanny. Day care is acceptable since the reality of two parents working is a well-known fact. Then address who will be parenting the child. Does the schedule allow both parents to care for the child? Will Grandma help out from time to time? Or will you use a day-care center part time, one you have investigated and feel comfortable with?" says Smith-Pliner. "It is great if you will be a full-time mom; then you can say you can't wait to start going to swim class with the baby or exercise class, for example." (All of these suggestions are also appropriate for Dear Birth Mother letters.)

Keep your video under ten minutes. Dress neatly and casually. Record it in a relaxed setting, such as in front of the fireplace, next to a pond, or on a swingset at the park. Include your children if applicable. The easiest way to produce the video is to have someone record it for you. One couple made their video themselves, but it took all day. One time they forgot to turn the camera on. Another time, only one-half of the father-to-be was in the picture, and he was the one speaking. Ask a friend to help. Or, if you would feel more comfortable with a stranger, hire a professional.

One of the best videos I viewed was of a mom and dad in front of the fireplace. The mother was holding their two-year-old while the father was talking sincerely about their family life and how much their religious beliefs meant to them. They then moved to the child's bedroom and the mother talked about how she and the child spent their days together and the things they planned to do with a new baby. The video concluded with all of them playing together on the floor. It was a very touching video and the very first they had ever made.

MAKING A LIFE BOOK

Instead of a personal résumé, you may be asked to make a life book (sometimes called a "photo letter") and submit it to your agency or attorney. A life book is like a photo résumé. It is not just an album with photographs. It is, however, another marketing strategy. Once again, you must decide what part of your lives you want to emphasize.

For a great-looking life book, use a scrapbook. Decide at which point in your life you want to begin your story. Couples who have dated since high school often like to start back then, using a prom picture, for instance, as their first photograph together. From there, they continue with pictures until they reach the present. Others may begin with pictures of their wedding day.

Using a scrapbook, instead of a photo album, allows you to be creative. Like the personal résumé, you want your life book to stand out from the rest. Little things like cutting your pictures to different sizes; using borders around the pictures or pages; or using watercolors, markers, or colored pencils and stencils can make a wonderful-looking life book.

Mentally divide your life book into sections, such as your wedding day, activities you enjoy together, your families, your social life, the holidays or an annual family reunion, picnics or special events you participate in. Then browse through your photographs and choose those you want to add to your book under the different categories. Under each picture write one line, like "celebrating our third wedding anniversary." Add a special ending. One family drew a picture frame on the very last page and under the empty frame they wrote "We are waiting for that special someone to complete our family." You may also include your Dear Birth Mother letter; make it the first entry in your life book. Before you know it, you will have a beautiful picture story of your life together to share with birth parents, and a wonderful keepsake to share with your child someday.

FINAL THOUGHTS

Private adoption is a viable alternative to agency adoption. But, unlike agency adoption, no one is going to hand you a baby. You must be very assertive and creative to pursue independent adoption. Familiarize yourself with the ins and outs of this approach and understand the risks, both emotionally and financially, before becoming involved.

Many agency social workers do not support independent adoption. They argue that the birth mother does not receive adequate counseling about other choices besides adoption. Without a doubt, many birth mothers who place privately do not receive counseling. Birth mothers need to be educated about the benefits of counseling and encouraged to receive it at the expense of the adoptive parents. Not only should they be told of their other choices, such as parenting the child, but they need to be aware of the types of feelings they will experience after birth, at placement, and when they terminate their parental rights. Adoptive parents should not think of counseling as an additional expense but, instead, as insurance. The woman who makes the assiduous decision for adoption, who understands the normal feelings she will experience after birth and placement, is less apt to change her mind. If you use an intermediary, be sure he understands the importance of counseling for the birth mother and ask that it be offered to her.

If you want to adopt a baby today, you have a good chance of succeeding independently. Try the strategies outlined in this chapter and create some new ones. Involve yourself in your adoption plan instead of sitting back and waiting. Work with your attorney and with your birth mother. Build trust and support into the relationship. As Dawn Smith-Pliner says, "If everyone is working in the best interest of the child then you will have a very harmonious group of people working together."

RECOMMENDED READING

Adamec, Christine, ed. *How to Adopt Your Baby Privately: The Nationwide Directory of Adoption Attorneys.* Palm Bay, FL: Adoption Advocates Press, 1992.

Michelman, Stanley B. and Meg Schneider with Antonia van der Meer. *The Private Adoption Handbook: The Complete Step-by-Step Guide to Independently Adopting a Baby.* New York: Dell, 1988.

Surviving the Wait

Adoption can be a long process from start to finish. First, you decide to adopt. Then you begin your research. Your research leads you to an adoption agency or adoption attorney. You submit an application, have your home study conducted, and then you WAIT.

Sounds simple, but the reality is that the journey from making the decision to adopt to officially waiting for a child may take many months, or a few years, to complete. Some of you may begin working with one agency only to find yourself applying to another agency a year later. Those pursuing intercountry adoption may begin with one foreign program and then have to change programs several months down the road due to circumstances beyond anyone's control. A few families may receive two, or even three, referrals before a child is actually placed. Those pursuing independent adoption in the United States may work with several prospective birth mothers before finding one who actually places her baby for adoption.

The point is that you will spend a great deal of time waiting before you actually begin The Wait. (The official wait starts when your adoption source says, "We will have a child for you in about six months or a year.") For some that wait may be months. For others, it may be a year or two or longer. No matter the length, all parents will wait. Waiting is part of the adoption process.

Now it may have taken a great deal of hard work and many months to arrive at The Wait, but at least you had something to do to occupy the time. When the official wait begins, your work ends. So what do you do now? Do you put your life on hold until you receive The Call? Should you plan a vacation? Continue your courses at the university? Agree to serve one more term as secretary for your favorite organization? Should you coach basketball again this year? Remodel the bathroom? And to make matters even more complicated, behind every "should" is a "what if?" What if the baby is born? What if our daughter comes home next month?

MANAGING THE TIME

What can you do to make your wait bearable? How can you survive it, maintain your sanity, and prepare for your child at the same time? Try some of the following suggestions offered by other prospective and adoptive parents.

1. Be extra good to yourself—The adoption process is stressful, time consuming, and expensive. Take time each day to relax; do something just for yourself, something you normally wouldn't do. Exercise, read a good book, take a long soothing bath, work in your garden, visit a friend, tour the local museum, plan a picnic, have a romantic dinner for two, or begin a new hobby. Pamper your spouse and spend time alone. Once your child arrives, life as you know it will never be the same.

2. Keep a journal—Record your adoption progress in a journal. Write about the lows and highs. Express your frustrations as you search for an adoption source and write about your joy when you find one. Picture life with your future son or daughter and write about the things you will do together. Record your hopes and dreams. The wonderful thing about a journal is that it will always be readily available when friends or family are not around to listen. And then when everything is behind you, think of the wonderful gift you have given yourself. A complete record of your journey to read over and over. It will be a wonderful keepsake to share years later, if you desire, with your child.

3. Build a support system—Surround yourself with supportive people. Adoptive parents have particularly broad shoulders to lean on. They fully understand what you are experiencing, as do other waiting parents. Make an effort to be with these people.

Seek out family, friends, clergy, and professionals who can empathize with you while you wait. Stay away from those who are unable to. "Every time I tried to talk to my mother about what was happening she never had much to say," says one adoptive mom. "One day I was particularly upset because the Interstate Compact Office in our state refused to give verbal permission [to pick up their baby] over the phone to the Interstate Office in the placing state. I was telling my mother what was happening when I realized she was not listening. When I asked her what was the matter she said, 'I find this all so boring, Katie.' Boy, I didn't need that from anyone and after that I didn't talk to her about the adoption until the baby arrived."

Most people will try to be helpful, and many will have suggestions, advice, or both to offer. "Our families tried so hard to be supportive. They were so sweet," says Janelle, an adoptive mom from Florida, "but our main support system was another adoptive couple. They were great! They called us every few days to see how we were doing and kept assuring us we would have a child someday soon."

4. Child-care classes—Awaiting the arrival of a baby? Many communities offer child-care classes for prospective adoptive parents. The classes cover such things as child development, common health problems, how to find a good pediatrician, baby-care basics (bathing, diapering), CPR, first aid, safety, nutrition, and the psychological and emotional adjustments involved in becoming parents through adoption. These classes also provide the opportunity to meet other prospective adoptive parents who also are waiting for a baby to arrive.

"The child-care classes were great," says Terri, an adoptive mom from Illinois. "We were waiting for a baby through private adoption and we met three other couples who were also waiting. We have all since adopted. Our children were born within months of each other and we have all remained very close over the past four years."

"Our adoption happened very quickly and we never had time to attend parenting classes. The first time I had to change my son's diaper was in the airport in front of the agency director," says 38-year-old Debbie. "My hands were shaking. I hadn't changed a diaper since seventh grade. The next morning I had to bathe him. I didn't even know where to begin. My sister-in-law came over and showed me what to do. I had to learn how to do everything."

Your support group may offer parenting classes. If not, members may be able to tell you where classes are available in your community. If they cannot, contact area hospitals, adoption agencies, community centers, or family service organizations.

5. Find a pediatrician—A pediatrician is a doctor who specializes in caring for children from birth to approximately sixteen years. Many parents of infants choose to have their children seen by pediatricians. Others take their children to their family physician. It does not matter how old or healthy your child is when he arrives, or how much medical background information you have been given. The truth is that when your child is placed, you will take him to be examined by your physician. New parents want to be assured that their child is healthy, or at least as healthy as they have been led to believe.

If you will be parenting an infant for the first time, you may want to begin looking for a pediatrician before your baby arrives. Start by talking to friends or relatives who have small children. Find out who they take their children to see. Ask co-workers, church friends, and neighbors. Even in a large city, you will be surprised to find that some of your friends and acquaintances take their children to the same physician. Ask them what they like or dislike about their child's doctor. Then ask your own physician who he recommends. Often, it is the same doctor or the same group of doctors.

Make an appointment to talk with the doctor or, at the very least, with the doctor's nurse. Find out approximately how many adopted children are seen in his practice. If your baby or youngster will be arriving from overseas, ask about the number of foreign-born adopted children the doctor sees. Ask how he feels about accepting a child with little or no medical background information because this can be very disturbing to some physicians. Inquire about appointment times. If your child is sick, will he see her the same day? Is there always someone on call, even at three o'clock in the morning? Are infants seen at different times than the older children? Is there a separate waiting room for sick children? No parent with a healthy child likes to sit down in the waiting room next to a child who is contagious.

When the time comes for the first checkup, explain the situation to whomever schedules your appointment. Be sure they understand that you will be arriving with an infant (or whatever age child you will be with) and that you will bring all of the medical papers you have been given. Ask them to note your circumstances surrounding this particular visit. This will help prevent uncomfortable exchanges from occurring.

One new mom relayed this story:

I called and made an appointment for our infant son. I explained that we were adopting and that our son would be twelve weeks old when he arrived.

On the day of the appointment, the nurse called out my son's name and I stood up and handed the nurse the medical papers we had received. As she walked away from us, she loudly asked, 'What is the name of the doctor you were seeing before?' I told her that everything she needed to know was in his file. She asked the same question again and I gave the same answer. She then asked the name of the hospital he was born in. Then she wanted to know if he was born vaginally. I told her I could not answer any of her questions because I had not read his file. Finally I had no choice but to tell her, in front of everyone, that we had adopted him a few days earlier.

Well, you would think that would have been the end, but it wasn't. In the examining room she asked if his 'real mom' had breast fed him. How was I supposed to know that? Then she wanted to know if it was a difficult birth. I told her I didn't know because I wasn't there. She continued the questions until I finally summoned enough nerve to ask her to leave the room.

Few people will encounter an insensitive nurse like this, but it does happen. Try to lay the groundwork before you arrive and remind the nurse, or receptionist, of the circumstances when you check in for your appointment.

6. **Volunteer your time**—Try to take your mind off the wait by doing something for someone else. Every charitable organization, hospital, day-care center, and nursing home needs volunteers. Offer your services even if you only have a few free hours a week. It will help you to forget about your worries for a while.

One waiting mom worked four hours a week at a home for children who had been removed from their homes by the court. Another mom worked with pregnant teens. Still another volunteered to work with the Girl Scouts. They all said they felt good about doing something for others and the work never failed to brighten their day.

7. Read—There are so many excellent books available on baby and child care. Take the time now to read them before your child arrives. Purchase those that seem particularly helpful and informative for reference. When your child awakes feverish at three o'clock in the morning, you will be glad you have them.

Take the time to read some books on raising adopted children. Read every book you can find because adoption does not end the day your child arrives. Arrival day is just the beginning. Adoption will affect you and your child for your entire life. Reading will help you know what to anticipate before questions are asked because they usually come at the most unexpected time.

There are also books about adoption for preschoolers, grade-school-age children, and teens. There's a listing of books on parenting an adopted child, as well as books for adopted children, in the bibliography. This listing is not meant to be inclusive. There are many books published on all aspects of adoption. Consult your library, the parenting resource materials listed in *OURS* magazine, and the book *Adoption: An Annotated Bibliography and Guide,* by Lois Ruskai Melina (London: Garland Publishing, Inc., 1987). See the appendices for adoption book distributors.

8. Learn how to answer questions—All adoptive parents will, at one time or another, be confronted with personal questions about their children and their adoption. Here's a short list of questions and comments you may eventually hear. Think about how you might reply.

- Do you know who his real parents are?
- What did the agency tell you about her parents?
- Were his parents married?
- How could they just give away their own flesh and blood?
- The only problem with adoption is that you never know what you are getting.
- Oh, you adopted! Gee, I am sorry.
- He's cute. Are you going to keep him?
- Her skin is so dark. What is she?
- How nice of you to adopt a baby that nobody wanted.
- You will probably get pregnant now. What will you do with him then?
- I bet you wish you could have had children of your own.
- Can you send her back if you decide you don't want her?
- How much did he cost you?
- I give you credit. I wouldn't want someone else's child. Doesn't it bother you?

- He's not from around here. Where did he come from?
- Can she speak English?

Once you become adoptive parents, you also become adoption educators. You will teach others about adoption for the rest of your life, so it is extremely important that you always use positive adoption language whenever you discuss the subject.

Most people do not know much about adoption, so they find it an intriguing subject. When they finally meet someone who has adopted, etiquette goes out the back door. They will bombard you with questions. Many of the questions will be harmless, others will be extremely personal, and some will shock you. You must learn how to deal with these questions in a polite, positive manner, while educating at the same time.

You will be surprised by the number of people who ask you questions, particularly after you first adopt. Within about six months or less, many of the questions stop because by then you have had a chance to talk with family, friends, and acquaintances about the adoption. You will find, however, that the questions never really end.

Every time your child sees a new doctor the adoption will be mentioned because there are always questions that cannot be answered. One mom said she was stunned when her child went to see a specialist. Before the appointment, they were asked to complete a twelve-page questionnaire and were only able to answer the first five questions. Even if you believe that it will never be necessary to inform your child's teachers of the adoption because your child "blends" with your family, the inevitable family tree project will surface. Your child will tell classmates that he was adopted. When yet another child enters your family through adoption, you will have even more questions to answer.

For your child's sake, learn the appropriate responses to those personal questions you might be asked. Remember background information you receive on your child is not information to be shared with anyone but your child. If questioned, politely tell people this information belongs to your child and it would be inappropriate for you to pass it along before you have shared it with her.

Always use the correct terminology when talking about adoption. Many adoptive parents use such terms as "birth mother," "birth father," or "birth parents" when referring to the child's first family; others use "biological" instead of "birth". Either is acceptable. However, saying "real parent" or "natural parent" is generally scorned by adoptive parents because it implies that the adoptive parent is somehow not real or natural.

So how do you learn to answer questions appropriately? How do you learn positive adoption language? One way to learn is by reading adoption books and subscribing to adoption magazines and newsletters. Just a few of the magazines and newsletters available include: *OURS: The Magazine of Adoptive Families,* available through Adoptive Families of America with membership; *AdoptNet,* a magazine available by subscription (write to P.O. Box 50512, Palo Alto, CA 94303); *Face Facts*, P.O. Box 28058, Northwood Station, Baltimore, MD 21239; *Roots and Wings*, 15 Nancy Terrace, Hackettstown, NJ 07840; and *Adopted Child*, a newsletter available by subscription (write to P.O. Box 9362, Moscow, ID 83843). An excellent book, *When Friends Ask about Adoption: Question and Answer Guide for Non-Adopted Parents and Other Caring Adults*, by Linda Bothun (Chevy Chase, MD: Swan Publications, 1987), is a resource you can share with family and friends.

Another way to learn positive adoption language is to spend time with experienced adoptive families and adoption professionals. Participate in your support group and attend adoption conferences. Conferences are held across the United States. Information on conferences can be obtained from parent support organizations, adoption agencies, adoption newsletters, and magazines. Some support groups hold miniworkshops within their community. Watch for information on local events.

9. Decide whether to decorate—Many parents decorate the child's room before the child arrives. If the child is older, many parents do the basics like add a fresh coat of paint or install new carpeting. Then, once their child arrives, they let the child choose his bedspread, window treatments, and pictures.

Many parents who are waiting for a baby through private adoption, are often hesitant to decorate a nursery since there is always a chance that a birth mother will decide to parent the child instead of placing her baby for adoption. In this situation, some prospective parents choose furniture and bedding ahead of time. When they know they will be picking up the baby the next day, they purchase the furnishings and often are able to have the room completed within a few hours.

10. Take a photography course—If you do not already own a camera, buy one and take a course in photography. Courses are usually available at a local university or through adult education classes.

All pictures are priceless, but those taken on arrival day are even more so. These pictures represent the beginning of your family and, once in the album, are an excellent way to introduce your child to adoption. Children love to look at pictures of themselves and enjoy hearing their adoption story for many years.

You can also use a baby book, along with a photo album, to document the adoption story. Baby books for adopted children are available at greeting card stores like Hallmark. A book for babies and older children, titled *My Story: An Adoption Baby Book*, by Christina M. Swan and Laura Richards, is available from Adoptive Families of America. The book is appropriate for United States- and foreign-born children. A Christian- or Jewish-influenced version is available.

11. Order arrival announcements—Yes, you can begin working on your announcements ahead of time. If you are expecting a baby and don't know the sex, choose a unisex card. One family had their envelopes addressed and stamped and completed the arrival notice on the way to pick up their infant. They met their baby in an airport, and before they boarded the plane for their trip home they dropped the announcements in the mail.

Design your own card and take it to the printer. On the day your child arrives home, call the printer with the details. Check *OURS: The magazine of adoptive families.* Many of its advertisers specialize in arrival announcements for adopted children of all ages from an assortment of countries.

12. Continue with your life—Remain active. Plan and take a vacation. Remodel your bathroom. Take the course at school you have been thinking about. Serve on the board of directors of your favorite charity. Accept the new job. In other words, do not put your life on hold. Many adoptive families have received their children with only one day's notice and they managed particularly well. You will too. One family had a vacation planned when the agency called about a baby four days before they were due to leave. They adopted the baby and still managed to get away for a few days.

Use some of this time to prepare for your child. If you work, check with your employer about an adoption leave or a leave of absence. Are you entitled to leave with pay? If you are adopting an infant through an agency that requires the mother to be at home with the baby for a specific time period, will they hold your job for you?

Check your medical insurance policy. Some policies cover an adopted child upon placement, including any health problems. Other policies may not cover a child until the adoption is finalized and even then may not cover pre-existing health conditions. Some agencies require your newly adopted child to be covered by medical insurance upon placement. If your policy does not cover your child at arrival, you will need to obtain additional coverage either from your present carrier or another company. Single parents may need to switch from an individual policy to a family policy.

Depending on your child's age, you may want to line up babysitters in advance. Even when the arrival is an infant, new parents should try to spend a few hours a week alone together. If your expected child will be a toddler and you will continue working, visit day-care centers and nursery schools. For the older child, talk with the staff at the school your child will attend. Try to get yourself organized before your child arrives home.

Children coming from overseas will require some additional preparation on your part. Find out as much information as you can about the culture your child is coming from. Life in an orphanage is different from living in a foster home. Will your child be used to sleeping in a large room with many other children? If so, she may not be too happy sleeping in her own room by herself no matter how "cute" the new room is. Children used to sleeping on the floor may not be pleased when they are tucked into bed.

If your child is a toddler or older, learn some basic words in his language so you can communicate. Try to find an adult in your community who speaks his language. It will help to have someone who can translate and talk with your child during those first few weeks or months. These are just a few issues you will have to deal with when your child arrives. It is imperative that you talk with other adoptive families who have adopted from abroad. They can give you a fairly accurate picture of what to expect and how to prepare yourself for the days and weeks ahead.

There are many things you can do to occupy your time during the wait. You are limited only by your imagination. Enjoy your waiting time by doing something you have always wanted to do. Prepare for your child and relax. Your wait will be over before you know it.

Afterword

I hope this handbook has convinced you adoption is possible and that you can adopt the type of child you seek, whether that child is from the United States or abroad, is healthy or has special needs, is an infant or an older child. Relying on what I've learned from assisting hundreds of families in their adoption efforts, I've covered both the usual and the unusual questions and circumstances pre-adoptive families have. But your situation may be extraordinary. If it is, I encourage you to continue your research because adoption is possible for most people, but especially for those people who are "doers."

I urge you to ask questions and request help along the route you choose to follow. There are millions of people in this country touched by adoption, and each year thousands of families adopt children. Actively seek help from adoptive parents and adoption professionals. Most will be happy to share information with you.

After you have adopted, when your child is safely home with you, do not abandon your support group. So often parents mistakenly believe they no longer need the support of other adoptive parents. As adoptive parents, you will always have unique issues to resolve. Other adoptive families can help. Your child should also interact with other adopted children to build self-esteem. It is a nice way for a child to learn that she is not the only child in the world who was adopted.

Not surprisingly, once you have adopted, other prospective parents will contact you for information and support. Reach out to those pre-adopters. Share your files of information with them. Help other families adopt a child. Advocate adoption in your community. Let others know that adoption builds wonderful families.

You have dreamed of having a child for a long time now, and you are about to begin the most incredible journey. I wish you much success as you start down the path. As Pearl S. Buck once said, "Our treasure is in our children, for in them is our future. And what a future!" Good luck! And may you have a happy, blessed, and fulfilling life with the beautiful children you adopt.

Bibliography

Adoptees and Birth Parents Making Contact

Gediman, Judith S. and Linda P. Brown. *Birth Bond: Reunions between Birthparents and Adoptees, What Happens After. . . .* Far Hills, NJ: New Horizons Press, 1991.

Adoption of Older Children and Children with Special Needs

"Black Children Are Adopted Less Often." *Behavior Today,* November 21, 1983.

Brockhaus, J. and R. Brockhaus. "Adopting an Older Child: The Emotional Process." *American Journal of Nursing* 82 (1982): 288–294.

Dunn, Linda, ed. *Adopting Children with Special Needs: A Sequel.* Washington, DC: North American Council on Adoptable Children, 1983.

Jewett, Claudia L. *Adopting the Older Child.* Boston: Harvard Common Press, 1978.

———. *Helping Children Cope with Separation and Loss.* Boston: Harvard Common Press, 1982.

Kennedy, Maggie. "Black Children up for Adoption Need Loving Homes." *Dallas Times Herald,* August 29, 1987.

Kravi, Patricia, ed. *Adopting Children with Special Needs.* Riverside, CA: North American Council on Adoptable Children, 1976.

Leof, Joan. "Adopting Children with Developmental Disabilities." Rockville, MD: National Adoption Information Clearinghouse.

Marks, Jane. "We Have A Problem." *Parents,* October 1987, 62–68.

McNamara, Joan and Bernard McNamara. *The Special Child Handbook.* New York: Hawthorn Books, 1977.

Veronico, A. "One Church, One Child: Placing Children with Special Needs." *Children Today,* March/April 1983, 6–10.

Adoption Support and Awareness (for Family and Friends)

Holmes, Pat. *Supporting an Adoption.* Wayne, PA: Our Child Press, 1982.

Adoption Terminology

Bothun, Linda. *When Friends Ask about Adoption: A Question & Answer Guide for Non-Adoptive Parents & Other Caring Adults.* Chevy Chase, MD: Swan Publications, 1987.

Agency Adoption

Alexander-Roberts, Colleen. "Adoption Agencies: How They Work." *AdoptNet* 4, no. 4 (July/August 1992): 32–33, 47.
Burgess, Linda C. *The Art of Adoption.* Rev. ed. New York: W.W. Norton and Company, 1981.

Baby Brokers

Alexander-Roberts, Colleen. "Baby Broker Agencies: How to Spot One." *AdoptNet* 4, no. 5 (September/October 1992): 34, 35.
Lee, Linda. "The Baby Brokers." *Woman's World,* August 25 1987, 6–7.

Children's Books

Brodzinsky, Anne. *The Mulberry Bird: Story of an Adoption.* Ft. Wayne, IN: Perspectives Press, 1986.
Bunin, Sherry and Catherine Bunin. *Is that Your Sister? A True Story of Adoption.* Wayne, PA: Our Child Press, 1992.
Freudber, J. and T. Geiss. *Susan and Gordon Adopt a Baby.* New York: Random House, 1989.
Girard, Linda. *Adoption Is for Always.* Niles, IL: Albert Whitman and Co., 1986.
Koch, Janet. *Our Baby: A Birth and Adoption Story.* Ft. Wayne, IN: Perspectives Press, 1986.
Krementz, Jill. *How It Feels to Be Adopted.* New York: Knopf, 1988.
Livingston, Carole. *Why Was I Adopted?* Secaucus, NJ: Lyle Stuart, 1986.
Lowe, Darla. *Story of Adoption: Why Do I Look Different?* Minneapolis, MN: East West Press, 1987.
Rosenberg, Maxine B. *Being Adopted.* New York: Lathrop, Lee, Shepard Books, 1984.
Schnitter, Jane T. *William Is My Brother.* Indianapolis, IN: Perspectives Press, 1991.
Stein, Stephanie. *Lucy's Feet.* Indianapolis, IN: Perspectives Press, 1992.
Tax, Meredith. *Families.* Boston: Little, Brown and Co., 1981.
Wasson, Valentina. *The Chosen Baby.* Philadelphia: J.B. Lippincott, 1977.
Welch, Sheila Kelly. *Don't Call Me Marda.* Wayne, PA: Our Child Press, 1990.
Wickstrom, Lois. *Oliver: A Story about Adoption.* Wayne, PA: Our Child Press, 1991.

General Adoption Information

Adamec, Christine and William Pierce. *The Encyclopedia of Adoption.* New York: Facts on File, 1991.

"As Adoptions Get More Difficult." *U.S. News and World Report,* June 25, 1984, 32.

Austin, Judy, ed. *Adoption: The Inside Story.* London: Barn Owl Publications, 1985.

Berman, Claire. "Adoption in America Today." *Families,* March 1982, 8–12.

Bodnar, Janet. "Adoption: The Long and Costly Road." *Kiplinger's Personal Finance Magazine,* August 1992, 68–74.

Gibbs, Nancy, Mary Cronin, Elizabeth Taylor, and James Willwerth. "The Baby Chase." *Time,* October 9, 1989, 86–89.

Gubernick, Lisa. "How Much is that Baby in the Window?" *Forbes,* October 14, 1991, 90–98.

Harris, Marlys. "Where Have All the Babies Gone?" *Money,* December 1988, 164–175.

Havemann, J. "Women Having Babies Less Often but Births Out-of-Wedlock Rise." *Los Angeles Times,* April 26, 1984.

Holmes, Pat. *Concepts in Adoption.* Wayne, PA: Our Child Press, 1984.

Lindsay, Jeanne and Catherine Monserrat. *Adoption Awareness: A Guide for Teachers, Counselors, Nurses, and Caring Others.* Buena Park, CA: Morning Glory Press, 1989.

National Committee for Adoption. *Adoption Factbook: United States Data, Issues, Regulations and Resources.* Washington, DC: National Committee for Adoption, 1989.

Pierce, William. "Taking Adoption Seriously." *Society,* July/August 1990, 23–24.

Plumez, Jacqueline. "Families: The Adoption Option." *Working Woman,* May 1983, 148+.

Quindlen, Anna. "Baby Craving." *Life,* June 1987, 23–24.

Riben, Marsha. *The Dark Side of Adoption.* Detroit: Harlo Press, 1988.

Smith, Dorothy W. and Laurie Nehls Sherwin. *Mothers and Their Adopted Children: The Bonding Process.* New York: Tiresias, 1983.

Home Studies

Smith, Debra. *The Adoption Home Study Process.* Rockville, MD: National Adoption Information Clearinghouse.

How-to-Adopt Resources

Adamec, Christine A. *There ARE Babies to Adopt: A Resource Guide for Prospective Parents.* New York: Pinnacle, 1991.

———. "Adopt a Boy." *OURS* 21, no. 4 (July/August 1988): 30–31.

Bolles, Edmund Blair. *The Penguin Adoption Handbook: A Guide to Creating Your New Family*. New York: Penguin Books, 1984.

Gilman, Lois. *The Adoption Resource Book*. Rev. ed. New York: Harper and Row, 1987.

Goodman, Eric K. "The Adoption Maze." *Glamour,* September 1984, 338–339, 406–409.

National Adoption Information Clearinghouse. "Adoption—Where Do I Start?" Rockville, MD: NAIC.

Plumez, Jacqueline Honor, Ph.D. *Successful Adoption*. Rev. ed. New York: Harmony House, 1987.

Powledge, Fred. *The New Adoption Maze and How to Get Through It*. St. Louis: C.V. Mosby, 1985.

Independent Adoption

Adamec, Christine, ed. *How to Adopt Your Baby Privately: The Nationwide Directory of Adoption Attorneys*. Palm Bay, FL: Adoption Advocates Press, 1992.

Carsola, A.T. and S.D. Lewis. "Independent Adoptions: The Preferred Adoption." *Family Law News* 4 (1981): 1–3.

Del Vecchio, Rick. "Children from the Classifieds." *The Columbus Dispatch,* October 24, 1990.

McRae, Susan. "Attorney Focuses Practice on Adoption Law." *The Los Angeles Daily Journal,* August 12, 1988.

Meezan, W., S. Katz, and E.M. Russo. *Adoption without Agencies: A Study of Independent Adoptions*. New York: Child Welfare League of America, Inc., 1978.

Michelman, Stanley B. and Meg Schneider with Antonia van der Meer. *The Private Adoption Handbook: A Step-by-Step Guide to Independently Adopting a Baby*. New York: Dell, 1988.

Ogintz, Eileen. "Baby Wanted: Call Viv. . . ." *Glamour,* August 1988, 160–168.

Sector, B. "Couples Seeking to Adopt a Baby Use Classified Ads." *Los Angeles Times,* May 24, 1987.

Stabiner, Karen. "The Baby Brokers." *Los Angeles Times Magazine,* August 14, 1988, 8–16, 35–38.

Infertility and Adoption

Johnston, Patricia Irwin. *Adopting After Infertility*. Indianapolis: Perspectives Press, 1992. Also discusses psychological issues.

———. *An Adoptor's Advocate*. Ft. Wayne, IN: Perspectives Press, 1984. Also discusses psychological issues.

Melina, Lois. "Pros, cons of adopting during infertility treatment." *Adopted Child* (newsletter), June 1986. Also discusses psychological issues.

Intercountry Adoption

Adamec, Christine A. "They Adopted from Afar." *Home Life*, January 1985, 26-29.

Boundy, Donna. "Importing Baby: The Fears, Frustrations and Joys of Foreign Adoption." *Women's World*, February 16, 1988.

"Children for Sale." *South*, December 1987, 9-12.

Erichsen, Jean Nelson- and Heino R. Erichsen. *How to Adopt Internationally*. The Woodlands, TX: Los Niños International Adoption Center, 1992.

Harder, Laura, with Karen S. Schneider. "From Bucharest with Love." *People Weekly*, September 24, 1990, 34-39.

International Concerns Committee for Children. *Report on Foreign Adoption*. Boulder, CO: ICCC, 1993.

____. *Report on Foreign Adoption*. Boulder, CO: ICCC, 1991.

____. *Report on Foreign Adoption*. Boulder, CO: ICCC, 1984.

O'Rourke, Lisa and Ruth Hubbell. "Adopting a Foreign Child through an Agency." Rockville, MD: National Adoption Information Clearinghouse.

Redlich, Susan. "Baby of Mine." *First*, July 8, 1991.

Register, Cheri. *Are Those Kids Yours? American Families with Children Adopted from Other Countries*. New York: The Free Press, 1991.

Wirth, Eileen M. and Joan Worden. *How to Adopt a Child from Another Country*. Nashville: Abingdon Press, 1993.

Wooley, Suzanne. "When It Comes to Adoption, It's a Wide, Wide World." *Business Week*, June 20, 1988, 164-165.

Learning Disabilities, ADHD, and Adopted Children

Alexander-Roberts, Colleen. *The ADHD Parenting Handbook*. Dallas: Taylor Publishing, 1994.

____. *ADHD and Teens*. Dallas: Taylor Publishing, 1995.

Bordwell, Martha, Ph.D. "The Link Between Adoption and Learning Disabilities." *OURS*, September/October, 1992, 22-25.

Openness in Adoption

Alexander-Roberts, Colleen. "Openness, Honesty and Trust: The Benefits of Open Adoption." *Ours*, November/December, 1989, 12-14.

Arms, Suzanne. *Adoption: A Handful of Hope*. Berkeley: Celestial Arts, 1990.

Caplan, Lincoln. *An Open Adoption*. New York: Farrar, Straus and Giroux, 1990.

Distelheim, Rochelle. "Two Mothers for Laura." *McCalls*, September 1987, 135-137.

Gritter, James L., ed. *Adoption without Fear.* San Antonio: Corona Publishing, 1989.

Hormann, Elizabeth. "New Forms of Adoption." *Mothering,* Spring 1986, 96–101.

Kozak, Victoria. "Real Mothers." *Mothering,* Spring 1986, 94–95.

Lindsay, Jeanne Warren. *Open Adoption: A Caring Option.* Buena Park, CA: Morning Glory Press, 1987.

Ogintz, Eileen. "Would You Choose These Parents to Raise Your Baby?" *Chicago Tribune,* September 18, 1988.

Pannor, Reuben and Annette Baran. "Open Adoption as Standard Practice." *Child Welfare* (Child Welfare League of America, Inc., New York), 63 no. 3, (May/June 1984).

Rappaport, Bruce. *The Open Adoption Book: A Guide to Adoption without Tears.* New York: Macmillan, 1992.

———. "The Normalization of Adoption." *New Adoption Journal* (Independent Adoption Center, Pleasant Hill, CA), Summer/Fall 1988.

Rillera, Mary Jo and Sharon Kaplan. *Cooperative Adoption: A Handbook.* Westminister, CA: Triadoption Publications, 1985.

Severson, Randolph. *A Letter to Adoptive Parents . . . On Open Adoption.* Dallas: Cygnet Designs, 1991.

Silber, Kathleen and Patricia Martinez Dorner. *Children of Open Adoption.* San Antonio: Corona Publishing, 1990.

Silber, Kathleen and Phylis Speedlin. *Dear Birthmother: Thank You for Our Baby.* San Antonio: Corona Publishing, 1983.

Theroux, Phyllis. "From the Arms of Another Mother." *Parents,* October 1986, 90–100.

Parenting Adopted Children

Bothen, Linda. *When Friends Ask about Adoption: Question and Answer Guide for Non-Adopted Parents and Other Caring Adults.* Chevy Chase, MD: Swan Publications, 1987.

Hallenbeck, Carol. *Our Child: Preparation for Parenting in Adoption.* Wayne, PA: Our Child Press, 1988.

Katz, Lilian G. "Adopted Children." *Parents,* January 1987, 116.

Komar, Marian. *Communicating with the Adopted Child.* New York: Walker and Company, 1991. Also discusses psychological issues.

Melina, Lois R. *Raising Adopted Children: A Manuel for Adoptive Parents.* New York: Harper and Row, 1986. Also discusses psychological issues.

———. *Making Sense of Adoption: A Parent's Guide.* New York: Harper and Row, 1989. Also discusses psychological issues.

Sachs, Andrea. "When the Lullaby Ends." *Time,* June 4, 1990, 82.

Schaffer, Judith and Christina Lindstrom. *How to Raise an Adopted Child.* New York: Crown, 1989. Also discusses psychological issues.

Schneider, Phyllis. "What It's Like to Adopt," *Parents,* November 1987, 167–70.

Whitley, Glenna. "When a Family Doesn't Work." *Dallas Life Magazine,* August 28, 1988, 11–20.

Personal Adoption Experiences (Adopted Persons)

Dusky, Lorraine. *Birthmark.* New York: M. Evans and Company, 1979.

Lifton, Betty Jean. *I'm Still Me.* New York: Knopf, 1986.

———. *Lost and Found: The Adoption Experience.* New York: Harper and Row, 1988.

———. *Twice Born: Memoirs of an Adopted Daughter.* New York: McGraw-Hill, 1975.

Maxtone-Graham, Katrina. *An Adopted Woman.* New York: Remi Books, 1983.

Reed, Robert. "They Picked Me." *Mothering,* Spring 1986, 91–92.

Personal Adoption Experiences (Adoptive Parents)

Alexander-Roberts, Colleen. "The Written Antidote: A Network of Friendships." *OURS,* January/February 1990.

Annarelli, J.M. "We Were Lucky to Get Our Baby." *USA Today,* March 9, 1981.

Blank, J.B. *Nineteen Steps up the Mountain: The Story of the DeBolt Family.* Philadelphia: Lippincott, 1976. Also covers adoption of children with special needs and older children.

Chase, Mary E. *Waiting for Baby: One Couple's Journey through Infertility to Adoption.* New York: McGraw-Hill, 1990. Also covers infertility and independent adoption.

Dorris, Michael. *The Broken Cord.* New York: Harper and Row, 1989. Also covers adoption of children with special needs.

Herst, J. "Adoption: Parents Provide Insights to Experience." *Denver Post,* May 27, 1984.

Jenkins, Joy. "One Couple's Crusade for Children." *Good Housekeeping,* November 1990, 90–92, 97–98.

Kline, D. "He's Ours . . . He's Really Ours!" *McCall's,* March 1984, 56+.

Kornheiser, Tony. *The Baby Chase.* New York: Atheneum, 1983.

Roberts, Colleen M. "Our Son Christopher." *OURS,* July/August 1986. Also includes how-to-adopt information.

Sheehy, Gail. *Spirit of Survival.* New York: William Morrow, 1986. Also covers adoption of older child.

Viguers, Susan T. *With Child: One Couple's Journey to Their Adopted Children.* San Diego: Harcourt Brace Jovanovich, 1986. Also covers infertility and international adoption.

Personal Adoption Experiences (Birth Parents)

Moore, Dorothy. "A Spirit of Love." *Mothering,* Spring 1986, 93.
Schaefer, Carol. *The Other Mother: A Woman's Love for the Child She Gave up for Adoption.* New York: Soho, 1991.

Postadoption Support

Macaskill, C. "Postadoption Support: Is It Essential?" *Adoption and Fostering* 9 (1985): 45–49.

Psychological Issues

Brodzinsky, David and Marshall Schechter, eds. *The Psychology of Adoption.* New York: Oxford University Press, 1990.
Brodzinsky, David M., Ph.D., Marshall D. Schecter, M.D., and Robin Marantz Henig. *Being Adopted: The Lifelong Search for Self.* New York: Doubleday, 1992.
Feigelman, William and Arnold R. Silverman. *Chosen Children: New Patterns of Adoptive Relationships.* New York: Praeger, 1983.
Kirk, H. David. *Adoptive Kinship: A Modern Institution in Need of Reform.* Rev. ed. Port Angeles, WA: Ben-Simon Publications, 1985.
Rosenberg, Elinor B. *The Adoption Life Cycle: The Children and Their Families through the Years.* New York: The Free Press, 1992.
Smith, Jerome and Franklin I. Miroff. *You're Our Child: The Adoption Experience.* Lanham, MD: Madison Books, 1987.
Sorosky, Arthur D., M.D., Annette Baran, and Reuban Pannor. *The Adoption Triangle: Sealed or Open Records: How They Affect Adoptees, Birth Parents, and Adoptive Parents.* San Antonio: Corona Publishing, 1989.

Single Adoptive Parents

Curto, Josephine J. *How to Become a Single Parent: A Guide for Single People Considering Adoption or Natural Parenthood Alone.* Englewood Cliffs, NJ: Prentice-Hall, 1983.
Dougherty, Sharon Ann. "Single Adoptive Mothers and Their Children." *The Philadelphia Inquirer,* June 13, 1990.
Groze, Victor K. and James A. Rosenthal. "Single Parents and Their Adopted Children: A Psychosocial Analysis." *Families in Society* 72, no. 2 (February 1991): 67–77.
Horne, Juliet. "Single Adopters in the U.S." *Adoption and Fostering* 8 (1984): 40–41.
Kramer, Judy. "36, Unmarried and Longing for a Child." *New Woman,* July 1987, 53–58.
Marindian, Hope. *The Handbook for Single Parents.* Chevy Chase, MD: Committee for Single Adoptive Parents, 1992.

Oliver, Stephanie Stokes. "Single Adoptive Fathers." *Essence* 12 (1988) 114–116, 146.

Prowler, Mady. "Single Parent Adoption: What You Need to Know." Rockville, MD: National Adoption Information Clearinghouse.

Sullivan, Marylou. "Perceptions of Single Adoptive Parents: How We View Ourselves, How Others View Us." *OURS* 22, no. 6 (November/ December 1989): 34–35.

State-By-State Adoption Agency Listings

International Concerns Committee for Children. *Report on Foreign Adoption.* Boulder, CO: ICCC, 1993.

National Adoption Information Clearinghouse. Rev. ed. *National Adoption Directory.* Rockville, MD, 1992.

Paul, Ellen. *Adoption Choices.* Detroit: Visible Ink, 1991.

Posner, Julia. *The Adoption Resource Guide.* Washington, DC: Child Welfare League of America, Inc., 1990.

State Laws

National Adoption Information Clearinghouse. *Adoption Laws: Answers to the Most-Asked Questions.* Rockville, MD: NAIC.

Women and Untimely Pregnancies

Deykin, E.Y., E. Campbell, and P. Patti. "The Postadoption Experience of Surrendering Parent." *American Journal of Orthopsychiatry* 54 (1984): 271–280.

Lindsay, Jeanne. *Pregnant Too Soon: Adoption Is an Option.* St. Paul, MN: EMC, 1980.

Wrenn, M. "Babies Having Babies." *Life* 6 (1983): 102–112.

Zimmerman, M. *Should I Keep My Baby?* Minneapolis: Bethany House, 1983.

Appendices

Adoption Attorneys

ALABAMA

David P. Broome
PO Box 1944
Mobile, AL 36633
(334) 432-9933

John W. Green, III
107 North Side Square
Huntsville, AL 35801
(205) 534-5671

ALASKA

R. Brock Shamberg
12350 Industry Way, Ste. 206
Anchorage, AK 99515
(907) 345-3855

Frederick T. Slone
3003 Minnesota Dr., Ste. 301
Anchorage, AK 99503
(907) 272-4471

ARIZONA

Bruce R. Cohen
2198 E. Camelback Rd., Ste. 365
Phoenix, AZ 85016
(602) 955-1515

Robert W. Finn
4400 E. Broadway, #801
Tucson, AZ 85715
(602) 881-1720

Dale R. Gwilliam
1400 E. Southern Ave., Ste. 1040
Tempe, AZ 85282
(602) 820-5534

Brooks T. Hozier
1221 E. Osborn, #106
Phoenix, AZ 80514
(602) 266-2667

Macre S. Inabinet
40 E. Virginia, Ste. 202
Phoenix, AZ 85004
(602) 263-5771

Rita A. Meiser
Two North Central, Ste. 1600
Phoenix, AZ 85004
(602) 262-5841

Kathryn A. Pidgeon
7500 N. Dreamy Draw Dr., Ste. 200
Phoenix, AZ 85020
(602) 371-1317

K. Terry Williams
222 S. Dobson, Ste. 302
Mason, AZ 85202
(602) 962-9014

ARKANSAS

Kaye H. McLead
620 W. Third, Ste. 210
Little Rock, AR 72201

CALIFORNIA

Philip Adams
220 Montgomery St.
San Francisco, CA 94104
(415) 421-1296

Barbara Bayliss
4525 Wilshire Blvd., #201
Los Angeles, CA 90010
(213) 664-5600

Martin Brandfon
620 Jefferson Ave.
Redwood City, CA 94065
(415) 594-9909

David H. Braum
16255 Ventura Blvd.,
 Ste. 704
Encino, CA 91436
(818) 501-8355

Vanessa Zecher Cain
111 N. Market St., Ste. 730
San Jose, CA 95113
(408) 995-3240

Alvin M. Coen
16152 Beach Blvd., Ste. 101
Huntington Beach, CA 92647
1-800-788-9594

Douglas R. Donnelly
926 Garden St.
Santa Barbara, CA 93101
(805) 962-0988

Steven C. Fishbein
1621 Executive Ct.
Sacramento, CA 95864
(916) 489-9300

Marc Gradstein
1204 Burlingame Ave., Ste.7
Burlingame, CA 94010
(415) 347-7041

David Keene Leavitt
9454 Wilshire Blvd., Penthouse
Beverly Hills, CA 90212
(310) 273-3151

Diane Michelsen
3190 Old Tunnel Rd.
Lafayette, CA 94563
(510) 945-1880

Michael M. Noyes
21515 Hawthorne Blvd., #1290
Torrance, CA 90503
(310) 543-1151

Linda S. Nunez
513 E. First St.,
 2nd Floor
Tustin, CA 92680
1-800-232-3678

Susan Peck
3190 Old Tunnel Rd.
Lafayette, CA 94563
(510) 945-1880

Allison R. Pharis
7770 Healdsburg Ave.
Sebastopol, CA 95472
(707) 823-7361

David J. Radis
1901 Ave. of the Stars,
 20th Floor
Los Angeles, CA 90067
(310) 552-0536

Lesley A. Siegel
3018 Willow Pass Rd., Ste. 201
Concord, CA 94519
(510) 676-3961

Jed Somit
1440 Broadway, Ste. 910
Oakland, CA 94612
(510) 839-3215

Janis K. Stocks
1450 Frazee Rd., Ste. 409
San Diego, CA 92108
(619) 296-6251

Ronald L. Stoddart
1698 Greenbrier Ln., Ste. 201
Brea, CA 92621
(714) 990-5100

Kelly J. Walker
520 Mission St.
Santa Cruz, CA 95060
(408) 685-8083

Robert R. Walmsley
615 Civic Center Dr. West,
 Ste. 300
Santa Ana, CA 92701
(714) 547-6226

Felice A. Webster
4525 Wilshire Blvd., #201
Los Angeles, CA 90010
(213) 664-5600

Steven Wessels
2209 J Street
Sacramento, CA 95816
(916) 446-6076

M.D. Widelock
5401 California Ave., #300
Bakersfield, CA 93309
(805) 325-6950

Nanci R. Worcester
853 Lincoln Way, Ste. 102
Auburn, CA 95603
1-800-523-6781

COLORADO

Pamela A. Gordon
468 Corona St.
Denver, CO 80218
(303) 777-6051

David C. Keene
5299 Dtc. Blvd., Ste. 1300
Englewood, CO 80111
(303) 688-6180

Susan B. Price
4600 S. Ulster
Denver, CO 80237
(303) 721-6077

Stephen H. Swift
733 E. Costilla St., Stes. A & B
Colorado Springs, CO 80903
(719) 520-0164

CONNECTICUT

Janet S. Stutling
68 S. Main St.
West Hartford, CT 06127
(203) 561-4832

DELAWARE

Joel D. Tenenbaum
3200 Concord Pike
PO Box 7329
Wilmington, DE 19803
(302) 477-3200

DISTRICT OF COLUMBIA

Mark T. McDermott
1300 Nineteenth St. NW,
   Ste. 400
Washington, DC 20036
(202) 331-1955

FLORIDA

Brant A. Bailey
4454 Central Ave.
St. Petersburg, FL 33711
(813) 323-7383

Michael B. Brown
One Beach Drive SE, Ste. 205
St. Petersburg, FL 33701
(813) 821-5507

Bennett C. Cohn
1400 Centerpark Blvd., Ste. 360
West Palm Beach, FL 33401
(407) 478-5292

Donald M. Darrach
9350 S. Dixie Hwy., PH.2
Miami, FL 33156
(305) 670-9994

Kathleen C. Fox
PO Box 1930
Alachua, FL 32615
(904) 462-5157

Irving Grass
142 Minuteman Causeway
PO Box 321569
Cocoa Beach, FL 32931
(407) 783-6720

Mikal W. Grass
142 Minuteman Causeway
PO Box 321569
Cocoa Beach, FL 32931
(407) 783-6720

Donald F. Jacobs
1214 E. Concord St.
Orlando, FL 32803
(407) 896-9400

Penny K. Jacobs
1214 E. Concord St.
Orlando, FL 32803
(407) 896-9400

Anthony B. Marchese
4010 Boy Scout Blvd., Ste. 590
Tampa, FL 33607
(813) 877-6643

Linda W. McIntyre
10239 W. Sample Rd.
Coral Springs, FL 33065
(305) 344-0990

Elena Moure-Domecq
1850 SW 8 St.
Miami, FL 33135
(305) 643-2900

Sanford Rockowitz
8900 SW 107 Ave., Ste. 206
Miami, FL 33176
(305) 595-8630

Paul N. Schaefer
2735 W. State Rd. 434, Ste. 1
Longwood, FL 32779
(407) 774-7122

Mary Ann Scherer
2734 E. Oakland Park
Ft. Lauderdale, FL 33306
(305) 564-6900

Susan L. Stockham
2520 S. Tamiami Tr.
Sarasota, FL 34239
(813) 957-0094

Cynthia Stump Swanson
500 E. University Ave., Ste. C
Gainesville, FL 32601
(904) 375-5602

Christine Welch
3800 W. Bay-to-Bay Blvd., #13
Tampa, FL 33629
(813) 835-6000

GEORGIA

Rhonda L. Fishvein
17 Executive Park Dr., #408
Atlanta, GA 30329
(404) 248-9205

HAWAII

Laurie A. Loomis
1300 Pacific Tower
1001 Bishop St.
Honolulu, HI 96813
(808) 524-5066

IDAHO

Bart D. Browning
PO Box 1846
Twin Falls, ID 83303
(208) 733-7180

Steve Smith
PO Box C
Sandpoint, ID 83864
(208) 263-3115

ILLINOIS

Daniel Azulay
35 E. Wacker Dr., Ste. 3300
Chicago, IL 60601
(312) 236-6965

Shelley B. Bostick
312 W. Randolph, Ste. 200
Chicago, IL 60606
(312) 541-1149

Susan F. Grammer
PO Box 111
Bethalto, IL 62010
(618) 259-2113

Michael W. Heller
Commerce Bank Bldg.,
    Ste. 916
Peoria, IL 61602
(309) 674-1007

Richard Lifshitz
120 N. LaSalle St., Ste. 2900
Chicago, IL 60602
(312) 236-7080

Kathleen Hogan Morrison
120 N. LaSalle St., Ste. 2900
Chicago, IL 60602
(312) 236-7080

Lawrence M. Raphael
77 W. Washington St.,
    Ste. 1018
Chicago, IL 60602
(312) 782-2546

Sally Wildman
180 N. LaSalle St.
Chicago, IL 60602
(312) 726-9214

INDIANA

Joel D. Kirsh
401 Pennsylvania Pkwy.,
    Ste. 370
Indianapolis, IN 46280
(317) 575-5555

Franklin I. Miroff
251 E. Ohio, Ste. 1000
Indianapolis, IN 46204
(317) 264-1040

KANSAS

Allan A. Hazlett
1608 SW Mulvane St.
Topeka, KS 66604
(913) 232-2011

Joseph N. Vader
108 E. Poplar
PO Box 1185
Olathe, KS 66051
(913) 764-5010

KENTUCKY

Carolyn S. Arnett
1500 Kentucky Home Life Bldg.
Louisville, KY 40202
(502) 584-0291

James A. Crumlin
608 W. Muhammad Ali Blvd.,
Ste. 503
Louisville, KY 40203
(502) 585-2374

Elisabeth Goldman
118 Lafayette Ave.
Lexington, KY 40502
(606) 252-2325

Donald C. Morris
1009 S. Fourth St.
Louisville, KY 40203
(502) 589-0543

W. Waverly Townes
730 W. Main St.,
Ste. 500
The Hart Block Bldg.
Louisville, KY 40202
(502) 583-7400

LOUISIANA

Edward A. Kaplan
1307 Texas Ave.
PO Box 12386
Alexandria, LA 71315
(318) 448-0831

Edith H. Morris
1515 Poydras St., Ste. 1870
New Orleans, LA 70112
(504) 524-3781

Frederick A. Wild III
206-B W. Harrison Ave.
New Orleans, LA 70112
(504) 482-2115

MAINE

Susan E. Bowie
66 Pearl St., Ste. 321
Portland, ME 04101
(207) 774-5621

MARYLAND

Jeffery E. Badger
124 E. Main St.
Salisbury, MD 21801
(410) 749-2356

Sara M. Donohur
414 Hungerford Dr., Ste. 456
(301) 340-9090

MASSACHUSETTS

Karen K. Greenberg
144 Gould St., Ste. 162
Needham, MA 02194
(617) 444-6611

Jeffrey M. Kaye
260 Haverhill St.
Lawrence, MA 01840
(508) 682-4413

Arthur H. Rosenberg
31 Arapahoe Rd.
West Newton, MA 02165
(617) 928-3683

Robert H. Weber
246 Walnut St.
Newton, MA 02160
(617) 964-7000

MICHIGAN

Herbert A. Brail
930 Mason
Dearborn, MI 48124
(313) 278-8775

MINNESOTA

Jody Ollyver DeSmidt
701 Fourth Ave. S., Ste. 650
Minneapolis, MN 55415
(612) 340-1150

Steven L. Gawron
2850 Metro Dr., Ste. 429
Bloomington, MN 55425
(612) 854-4483

Amy M. Silberberg
175 E. Fifth St., Ste. 763
St. Paul, MN 55101
(612) 228-1455

Judith D. Vincent
111 Third Ave. S.
Mill Place, Ste. 240
Minneapolis, MN 55401
(612) 332-7772

MISSISSIPPI

Lisa Milner
511 E. Pearl St.
Jackson, MS 39201
(601) 948-8800

MISSOURI

Robert A. Cox
6822 Delmar Blvd.
St. Louis, MO 63130
(314) 862-2000

Catherine W. Keefe
120 S. Central Ave., Ste. 1505
Clayton, MO 63105
(314) 727-7050

NEBRASKA

Susan K. Sapp
1900 FirsTier Bank
Lincoln, NE 68508
(402) 474-6900

NEW HAMPSHIRE

Ann McLane Kuster
Two Capital Plaza
PO Box 1500
Concord, NH 03302-1500
(603) 226-2600

Valerie C. Raudonia
Seven Auburn St.
Nashua, NH 03060
(603) 883-3831

NEW JERSEY

Craig B. Bluestein
One Greentree Centre,
  Ste. 201
Marlton, NJ 08053
(609) 988-5513

Jarrold N. Kaminsky
3084 State Hwy. 27, Ste. 3
Kendall Park, NJ 08824
(908) 821-2889

Anne M. Zahn
2 Janet Ct.
Milltown, NJ 08850
(908) 846-3715

NEW YORK

Raymond J. Dauge
200 Empire Bldg.
472 S. Salina St.
Syracuse, NY 13202
(315) 422 2052

Cynthia Perla Meckler
8081 Floss Lane
Buffalo, NY 14051
(716) 688-1540

Stanley B. Michelman
One Blue Hill Plaza,
  Ste. 1146
Pearl River, NY 10965
(914) 735-9650

Susanne Nichols
11 Martime Ave., 11th Floor
White Plains, NY 10606
(914) 949-7755

Brendan C. O'Shea
11 N. Pearl St., 15th Floor
Albany, NY 12207
(518) 432-7511

Lucille Rosenstock
11 Martine Ave.
White Plains, NY 10606
(914) 949-7755

Benjamin J. Rosin
630 Third Ave., 15th Floor
New York, NY 10017
(212) 972-5430

Amy Klein Szymoniak
5888 Main St.
Williamsville, NY 14221
(716) 632-2546

Eli I. Taub
705 Union St.
Schenectady, NY 12305
(518) 370-5515

Golda Zimmerman
117 S. State St.
Syracuse, NY 13202
(315) 475-3322

NORTH CAROLINA

Maura Gavigan
6832 Morrison Blvd.
Charlotte, NC 28211
(704) 364-0010

F. Kevin Gorham
220 N. Eugene St.
Greensboro, NC 27401
(910) 272-8149

OHIO

Hal Hanna
700 N. Main St.
PO Box 25
Bowling Green, OH 43402
(419) 352-6501

Jill Hayes
3361 Executive Pkwy,
    Ste. 100
Toledo, OH 43606
(419) 536-8600

Mary E. Smith
1200 Edison Plaza
300 Madison Ave.
Toledo, OH 43604
(419) 243-6281

James E. Swaim
318 W. Fourth St.
Dayton, OH 45402
(513) 223-5200

OKLAHOMA

Cynthia Calibani
2109 Cache Rd., Ste. C
Lawton, OK 73505
(405) 248-1511

John M. O'Connor
2900 Bank 4th Center
Tulsa, OK 74119
(918) 587-0101

Jack H. Petty
6666 NW 39th Expressway
Bethany, OK 73008
(405) 787-6911

Peter K. Schaffer
2600 City Place
204 N. Robinson Ave.
Oklahoma City, OK 73102
(405) 239-7707

Michael E. Yeksavich
4821 S. Sheridan, Ste. 208
Tulsa, OK 74145
(918) 665-7477

Phyllis L. Zimmerman
15 W. Sixth St., Ste. 1220
Tulsa, OK 74119
(918) 582-6151

OREGON

Catherine M. Dexter
921 SW Washington, Ste. 865
Portland, OR 97062
(503) 222-2474

John R. Hassen
PO Box 670
Medford, OR 97501
(503) 779-8550

Laurence H. Spiegel
PO Box 1708
Oswego, OR 97035
(503) 635-7773

PENNSYLVANIA

Steven G. Dubin
The Benson Manor, Ste. 110
101 Washington Ln.
Jenkington, PA 19046
(215) 885-1210

Debra M. Fox
6624 Morris Park Rd.
Philadelphia, PA 19151
(215) 879-5003

Samuel C. Totaro, Jr.
Four Greenwood Sq., Ste. 100
Bensalem, PA 19020
(215) 244-1045

SOUTH CAROLINA

Richard C. Bell
820 Johnnie Dodds Blvd.
Charleston County
Mt. Pleasant, SC 29464
(803) 884-5103

Pamela E. Deal
PO Box 1764
Clemson, SC 29633
(803) 654-1669

Thomas P. Lowndes, Jr.
18 Broad St., Ste. 507
Charleston, SC 29401
(803) 573-7575

Fletcher D. Thompson
PO Box 1853
Spartanburg, SC 29304
(803) 573-7575

TENNESSEE

Julie A. Grinalds
203 S. Shannon, Ste. 100
Jackson, TN 38301

Diana L. Schmied
6471 Stage Rd., Ste. 201
Bartlett, TN 38184
(901) 388-6659

TEXAS

Vika Andrel
4005 Manchaca, Ste. 108
Austin, TX 78704
(512) 448-4605

Susan I. Paquet
1701 River Run Rd.,
 Ste. 1021
Ft. Worth, TX 76107
(817) 338-4854

M. Brooks Royall
13430 NW Fwy., Ste. 150
Houston, TX 77040
(713) 462-6500

Mark Jordan Siegal
3607 Fairmount
Dallas, TX 77040
(214) 520-0000

Ronald E. Walker, Jr.
504 S. Polk, Ste. 102
Amarillo, TX 79101
(806) 372-3477

Linda Zuflacht
8703 Wurzbach Rd.
San Antonio, TX 78240
(210) 699-6088

VERMONT

Susan L. Fowler
289 College St.
Burlington, VT 05401
(802) 863-2818

Edward L. Winpenny
25 Main St.
Poultney, VT 05764
(802) 287-9110

VIRGINIA

Jennifer A. Brust
2000 N. 14th St.,
 Ste. 100
Arlington, VA 05764
(703) 525-4000

Robert H. Klima
9257 Lee Ave.,
 Ste. 201
Manassas, VA 22110
(703) 361-5051

William Reilly Marchant
316 W. Broad St.
Richmond, VA 23220
(804) 644-0711

Rodney M. Poole
2800 Patterson Ave.,
 Ste. 100
Richmond, VA 23221
(804) 358-6669

Nancy D. Poster
9909 Georgetown Pike
PO Box 197
Great Falls, VA 22066
(703) 759-1560

Teresa L. Temple
2800 Patterson Ave., Ste. 100
Richmond, VA 23221
(804) 358-6669

Ellen S. Weinman
15 S. College Ave.
Salem, VA 24153
(703) 389-3825

WASHINGTON

Rita L. Bender
1301 5th Ave., Ste. 3401
Seattle, WA 98101
(206) 623-6501

Caroline D. Davis
1200 Fifth Ave.
IBM Bldg., Ste. 1925
Seattle, WA 98101
(206) 628-0890

J. Eric Gustafson
PO Box 1689
Yakima, WA 98907
(509) 248-7220

Thomas J. Taylor
344 Cleveland Ave., Ste. G
Olympia, WA 98501
(206) 943-9557

Eric B. Watness
101 Yesler Way, Ste. 603
Seattle, WA 98104
(206) 628-0310

WISCONSIN

Susan M. DeGroot
7617 Mineral Point Rd.
PO Box 5510
Madison, WI 53705

Stephen W. Hayes
411 E. Wisconsin Ave., Ste. 700
Milwaukee, WI 53202
(414) 276-1122

Judith S. Newton
Three S. Pickney St., Ste. 1000
Madison, WI 53703
(608) 259-2646

Victoria J. Schroeder
N9 W31864 Cobblestone
Delafield, WI 53018
(414) 646-2054

WYOMING

Peter J. Feeney
PO Box 437
Casper, WY 82602
(307) 266-4422

William D. Hjelmstad
300 S. Wolcott, Ste. 240
Casper, WY 82601
(307) 577-0934

Phillip T. Willoughby
300 N. Ash St.
Casper, WY 82601

Adoption Book Publishers and Distributors
(When calling or writing, ask for a catalog)

Adoption Advocates Press
1921 Ohio St. NW, Ste. C
Palm Bay, FL 32907
(407) 724-0815

Perspective Press
PO Box 90318
Indianapolis, IN 46290
(317) 872-3055

Tapestry Books
One Country Club Dr.
Ringoes, NJ 08551
1-800-765-2367

Adoptive Parent Support Organizations

Alabama

Adoption Connection
Nann Worel
1500 Hillcrest Rd., #928
Mobile, AL 36695-3963

Parents Adopting Children Together
Elissa Jones
301 Deer Run Rd.
Auburn, AL 36380

Arizona

Extensions
Randi Sweet
7835 E. Glenrosa Ave. #4
Scottsdale, AZ 85251–4145

Arkansas

River Valley Adoption Support
    Group
Elizabeth & Steve Franks
1005 W. 18th Terrace
Russellville, AR 72801-7025

California

Adoption Support & Information
    Group
David Baum
16255 Ventura Blvd.,
    Ste. 704
Encino, CA 91436-2312

F.A.C.E.S.
Bonnie Malouf
June Davies
2510 Smith Grade
Santa Cruz, CA 95060-9733

FAIR
379 Palo Alto Ave.
Mountain View, CA 94041-1117

For the Children
Bob & Donna King
13074 Larkhaven Dr.
Moreno Valley, CA 92553-5689

Hand in Hand
Chris Winston
874 Phillip Ct.
Eldorado Hills, CA 95762

Inter-Country Adoption Network
Nancy Tapia
7450 Kelvin Ave.
Canoga Park, CA 91306-2726

North Coast Adoptive Families
Colleen Morris
2136 Parrish Dr.
Santa Rosa, CA 95404-2323

Orange County Parent Association
Gerry Mazur
39 Foxboro
Irvine, CA 92714-7524

Ours Through Adoption
Judy Pietz
Box 85152-343
San Diego, CA 92138

PACT
Susanne Rose
3904 Via Cardelina
Palos Verdes Estates, CA 90274

Parents of Peruvian Adoptees
Jan McFarlane
2067 Meridian Ave., Apt. 8
South Pasadena, CA 91030-4245

San Mateo Adoptive Families
Carol Regalia
2136 Whipple Ave.
Redwood City, CA 94062

Solano Cty. Adoption Support
Group
Cheryl Richno
212 Sunhaven Dr.
Fairfield, CA 94533-5892

T.E.A.M. Together Expecting A
Miracle
1300 Astoria Pl.
Oxnard, CA 93030-8617

Colorado

Adoptive Families of Denver Inc.
Pam Sweetser
2052 Elm St.
Denver, CO 80207

Rocky Mountain Adoption
Exchange
Mary Sullivan
925 S. Niagara St., Ste. 100
Denver, CO 80224-1658

Connecticut

Adoptive Parents Exchange Group
D. Stroffolino & D. Mulrey
6 Putnam Park Rd.
Bethel, CT 06801-2221

Intl. Adoptive Families
Jeanne Allard
433 Quarry Brook Dr.
South Windsor, CT 06074-3598

LAPA Latin American Parents
Association
Christine Hamilton
55 Jeremiah Rd.
Sandy Hook, CT 06482-1417

Delaware

Adoptive Families with
Information & Support
Mary Lou Edgar
2610 Northgate Rd.
Wilmington, DE 19810

District of Columbia

North Virginia F.A.C.E.
Eliza Button
103 15th St. NE
Washington, DC 20002-6505

Florida

Adoption Support Network
Mrs. Christy Whitehead
15183 Normandy Blvd.
Jacksonville, FL 32234

Families Through Adoption
Kathy Timmens
Box 420085
Naples, FL 33942-0002

Gatherings of Int'l Adoptive
Families
Lori Stolt Bollman
2923 SW 5th Pl.
Cape Coral, FL 33914-4610

Hope: Share-N-Care
Kimberly Hale & Jerry Woodbridge
4062 Greenwillow Ln. E.
Jacksonville, FL 32211-1638

Parents Adopting Children
Everywhere
Rebecca Mattox
1240 Meadowbrook Rd. NE
Palm Bay, FL 32905

Special Needs Adoption Support
Group
Nancy Ellison
15913 Layton Ct.
Tampa, FL 33647

Georgia

Adopted Kids & Parents
Marsha Kennedy
4137 Bellflower Ct.
Roswell, GA 30075

Clarke Cty. Adoption Resource
    Exchange
Box 6311
Athens, GA 30604-6311

Hawaii

Forever Families
Peggy Kuharcik
7719 Waikapu Loop
Honolulu, HI 96825

Resolve Of Hawaii–Kaui Site
3721 Omao
Koloa, HI 96756

Illinois

Adoptive Families Today
Kathy Casey
Box 1726
Barrington, IL 60011-1726

Central Illinois Adoptive Families
Candace Ogden
2206 Oakwood Ave.
Bloomington, IL 61704-2414

Child International
Maureen Kay
4121 Crestwood Dr.
Northbrook, IL 60062-7544

Fox Valley Adoption Support Group
Joanne Green
111 Adobe Dr.
Aurora, IL 60506-1603

Ours of Northern Illinois
Janet Allen
12510 Thistle Ridge Ct.
Roscoe, IL 61073

Stars of David
Susan Katz
3175 Commerical Ave.,
    Ste. 100
Northbrook, IL 60062-1915

Indiana

Adoptive Family Network
Karen Altergott
306 Sharon Rd.
W. Lafayette, IN 47906

Illiana Adoptive Parents
Ann Grant
8240 Beech Ave.
Munster, IN 46321-1405

Ours by Adoption
Lee Ann & Michael Fifer
RR 3, 104 S. Water St.
Monroeville, IN 46773-9301

Iowa

Adoptive Families of
    Greater Des Moines
Sue Whitlock
1005 N. C Street
Indianola, IA 50125-1327

Iowa City Int'l Adopt. Families
Chris Forcucci
1328 Melrose Ave.
Iowa City, IA 50125-1327

Iowa Parents of East Indian
    Children
Carol Bottom
206 N. Center St.
Marshalltown, IA 50158
(515) 752-6682

Kentucky

Adoptive Parents Guild
Pamela Raidt
1888 Douglas Rd.
Louisville, KY 40205

Kentuckian Families for Adoption
Eileen Deren
10417 Scarlet Oaks Ct.
Louisville, KY 40241-1714

Maryland

Adoptive Family Network
Jennifer Geipe
Box 7
Columbia, MD 21045

Children in Common
Janice Pearse
Box 21016
Baltimore, MD 21228-0516

Delmarva F.A.C.E.
Gloria J. Wilson
32810 Long Rodge Rd.
Parsonburg, MD 21849

Massachusetts

Bershire County Open Door Society
Carol & David Weissbrod
1866 Washington Mountain Rd.
Washington, MA 01223

Latin American Adoptive Families
Marilyn Rowland
23 Evangeline Rd.
Falmouth, MA 02540

Open Door Society of
    Massachusetts Inc.
Joan Clark
Box 1158
Westborough, MA 01581-6158

Michigan

Adoption Resource Group
Dennis & Micki Silva
319 Mason Ave.
Hancock, MI 49930-2130

Concerned Citizens for
    International Adoption
Box 1083
Portage, MI 49081-1083

European Adoptive Families of
    Michigan
Deborah Lawless
47540 Saltz Rd.
Canton, MI 48187-4826

Families for International Children
Doug Vanderlaan
6475 28th St. SE, #124
Grand Rapids, MI 49546-6952

The Family Tree
Janis J. Weaver
27821 Santa Barbara Dr.
Lathrup Village, MI 48076-3355

Greater Lansing Ours by Adoption
John Bankson
Box 25161
Lansing, MI 48909-5161

LAFTA
Mrs. Sabina Seidel
608 Marcelletti Ave.
Paw Paw, MI 49079-1219

Michigan Assn. of Single Adoptive
    Parents
Janet Way
7412 Coolidge Ave.
Center Line, MI 48015-2044

PACE
Tina Pawlak
1305 Seminole
Holland, MI 49424

Today's Families, Inc. APSG
Janice Jordan Skrobot
18326 Middlebelt Rd., #8
Linvonia, MI 48152-5007

Minnesota

Adoption Connection
Susan Boyle
210 Shorewood Dr.
International Falls, MN 56649-2108

Families of Multi Racial Adoptions
Jean & Gary Zandstra
2057 Roe Crest Dr.
Mankato, MN 56003-3434

Families Supporting Adoption
Joyce Anderson
11462 Crow Hassan Park Rd.
Hanover, MN 55341-9404

Northland Families Through
    Adoption
Angela Lagarde
518 Lagarde Rd.
Wrenswall, MN 55797

Parents of Indian Children
Lynn Malfield
1395 Simpson St.
St. Paul, MN 55108-2439

Parents of Latin American Children
Bernice Tenquist
16665 Argon St. NW
Anoka, MN 55304-1606

Rochester Area Adoptive Families
Nancy Johnson
Box 6914
Rochester, MN 55903
(507) 281-0747

Montana

Adoptive Families of Montana
Becky McDonald
1499 Cobb Hills Rd.
Bozeman, MT 59715

Montana Post Adoption Center
Frank Lane
Box 634
Helena, MT 59624-0634

Yellowstone International Families
Sherrie Pogue
5028 Rimrock Rd.
Billings, MT 59106

Nebraska

Families Through Adoption
Lori Erickson
1619 Coventry Ln.
Grand Island, NE 68801-7025

Kearney Area Adoption Assn.
14960 W. Cedarview Rd.
Wood River, NE 68883-9320

Open Hearts Adoption Support
  Group
Kay Lytle
4023 S. 81st St.
Lincoln, NE 68506

New Hampshire

Open Door Society Of N.H.
Debbie Herbert
Box 709
Goshen, NH 03752-0709

Open Door Society of N.H.
Box 792
Derry, NH 03038-0792

New Jersey

Adoptive Parents for Open Records
Joan & John Crout
625 St. Marks Ave.
Westfield, NJ 07090

Camden County Faces
Susan Grella
130 Mansfield Blvd. S.
Cherry Hill, NJ 08034-3615

Concerned Parents for Adoption
Patricia Persons
Box 179
Whippany, NJ 07981-0179

Jersey Shore Families by Adoption
Jan A. Devaney
507 Laurelwood Dr.
Lanoka Harbor, NJ 08734

Latin American Parents Assn.,
  NJ Chapter
Leslie Brookes
Box 2013
Brick, NJ 08723-1074

Links
Sally Vroom
91 Carlton Ave.
Washington, NJ 07882

New Mexico

Parents of Intercultural Adoption
Anne O'Rourke
Box 91175
Albuquerque, NM 87199-1175

New York

Adoption Resource Network Inc.
Cindy Fleischer & Lisa Maynard
Box 178
Pittsford, NY 14534

Adoptive Families of Older Children
Roberta & Alan Bentz-Letts
149-32A Union Tpke.
Flushing, NY 11367

Adoptive Parents Committee,
  NY Chapter
Sam Pitkowsky
Box 3525
New York, NY 10008-3525

Council of Adoptive Parents
Terry Savini & Martha Cameron
Box 964
Penfield, NY 14526-0964

Families Interested in Adoption Inc.
Sue Schultz
Box 56
Buffalo, NY 14231-0056

Families Through Adoption
Cheryl Anderson
301 Middle Rd.
Oneida, NY 13421-2812

International Adoptive Families
Sharon Burgess
Box 13903
Albany, NY 12212-3903

Ours Through Adoption
Peggy Metzger
Box 2054
Buffalo, NY 14240

Upstate NY Single Adoptive Parents
Florence Adams
30 Shaker Dr.
Loudonville, NY 12211-1843

North Carolina

Captial Area Families for Adoption
Pauline McNeill
4616 Thendara Way
Raleigh, NC 27612-6350

Carolina Adoptive Families
Vonnie Bishop
1005 Black Oak Dr.
Matthews, NC 28105-5501

Coastal Hearts of Adoptive Families
Deborah Lillie
6002 McClean Dr.
Emerald Isle, NC 28549

The Spice Rack
Lynn & Jerry Beard
604 Rollingwood Dr.
Greensboro, NC 27410-4520

Tri-Adopt
Ann Nashold
Box 51331, Shannon Plaza
Durham, NC 27717-1331

North Dakota

The Adoption Forum
Kim Rau
2136 Grant Dr.
Bismark, ND 58501-2355

Ohio

Adoptive Families of
Greater Cincinnati
Peggy Schramm
4 Revel Ct.
Cincinnati, OH 45217-1916

Adoptive Families Support Assn.
John Seavers
Box 91247
Cleveland, OH 44101-3247

Families Through Adoption
Mary Ellen Pyke
Box 2521
Akron, OH 44309

Korean Family Connection
Diane M. Gersten
5067 Lakeside Dr.
Mason, OH 45040-1767

New Roots
Sharon Reelhorn
Box 14953
Columbus, OH 43214-0953

Oklahoma

Adoptive Families Support Assn.
2009 W. Dena Dr.
Edmond, OK 73034

Adoptive Parents of
Central Oklahoma
Lonna Yeary
1237 Mountain Brook Dr.
Norman, OK 73072-3446

Cradle of Lawton
Jan Howenstine
902 NW Kingswood Rd.
Lawton, OK 73505-4130

Oregon

Adoption Network
Linnie Sohler
2251 Dry Creek Rd.
Mosier, OR 97040-9788

Adoptive Families Unlimited
Dianne Reinmuth
Box 40752
Eugene, OR 97404

NAFA
Kathy Johnson
Box 25355
Portland, OR 97225-0356

Pennsylvania

Families Through Adoption
Kathy Graham
4109 Kingswood Ct.
Harrisburg, PA 17112

Families Together
Susan Pedaline
Apollo Ln.
Rochester, PA 15074

International Families Through
   Adoption
Christy Yatzor
416 Primrose Dr.
Sarver, PA 16055-9577

Latin American Adoptive Families
Amy Lindner-Lesser
117 E. Greenwood Ave.
Lansdowne, PA 19050-1625

Parents of Adopted African
   Americans
Robert & Barbara Lewis
544 W. 31st Street
Erie, PA 16508-1743

Parents of Adoptive Int'l Children
Barbara Schlegel
1184 Jaime Lyn Dr.
Downingtown, PA 19335

South Carolina

Piedmont Adoptive Families
Karen Kearse
Box 754
Spartanburg, SC 29304-0754

SC COAC
Linda Williams
Box 1453
Greenville, SC 29602-1453

South Dakota

Families Through Adoption
Twyla Baedke
Box 851
Sioux Falls, SD 57101

Tennessee

Mid-South Families Through
   Adoption
Regina Fausett
3031 Lauren Dr.
Bartlett, TN 38133

N.E. Tennessee Adoption Support
   Group
Diane Ress
736 Island Rd.
Kingsport, TN 37664-4200

Ours of Middle Tennessee
Charles & Wanda Beck
3557 Bethlehem Rd.
Springfield, TN 37172

Texas

Adopting Children Together, Inc.
Debbie Sanders
Box 120966
Arlington, TX 76012-0966

Adoptive Families Together
Margaret Nichols
Box 272963
Houston, TX 77277-2963

Austin Kids From All Cultures
Pam & Ron Matthews
4508 Sinclair Ave.
Austin, TX 78756-3017

Council on Adoptable Children of
   Dallas
Box 141199, Dept. 500
Dallas, TX 75214-1199

Families Through Adoption
Bill Betzen
Box 190507
Dallas, TX 75219-0507

Open Arms
Lisa Archer
1615 Jo Ann Lane
Sugar Land, TX 77478-2366

Parents Aiding & Lending Support
Donna Thompson
3709 Canterbury Dr.
Baytown, TX 77521-2807

Vermont

The Chosen Children from
   Romania
K. Mark Treon
Box 401
Barre, VT 05641-0401

Friends in Adoption
Box 7270, Buxton Ave.
Middletown Springs, VT 05757

Virginia

Asia Family & Friends
Margie Perscheid
1906 Sword Ln.
Alexandria, VA 22308-2445

Assn. of Single Adoptive Parents of
   VA
408 Henry Clay Rd.
Ashland, VA 23005-1411

Blue Ridge Adoption Group
Janet Scheid
1453 Wolf Creek Dr.
Vinton, VA 24179-2800

Families for Russian & Ukrainian
   Adoptions
Linda H. Crumpecker
Box 2944
Merrifield, VA 22116-2944

North Virginia F.A.C.E.
Karol Quinn
6315 Gromley Pl.
Springfield, VA 22152

Romanian Children's Connection
Mary Thomas
1206 Hillside Terrace
Alexandria, VA 22302

Washington

AIAA Adoptive Parent Support Group
Kristi Greene
2711 S. Manito Blvd.
Spokane, WA 99203-2540

Families Through Adoption of WA
Lynn Thompson
11323 SE 218th Pl.
Kent, WA 98031-2123

Families With Children From China
Sarah Young
12224 SE 210th Pl.
Issaquah, WA 98027

North Central Washington
   Adoption Support Network
Cheryl Bailey
Box 3731
Wenatchee, WA 98807-3731

West Virginia

AFFA
Rick Watson
Box 2775
Charleston, WV 25330-2775

Wisconsin

Adoptive Parent Support Group of
   S. Wisconsin Inc.
Sharon Koenig
4206 Manitou Way
Madison, WI 53711-3704

Fox Valley Friends in Adoption
Shirley A. Schmidt
1032 Forestedge Dr.
Kaukauna, WI 54130-2958

Love Through Adoption
Phil & Linda Bertz
809 S. Apple Ave.
Marshfield, WI 54449

Ours Through Adoption
Judy Josse
4232 Garden Dr.
Racine, WI 53403-3900

Ours Through Adoption of
   NE Wisconsin
Mary Freberg
990 Hickory Hill Dr.
Green Bay, WI 54304-258

St. Croix Valley Korean-American
  Cultural Society
Kerry L. Geurkink
383 N. Glover Rd.
Hudson, WI 54016

Wyoming

Northern Wyoming Adoptive
  Parents, Inc.
Irene Tate
Box 788
Basin, WY 82410-0788

General Adoption Resources

*Information through page 209 courtesy of National Adoption
Information Clearinghouse; Rockville, Maryland.*

United States Immigration and Naturalization Service District Offices

Eastern

District of Columbia .... 4420 N. Fairfax Dr., Arlington, VA 22203
Maine..................... 739 Warren Ave., Rm. 316, Portland, ME 04103
Maryland................. Equitable Bank Center, 12th Floor, Tower 1,
                          100 S. Charles St., Baltimore, MD 21201
Massachusetts .... JFK Federal Bldg., Government Center, Rm. 1700,
                          Boston, MA 02203
New Jersey .... 970 Broad St., Newark, NJ 07102
New York................ 26 Federal Plaza, New York, NY 10278
                          130 Delaware Ave., Buffalo, NY 14202
Pennsylvania .... 1600 Callowhill St., Philadelphia, PA 19103
Puerto Rico.............. Carlos Chardon St., Hato Rey, PR 00917

Northern

Colorado................. 4730 Paris St., Denver, CO 80239
Illinois.................... 10 W. Jackson Blvd., Ste. 600, Chicago, IL 60604
Minnesota .... 2901 Metro Dr., Ste. 100, Bloomington, MN 55425
Missouri................. 9747 N. Conant Ave., Kansas City, MO 64153
Montana .... 2800 Skyway Dr., Helena, MT 59601
Ohio..................... AJC Federal Bldg., 1240 E. 9th St., Rm. 1917,
                          Cleveland, OH 44199
Oregon .... Federal Bldg., 511 NW Broadway,
                          Portland, OR 92709
Washington.............. 815 Airport Way South, Seattle, WA 98134

Southern

Florida................... 7880 Biscayne Blvd., Miami, FL 33138
Georgia.................. Postal Service Bldg., 77 Forsyth St. SW, Rm. G-85,
                          Atlanta, GA 30303
Louisiana................ Postal Service Bldg., 701 Loyola Ave.,
                          New Orleans, LA 70113
Texas .... 8101 N. Stemmons Fwy., Dallas, TX 75247
                          509 N. Belt, Houston, TX 77060
                          8940 Four Winds Dr., San Antonio, TX 78239
                          2102 Teege Ave., Harlingen, TX 78550

Western

Arizona...................2035 N. Central St., Phoenix, AZ 85004
California ....300 N. Los Angeles St., Los Angeles, CA 90012
                                880 Front St., Ste. 1234, San Diego, CA 92188
                                630 Sansome St., Rm. 232, San Francisco, CA 94111
                                24000 Avila Rd., PO Box 30080,
                                    Laguna Miguel,CA 92607-0080
Hawaii....................PO Box 461, 595 Ala Moana Dr.,
                                Honolulu, HI 96809

National Organizations Concerned with Adoptions

There are a number of national organizations that provide services
or undertake activities related to adoption. The following are some
of the most common activities:

• Standard Setting for Agency Services	S
• Information and Referral	I
• Publications and Materials	P
• Consultation and Technical Assistance	C
• Education and Training	E
• Advocacy and Public Policy	A
• Support Network	SN
• Exchange Services	X

The following national organizations are listed with their major
activities identified by the letter codes above:

Adopt a Special Kid 2201 Broadway, Ste. 702 Oakland, CA 94105 (510) 451-1748	A, E, I, X
Adoption Exchange Association 925 S. Niagara St., Ste. 100 Denver, CO 80224 (303) 333-0845	S, C, E
Adoptive Families of America (formerly OURS) 3333 Hwy. 100 N. Minneapolis, MN 55422 (612) 535-4829	P, C, SN, A, E
American Bar Association Center on Children and the Law 740 15th St. NW Washington, DC 20005 (202) 662-1000	P, C, E, A

American Public Welfare Association   P, C, A, S
810 First St. NE, Ste. 500
Washington, DC 20002-4205
(202) 682-0100

Children Awaiting Parents, Inc.   P, C, X
700 Exchange St.
Rochester, NY 14608
(716) 232-5110

Child Welfare Institute   C, E, S
2 Midtown Plaza
1365 Peachtree St. NE, Ste. 900
Atlanta, GA 30309-2956
(404) 876-1934

Child Welfare League of America   S, I, P, C, E, A
440 First St. NW, Ste. 310
Washington, DC 20001
(202) 638-2952

National Adoption Center   I, P, C, A, X
1500 Walnut St., Ste. 701
Philadelphia, PA 19102
1-800-TO-ADOPT or (215) 735-9988

National Adoption Information Clearinghouse   I, P
Cygnus Corporation
5640 Nicholson Lane, Ste. 300
Rockville, MD 20852
(301) 231-6512

National Committee for Adoption   I, P, C, E, A
1930 17th St. NW
Washington, DC 20009
(202) 328-1200

National Federation for Open Adoption Education   S, C, E
391 Taylor Blvd., Ste. 100
Pleasant Hill, CA 94523
(510) 827-2229

Branch Office: S, C, E
1607 S. Madison
Muncie, IN 49302
(317) 286-3721

National Foster Parent Association   SN, I, P
c/o 226 Kilts Dr.
Houston, TX 77024
(713) 467-1850

Nat'l Resource Center for Special Needs Adoption   C, E, P, S
16250 Northland Dr., Ste. 120
Southfield, MI 48075
(313) 443-7080

North American Council on Adoptable Children   I, C, E, P, A, SN
970 Raymond Ave., Ste. 106
St. Paul, MN 55114-1149
(612) 644-3036

One Church One Child
2811-2-E Industrial Plaza Dr., Rm. 114
Tallahassee, FL 32301
(904) 488-8251

Resources for Special Populations

Single Adoptive Parents

Committee for Single Adoptive Parents, Inc.   I, P, SN
PO Box 15084
Chevy Chase, MD 20825

Assistance with Fertility Problems

Resolve, Inc.   I, P, E, A, SN
1310 Broadway
Somerville, MA 02144-1731
(617) 623-1156

Jewish Adoptive Parents

Stars of David   I, P, SN
Ileen & Stuart Schwartz
Acting National Presidents
PO Box 1023
Denville, NJ 07834
(201) 627-7752

Adoptive Parents of Latin American Children

Latin American Parents Association   I, SN
PO Box 523
Unionville, CT 06085
(203) 270-1424

Adopted Persons, Adoptive Parents, and Birth Relatives

Adoptee Liberty Movement Assn. (ALMA)   I, C, E, A, P, SN
PO Box 727, Radio City Station
New York, NY 10101-0727
(212) 581-1568

American Adoption Congress   I, C, E, A, P, SN
100 Connecticut Ave. NW, Ste. 9
Washington, DC 20036
1-800-274-6736

Birthparent Connection   I, P, SN
PO Box 230643
Encinitas, CA 92023-0643
(619) 753-8288

Concerned United Birthparents   I, E, A, P, SN
2000 Walker St.
Des Moines, IA 50317
1-800-822-2777 or (515) 263-9558

Council for Equal Rights in Adoption   I, E, A, P, SN
401 E. 74th St., Ste. 17D
New York, NY 10021
(212) 988-0110

International Soundex Reunion Registry   I, C
PO Box 2312
Carson City, NV 89702
(702) 882-7755

Post Adoption Center for Education & Research   I, E, A, P, SN
(PACER)
PO Box 309
Orinda, CA 94563
(510) 935-6622

Adopted Children with Disabilities

Advocates for Deaf & Hard of Hearing Youth, Inc.   A, SN
PO Box 75949
Washington, DC 20013
(202) 651-5160

Alliance of Genetic Support Groups   I, SN
35 Wisconsin Circle, Ste. 440
Chevy Chase, MD 20815
1-800-336-GENE or (301) 652-5553

Children with AIDS Project of America   I, A, SN, X
PO Box 83131
Phoenix, AZ 85071-3131
1-800-866-AIDS or (602) 256-7510

Little People of America Adoption Committee   I, SN, X
Adoption Committee Chairperson
c/o Nancy Rockwood
1210 Woodland Park Dr.
Hurst, TX 76053-3882
1-800-LPA-ADOPT

National Assn. for Perinatal Addiction   I, P, C
Research and Education
200 N. Michigan, 3rd Floor
Chicago, IL 60601
(312) 541-1272

National Federation of the Blind   I, SN, X
Network on Adoption and Blindness
1800 Johnson St.
Baltimore, MD 21230
(410) 659-9314

BRANCH OF THE FEDERAL GOVERNMENT CONCERNED WITH ADOPTION

Department of Health and Human Services
Administration on Children and Families
Adoptions Opportunities Branch, Children's Bureau
PO Box 1182
Washington, DC 20201
(202) 401-9200

International, National, and Regional Adoption Exchanges and Photo Listings

International

International Concerns Committee
for Children Listing Service
911 Cypress Dr.
Boulder, CO 80303
(303) 494-8333

National

AASK America Adoption Exchange
657 Mission St., Ste. 601
San Francisco, CA 94105
(415) 543-2275

Children Awaiting Parents, Inc.
700 Exchange St.
Rochester, NY 14608
(716) 232-5110

Jewish Children's Adoption
Network
PO Box 16544
Denver, CO 80216
(303) 573-8113

National Adoption Center
1500 Walnut St., Ste. 701
Philadelphia, PA 19102
1-800-TO-ADOPT or (215) 735-9988

National American Indian Adoption
Service
Three Feathers Associates
PO Box 5508
Norman, OK 73070
(405) 360-2919

Regional

Adopt a Special Kid (AASK) Midwest
1025 N. Reynolds Rd., Ste. 201
Toledo, OH 43615
(419) 534-3350
Note: Covers Illinois, Indiana, Iowa,
Michigan, Minnesota, Ohio,
Wisconsin

Adoption Center of Delaware Valley
1500 Walnut St., Ste. 701
Philadelphia, PA 19102
1-800-TO-ADOPT or (215) 735-9988
Note: Covers Delaware, District of
Columbia, Maryland, New Jersey,
Pennsylvania, Virginia, West
Virginia

The Adoption Exchange
925 S. Niagara St., Ste. 100
Denver, CO 80224
(303) 333-0845
Note: Covers Colorado, Missouri,
Nevada, New Mexico, South
Dakota, Utah, Wyoming

Massachusetts Adoption Resource
Exchange, Inc.
867 Boylston St.
Boston, MA 02116
(617) 536-0362
Note: Covers Connecticut, Maine,
Massachusetts, New Hampshire,
Rhode Island, Vermont

Northwest Adoption Exchange
7th Ave., Ste. 409
Seattle, WA 98101
(206) 292-0082
Note: Covers Alaska, Idaho, Nevada,
Oregon, Utah, Washington

Branches:

610 Gold SW
Albuquerque, NM 87102
1-800-888-6966 or (505) 296-4017

610 E. South Temple
Salt Lake City, UT 84102
(801) 359-7700

Southeastern Exchange of the
United States (SEE US)
PO Box 1453
Greenville, SC 29602
(803) 242-0460
Note: Covers Alabama, Florida,
Georgia, Kentucky, Mississippi,
North Carolina, South Carolina,
Tennessee

Three Rivers Adoption Council
307 4th Ave., Ste. 710
Pittsburgh, PA 15222
(412) 471-8722
Note: Covers Delaware, District of
Columbia, Maryland, New Jersey,
Pennsylvania, Virginia, West
Virginia

Tri-State Adoption Exchange
Department of Human Services
221 State St.
Augusta, ME 04333
(207) 287-3707
Note: Covers Maine, New
Hampshire, Vermont

Magazines and Newsletters of Interest to Adoptive and Birth Families

You may subscribe to some of these publications directly. Others are published by membership organizations that you must join in order to receive the publication. Call or write the publication office of your interest for details.

Add-Option
Aid to Adoption of Special Kids
657 Mission St., Ste. 601
San Francisco, CA 94105
(415) 543-2275

Adoptalk
North American Council on
    Adoptable Children
970 Raymond Ave., Ste. 106
St. Paul, MN 55114-1149
(612) 644-3036

Adopted Child Newsletter
PO Box 9362
Moscow, ID 83843
(208) 882-1794

The Adoption Advocate's
NEWSletter
Adoption Advocate's Press
1921 Ohio St. NE, Ste. 5
Palm Bay, FL 32907
(407) 725-6379

Adoption Therapist
4209 McKinney Ave., Ste. 200
Dallas, TX 75205
(214) 526-8721

Adoption Therapy Coalition
Journal
PO Box 1392
Rockville, MD 20850
(301) 869-4806

The Decree
American Adoption Congress
100 Connecticut Ave. NW, Ste. 9
Washington, DC 20036
1-800-274-6736 or (202) 483-3399

FACE Facts
Families Adopting Children
    Everywhere
PO Box 28058
Northwood Station
Baltimore, MD 21239
(410) 488-2656

National Adoption Reports
National Council for Adoption
1930 17th St. NW
Washington, DC 20009
(202) 328-1200

Open Adoption
National Federation for Open
    Adoption Education
391 Taylor Blvd., Ste. 100
Pleasant Hill, CA 94523
(510) 827-2229

PACT Press
3450 Sacramento St., Ste. 239
San Francisco, CA 94118
(510) 530-7225

People Searching News
PO Box 10044
Palm Bay, FL 32910-0444
(407) 768-2222

Reunions, The Magazine
PO Box 11727
Milwaukee, WI 53211-1727
(414) 263-4567

Roots and Wings
30 Endicott Drive
Great Meadows, NJ 07838
(908) 637-8828

Private Adoption Agencies

Call your state's department of social services to obtain a listing of all the agencies in your state.

Alabama

Alabama Baptist Children's Home
1404 16th Ave. SE
PO Box 1805
Decatur, AL 35602

Association for Guidance, Aid,
  Placement, & Empathy
(AGAPE)
PO Box 850663
Mobile, AL 36685

Catholic Family Services
PO Box 745
Huntsville, AL 35801

Catholic Social Services
2164 11th Ave. South
Birmingham, AL 35265

Children's Aid Society
3600 8th Ave. South
Birmingham, AL 35212

Lifeline Children's Services
2908 Pumphouse Rd.
Birmingham, AL 35233

New Women Adoption Agency
1515 4th Ave. South
Birmingham, AL 35233

Villa Hope
4 Office Park Circle, Ste. 303
Birmingham, AL 35223

Alaska

Catholic Social Services
3710 E. 20th Ave., Ste. 1
Anchorage, AK 99508

Fairbanks Counseling & Adoption
753 Gaffney Rd.
Box 71544
Fairbanks, AK 99707

Hope Cottages, Inc.
2805 Bering St.
Anchorage, AK 99518

Kawerak Adoption Agency
PO Box 948
Nome, AK 99762

Arizona

Adopt a Special Kid (AASK) of
  Arizona
234 North Central, Ste. 127
Phoenix, AZ 85004

Arizona Children's Home
4621 N. 16th St., Ste. F-608
Phoenix, AZ 85016

Birth Hope Adoption Agency
3225 North Central, Ste. 1217
Phoenix, AZ 85004

Catholic Social Services of Phoenix
1825 W. Northern Ave.
Phoenix, AZ 85021

Christian Family Care Agency
3603 N. 7th Ave.
Phoenix, AZ 85013

Dillon Southwest
PO Box 3535
Scottsdale, AZ 85257

Hand in Hand International
  Adoptions
3102 N. Country Club
Tucson, AZ 85716

House of Samuel
2430 N. Sycamore
Tucson, AZ 85712

LDS Social Services
235 S. El Dorado
Mesa, AZ 85204

Arkansas

Bethany Christian Services
1100 N. University Ave., Ste. 209
Little Rock, AR 72207

Catholic Adoption Services
2415 N. Tyler
Little Rock, AR 72207

Friends of Children, Inc.
2024 Arkansas Valley Dr., Ste. 804
Little Rock, AR 72212

Searcy Children's Home
900 N. Main
Searcy, AR 72143

California

ACCEPT
339 S. San Antonio Rd.
Los Altos, CA 94022

Adopt International
121 Springdale Way
Redwood City, CA 94062

Adoption Center, Headquarters
391 Taylor Blvd., Ste. 100
Pleasant Hill, CA 94523

Adoption Horizons
302 4th St., 2nd Floor
Eureka, CA 95501

Adoption Services International
2021 Sperry Ave., Ste. 41
Ventura, CA 93003

Adoptions Unlimited
11800 Central Ave., Ste. 110
Chino, CA 91710

Bay Area Adoption Services, Inc.
465 Fairchild Dr., Ste. 215
Mountain View, CA 94043

Bethany Christian Services
Northern Region
3048 Hahn Dr.
Modesto, CA 95350

Bethany Christian Services
Southern Region
9928 Flower St., Ste. 202
Bellflower, CA 90706-5453

Black Adoption Placement &
    Research Center
1801 Harrison St., 2nd Floor
Oakland, CA 94612

Catholic Charities Adoption Agency
349 Cedar St.
San Diego, CA 92101-3197

Children's Home Society of
    California
Headquarters
1300 W. 4th St.
Los Angeles, CA 90017-1475

Families First
1909 Galileo Ct.
Davis, CA 95616

Family Builders by Adoption
1230 2nd Ave.
Oakland, CA 94606

Family Network
284 Foam St., Ste. 103
Monterey, CA 95355

Future Families
3233 Valencia Ave., Ste. A-6
Aptos, CA 95003

Hand in Hand Foundation
2401 Robertson Rd.
Soquel, CA 95073

Heritage Adoption Services
2214 Capital Ave., Ste. 2
Sacramento, CA 95816

Indian Child & Family Services
28441 Rancho California Rd., Ste. J
Temecula, CA 92590

Institute for Black Parenting
3233 Arlington Ave., Ste. 202
Riverside, CA 92506

Jewish Family & Children Services
Adoption Program
1600 Scott St.
San Francisco, CA 94115

LDS Social Services
4320 Stevens Creek Blvd., Ste. 129
San Jose, CA 95129

Life Adoption Services
440 W. Main St.
Tustin, CA 92680

Lilliput Children's Services
1540 River Park Dr., Ste. 107
Sacramento, CA 95815

North Bay Adoptions
9068 Brooks Rd. South
Windsor, CA 95202

Sierra Adoption Services
8928 Volunteer Ln., Ste. 240
Sacramento, CA 95826

Vista Del Mar Child Care Services
3200 Motor Ave.
Los Angeles, CA 90034

Colorado

Adoption Alliance
3010 S. Jamaica Court, Ste. 106
Aurora, CO 80014

Adoption Center of America
1119 N. Wahsatch, Ste. 2
Colorado Springs, CO 80903

Adoption Centre
6535 S. Dayton, Ste. 1950
Englewood, CO 80111

Adoption Consultants, Inc.
200 Union Blvd., Ste. G-16
Lakewood, CO 80228

The Adoption Option
2600 S. Parker Rd., Ste. 2-320
Aurora, CO 80014

Adoption Service, Inc.
2212 W. Colorado Ave.
Colorado Springs, CO 80904

Christian Family Services
1399 S. Havana St., Ste. 204
Aurora, CO 80012

Colorado Adoption Center
1136 E. Stuart St., Ste. 2040
Fort Collins, CO 80525

Creative Adoptions
2546 W. Main St., Ste. 100
Littleton, CO 80120

Designated Adoption Services of
   Colorado, Inc.
14420 Vance St., Ste. 202
Lakewood, CO 80215

Family Ties Adoption Agency
7257 Rogers St.
Golden, CO 80403

Hand in Hand
1617 W. Colorado Ave.
Colorado Springs, CO 80904

Loving Homes
2406 N. Grand Ave.
Pueblo, CO 81003-2406

Luthern Social Services of Colorado
3707 Parkmoor Village Dr., Ste. 101
Colorado Springs, CO 80917

Parent Resource Center
7025 Tall Oak Dr.
Colorado Springs, CO 80919

The Whole Family
190 E. 9th Ave., Ste. 200
Denver, CO 80203

Connecticut

Catholic Charities of Diocese of
   Norwich
11 Bath St.
Norwich, CT 06360

Children's Center
1400 Whitney Ave.
Hamden, CT 06514

Family and Children's Aid of
   Mid-Fairfield County
9 Mott Ave.
Norwalk, CT 06850

Family Life Center
79 Birch Hill
Weston, CT 06833

Franciscan Family Care Center
267 Finch Ave.
PO Box 417
Meriden, CT 06450

Highland Heights
651 Prospect St., Box 1224
New Haven, CT 06505

International Alliance for Children
23 S. Main St.
Milford, CT 06776

Jewish Family Services
2370 Park Ave.
Bridgeport, CT 06604

Jewish Family Services of
New Haven
1440 Whalley Ave.
New Haven, CT 06515

LDS Social Services
57 Quornhunt Rd.
West Simsbury, CT 06092

Lutheran Social Services
2139 Silas Deane Hwy., Ste. 201
Rocky Hill, CT 06082

Thursday's Child
227 Tunxis Ave.
Bloomfield, CT 06002

Wheeler Clinic, Inc.
91 Northwest Dr.
Plainville, CT 06062

Wide Horizons
99 W. Main St., Ste. 311
New Britain, CT 06051

Delaware

Adoptions from the Heart
Ste. 18A, Trolley Square
Wilmington, DE 19806

Bethany Christian Services
308 Possum Park Rd.
Newark, DE 19711

Catholic Charities
4th St. and Greenhill Ave.
Wilmington, DE 19805

Child & Home Study Associates
101 Stone Crop Rd.
Wilmington, DE 19810

Welcome House, Inc.
910 Barley Dr.
Wilmington, DE 19807

District of Columbia

Adoption Service Information
Agency
7720 Alaska Ave. NW
Washington, DC 20012

American Adoption Agency
1228 M St. NW 2nd Floor
Washington, DC 20005

Barker Foundation
1200 18th St. NW, Ste. 312
Washington, DC 20036

Catholic Charities
1438 Rhode Island Ave. NE
Washington, DC 20018

Children's Adoption Support
Services
3824 Legation St. NW
Washington, DC 20015

Cradle of Hope Adoption Center
1815 H St. NW, Ste. 1050
Washington, DC 20006

Datz Foundation
4545 42nd St. NW, Ste. 209
Washington, DC 20016

International Families, Inc.
5 Thomas Circle, NW
Washington, DC 20005

Lutheran Social Services
4406 Georgia Ave., NW
Washington, DC 20011

New Families Foundation
3615 Wisconsin Ave., NW
Washington, DC 20016

World Child, Inc.
4300 16th St., NW
Washington, DC 20011

Florida

Adoption Centre
341 N. Maitland Ave., Ste. 260
Maitland, FL 32751

Adoption Services, Inc.
3003 S. Congress Ave., Ste. 1C11F
Palm Springs, FL 33461

All About Adoptions
501A E. New Haven Ave.
Melbourne, FL 32901

Bond of Love Adoption Agency
10235 W. Sample Rd., Ste. 103
Coral Springs, FL 33065

Catholic Community Services, Inc.
1300 S. Andrews Ave.
Fort Lauderdale, FL 33316

Catholic Social Services
1771 N. Semoran Blvd.
Orlando, FL 32807

Centre for Innovative Solutions
1776 N. Pine Island Rd., Ste. 126
Plantation, FL 33322

Children's Home Society of Florida,
    Central Administrative Office
3027 San Diego Rd.
PO Box 10097
Jacksonville, FL 32207

Chosen Children
3924 A Ave.
Lake Worth, FL 33461

Christian Adoption Services
220 S. Dixie Hwy., #4
Lake Worth, FL 33460

Family Enrichment Center
6013 N. 40th St.
Tampa, FL 33610

Family Service Center of
    Pinellas County
2960 Roosevelt Blvd.
Clearwater, FL 34620

Florida Baptist Family Ministries
1030 Central Ave.
PO Box 1870
Lakeland, FL 33802

Florida Sheriff's Youth Ranch
3180 County Rd. 102
Safety Harbor, FL 34695

Jewish Family & Community
    Services
3601 Cardinal Point Dr.
Jacksonville, FL 32257

Jewish Family & Community
    Services of Greater Miami, Inc.
1790 S.W. 27th Ave.
Miami, FL 33145

LDS Social Services
1020 N. Orlando Ave., Ste. F
Winter Park, FL 32789

LifeNet, Inc.
PO Box 16797
Temple Terrace, FL 33867-6796

Lutheran Ministries of Florida
2456 Jackson St.
Fort Myers, FL 33901

Northside Centers, Inc.
Professional Parenting Program
12512 N. Bruce B. Downs Blvd.
Tampa, FL 33612-3807

Suncoast International Adoptions,
    Inc.
PO Box 332
Indian Rocks, FL 34635-0332

Therapeutic Group Home
317 S. Seacrest Blvd.
Boynton Beach, FL 33462

Universal Aid for Children, Inc.
1600 S. Federal Hwy., 2nd Floor
Hollywood, FL 33020

Georgia

Adoption Planning, Inc.
17 Executive Park Dr., Ste. 480
Decatur, GA 30029

Adoption Services, Inc.
PO Box 155
Pavo, GA 31778

Bethany Christian Services
1852 Century Pl., Ste. 165
Atlanta, GA 30345

Catholic Social Services, Inc.
Adoption Program
680 W. Peachtree St. NW
Atlanta, GA 30308

Covenant Care Services, Inc.
363 Pierce Ave., Ste. 202
Macon, GA 31204

Families First
1105 W. Peachtree St.
Atlanta, GA 30309

Family Counseling Center/CSRA,
    Inc.
603 Ellis St.
Augusta, GA 30901

Friends of Children, Inc.
5064 Roswell Rd. NE,
Ste. B-201
Atlanta, GA 30342

Jewish Family Services, Inc.
Cradle of Love Adoption
    Counseling and Services
1605 Peachtree St. NE
Atlanta, Ga 30309

LDS Social Services
4832 N. Royal Atlanta Dr.
Tucker, GA 30084

Lutheran Ministries of Georgia
726 W. Peachtree St. NW
Atlanta, GA 30308

Open Door Adoption Agency, Inc.
116 E. Monroe
PO Box 4
Thomasville, GA 31792

Parent and Child Development
    Services
21 E. Broad St.
Savannah, GA 31401

Partners in Adoption, Inc.
1050 Little River Ln.
Alpharetta, GA 30201

Hawaii

Catholic Services to Families
200 N. Vineyard Blvd., 3rd Fl.
Honolulu, HI 96817

Child and Family Services
200 N. Vineyard Blvd., Ste. 20
Honolulu, HI 96817

Crown Child Placement
    International, Inc.
75-5851 Kuakini Hwy.
Kailua-Kona, HI 96740

Hawaii International Child
    Placement and Family Services,
    Inc.
1208 Laukahi St.
Honolulu, HI 96821

LDS Social Services
Hawaii Honolulu Agency
1500 S. Beretonia St.,
Ste 403
Honolulu, HI 96826

Idaho

Children's Aid Society of Idaho
2308 N. Cole, Ste. E
Boise, ID 83704

Community Counseling Services of
    Idaho, Inc.
6054 W. Emerald
Boise, ID 83704

LDS Social Services
10740 Fairview, Ste. 100
Boise, ID 83704

Lutheran Social Services of
    Washington and Idaho
2201 Government Way, #H
Coeur d'Alene, ID 83814

Illinois

Baby Fold
108 E. Willow St.
Normal, IL 61761

Bensenville Home Society
331 S. York Rd.
Bensenville, IL 60106

Bethany Christian Services
9730 S. Western,
Ste. 203
Evergreen Park, IL 60642

Catholic Charities—Chicago
    Archdiocese
126 N. DesPlaines
Chicago, IL 60661

Counseling and Family Service
1821 N. Knoxville Ave.
Peoria, IL 61603

Cradle Society
2049 Ridge Ave.
Evanston, IL 60201

Evangelical Child and Family
Agency
1530 N. Main
Wheaton, IL 60187

Family Resource Center
5820-30 N. Clark
Chicago, IL 60660

Glenkirk
2501 N. Chestnut
Arlington Heights, IL 60004

Hobby Horse House
325 W. State
PO Box 1102
Jacksonville, FL 62651
(217) 243-7708

Illinois Baptist Maternity and
Adoption Services
4243 Lincolnshire Dr.
Mt. Vernon, IL 62864

Jewish Children's Bureau
1 S. Franklin St.
Chicago, IL 60606

Lutheran Social Services of Illinois
701 Devonshire, Ste. 204, Box C-9
Champaign, IL 61820

PSI Services, Inc.
111 E. Wacker Dr., Ste. 2500
Chicago, IL 60601

St. Mary's Services
717 W. Kirchoff Rd.
Arlington Heights, IL 60005

Sunny Ridge Family Center
2 S. 426 Orchard Rd.
Wheaton, IL 60187

Volunteers of America
224 N. Desplaines, Ste. 500
Chicago, IL 60661

Indiana

Adoption Alternatives
116 S. Taylor
South Bend, IN 46601

Adoption Resources Services, Inc.
724 W. Bristol, Ste. E
Elkhart, IN 46514

Adoption Services, Inc.
3050 N. Meridian St.
Indianapolis, IN 46208

Adoption Support Center
6331 N. Carrolton Ave.
Indianapolis, IN 46220

Americans for African Adoptions,
Inc.
8910 Timberwood Dr.
Indianapolis, IN 46234

Baptist Children's Home
354 West St.
Valparaiso, IN 46383

Bethany Christian Services
6144 N. Hillside Ave., Ste. 10
Indianapolis, IN 46220

Catholic Charities
315 E. Washington
Fort Wayne, IN 46802

Catholic Charities
120 S. Taylor St.
South Bend, IN 46601

Childplace, Inc.
2420 Hwy. 62
Jeffersonville, IN 47130

Children's Bureau of Indianapolis
426 English Foundation Bldg.
615 N. Alabama St.
Indianapolis, IN 46204

Chosen Children Adoption
Services
204 Pearl St.,
Ste. 200
New Albany, IN 47150

Coleman Adoption Agency
419 English Foundation Bldg.
615 N. Alabama St.
Indianapolis, IN 46204

Compassionate Care
253 N. Main St.
Oakland City, IN 47660

Family and Children's Services
Mid-Town Center
305 S. 3rd St.
Evansville, IN 47708

G.L.A.D.
5000 1st Ave.
Evansville, IN 47711

Lutheran Social Services
330 Madison Ave.
PO Box 11329
Fort Wayne, IN 46857-1329

St. Elizabeth's Home
2500 Churchman Ave.
Indianapolis, IN 46203

Sunny Ridge Family Center
9105-A Indianapolis Blvd.
Highland, IN 46322

The Villages, Inc.
2346 S. Lynhurst Dr.,
Ste. H201
Indianapolis, IN 46241

Iowa

American Home Finding
Association
217 E. Fifth St.
PO Box 656
Ottumwa, IA 52501

Baptist Children's Home & Family
Ministries
224-1/2 Northwest Abilene Rd.
Ankeny, IA 50021

Bethany Home
1606 Brady, Ste. 309
Davenport, IA 52803

Catholic Social Service
601 Grand Ave.
Des Moines, IA 50309-2501

Children's & Family Services of
Iowa
1111 University Ave.
Des Moines, IA 50314

Crittenton Center
1105 28th St.
Sioux City, IA 51104

Family Resources, Inc.
115 W. Sixth St.
PO Box 190
Davenport, IA 52803

Gift of Love International
Adoptions, Inc.
PO Box 447
5750 Columbine Dr.
Johnston, IA 50131

Hillcrest Family Services
205 12th St. SE
Cedar Rapids, IA 52403-4028

LDS Social Services
Iowa Des Moines Agency
3301 Ashworth Rd.
PO Box 65713
West Des Moines, IA 50625

Lutheran Social Service of Iowa
3116 University Ave.
Des Moines, IA 50311

Young House, Inc.
724 North Third
Burlington, IA 52601

Kansas

Adams Center
6000 High
Mission Hills, KS 66208

Adoption & Counseling Services
10045 Hemlock
Overland Park, KS 66212

Baumann, Powell, & Stonestreet
Independent Adoptions
5847 SW 29th St.
Topeka, KS 66614

Catholic Social Service
437 N. Topeka
PO Box 659
Wichita, KS 67201

Child Placement Services, Inc.
15520 S. Ridgeview
Olathe, KS 66062

Christian Family Services, Inc.
10901 Granada 3102
Overland Park, KS 66211-1411

Family Life Services Adoption
Agency
115 E. Chestnut Ave.
Arkansas City, KS 67005

Gentle Shepherd Child Placement
Agency
6310 Lamar Ave., Ste. 140
Overland Park, KS 66202

Highlands Child Placement Service,
Inc.
5506 Cambridge
Kansas City, KS 67208

Kansas Children's Service League
2053 Kansas Ave.
Topeka, KS 66605

Kansas Children's Service League
Black Adoptions Project
Gateway Centre II, Ste. 729
Fourth & State Ave.
PO Box 17-1273
Kansas City, KS 66117

LDS Social Service
7100 Hadley
PO Box 4040
Shawnee Mission, KS 66212

Lighthouse of Kansas
(*under Youth for Christ Charter*)
4715 Rainbow Blvd.
Shawnee Mission, KS 66205

Lutheran Social Services
Adoption for Black Children
1855 N. Hillside
Wichita, KS 67214

Native American Family Services,
Inc.
PO Box 206
Horton, KS 66439

The Villages, Inc.
2209 SW 29th St.
Topeka, KS 66611-1925

Kentucky

Adoption Advocates
745 W. Main St.
Louisville, KY 40202

Adoptions of Kentucky
One River Front Plaza,
Ste. 1708
Louisville, KY 40202

Catholic Social Service Bureau
3629 Church St.
Covington, KY 40208

Jewish Family & Vocational Service
3640 Dutchmans Ln.
Louisville, KY 40205

Kaleidescope Adoptions
International
1890 Lyda Ave.
Bowling Green, KY 42104

Louisiana

Adoption Options
1724 N. Burnside, Ste. 7
Gonzales, LA 70737

Associated Catholic Charities of
New Orleans, Inc.
1231 Prytania St.
New Orleans, LA 70130

Beacon House, Inc.
750 Louisiana Ave., Ste. C
Port Allen, LA 70767

Children's Bureau of New Orleans,
Inc.
1001 Howard Ave., Ste. 2800
Plaza Tower
New Orleans, LA 70113

Jewish Children's Regional Service
PO Box 15225
New Orleans, LA 70175

LDS Social Services
2000 Old Spanish Trail,
Ste. 115
Slidell, LA 70458

Louisiana Child Care & Placement
Services, Inc.
9080 Southwood Dr.
Shreveport, LA 71118

New Family Adoption Services, Inc.
118 Ridgelake Dr.
Metairie, LA 70001-5312

Special Delivery Adoption Services, Inc.
7809 Jefferson Hwy., Ste. D-1
Baton Rouge, LA 70809

St. Elizabeth Foundation
8054 Summa Dr.
Baton Rouge, LA 70809

St. Gerard's Adoption Network, Inc.
100 S. Vivian St.
PO Drawer 1260
Eunice, LA 70535

Maine

Good Samaritan Agency
450 Essex St.
Bangor, ME 04401

International Adoption Services Centre
PO Box 55
Alna, ME 04535

Maine Adoption Placement Service
Market Square
Houlton, ME 04730

Maine Adoption Placement Service
306 Congress St.
Portland, ME 04101

Sharing in Adoption
RR 1, Box 4W
Gorham, ME 04038

St. Andre Home, Inc.
283 Elm St.
Biddeford, ME 04005

Maryland

Adoption Resource Center
6630 Baltimore National Pike, Ste. 100 B
Baltimore, MD 21228

Adoptions Forever
5830 Hubbard Dr.
Rockville, MD 20852

Adoptions Together
3837 Farragut Ave.
Kensington, MD 20895

Bethany Christian Services
1641 Rt. 3 North, Ste. 205
Crofton, MD 21114

Children's Choice
213-219 W. Main St., 2nd Fl.
Salisbury, MD 21801-4906

Jewish Family Service
5750 Park Heights Ave.
Baltimore, MD 21215

New Partners, Inc.
International Relief for Children
8905 Bradley Blvd.
Potomac, MD 20854

Massachusetts

Adoption Center
55 Wheeler St.
Cambridge, MA 02138

Adoptions with Love, Inc.
One Wells Ave.
Newton, MA 02159

Alliance for Children, Inc.
110 Cedar St.
Wellesley, MA 02181

Bethany Christian Services
1538 Turnpike St.
North Andover, MA 01845

Boston Adoption Bureau, Inc.
14 Beacon St., Ste. 620
Boston, MA 02108

Cambridge Adoption & Counseling Association, Inc.
PO Box 190
Cambridge, MA 02142

Catholic Charitable Bureau of Boston
10 Derne St.
Boston, MA 02114

Children's Aid & Family Services of Hampshire County, Inc.
8 Trumbull Rd.
Northampton, MA 01060

Concord Family Service Society, Inc.
Community Agencies Bldg.
Concord, MA 01742

DARE Family Services
3 Monument Square
Beverly, MA 01915

DARE Family Services
265 Medford St., Ste. 200
Somerville, MA 01104

ECHO
29 Devonshire Rd.
PO Box 14222
Cheshire, MA 01228

Italian Home for Children, Inc.
Family Resource Program
1125 Centre St.
Jamaica Plain, MA 02130

Jewish Family & Children's
  Service
31 New Chardon St.
Boston, MA 02114

LDS Social Services of
  Massachusetts
45 Holden St.
PO Box 334
Cambridge, MA 02138

Lutheran Child & Family Services of
  Massachusetts
23 Institute Rd.
Worcester, MA 01608

New England Home for Little
  Wanderers
850 Boylston St., Ste. 201
Chestnut Hill, MA 02167

Project Impact, Inc.
25 West St.
Boston, MA 02111

Wide Horizons for Children
282 Moody St.
Waltham, MA 02154

Michigan

Adoption Associates
6491 San Ru Ave.
Jenison, MI 49428

Adoption Cradle
554 Capital Ave. SW
Battle Creek, MI 49015

Americans for International Aid &
  Adoption
877 S. Adams St., Ste. 106
Birmingham, MI 48009

Bethany Christian Services
6995 W. 48th
PO Box 173
Fremont, MI 49412

Bethany Christian Services
901 Eastern Ave. NE
Grand Rapids, MI 49503

Bethany Christian Services
32500 Concord Dr., Ste. 250
Madison Heights, MI 48071

Catholic Family Services
1819 Gull Rd.
Kalamazoo, MI 49001

Catholic Human Services
1000 Hastings St.
Traverse City, MI 49684

Child & Family Services of Michigan
4801 Willoughby, Ste. 1
Holt, MI 48842

Child & Family Services of Michigan
2157 University Park Dr.
PO Box 348
Okemos, MI 48805

Children's Aid Society
7700 Second Ave.
Detroit, MI 49423

Children's Hope Adoption Services
7823 S. Whiteville Rd.
Shepherd, MI 48883

Christian Cradle
416 Frandor, Ste. 205
Lansing, MI 48912

Christian Family Services
17105 W. 12 Mile Rd.
Southfield, MI 48076

Ennis Center for Children
20100 Greenfield Rd.
Detroit, MI 48235

Evergreen Children's Services
21590 Greenfield Rd.
Oak Park, MI 48237

Family Adoption Consultants
310 W. University
Rochester, MI 48307

Homes for Black Children
2340 Calvert
Detroit, MI 48206

Jewish Family Services
24123 Greenfield
Southfield, MI 48075

Keane Center for Adoption
937 Mason
Dearborn, MI 48124

LDS Social Services
37634 Enterprise Court
Farmington Hills, MI 48331

Michigan Indian Child Welfare
Agency
1345 Monrow Ave. SW
Grand Rapids, MI 49505

Orchards Children's Services
2990 W. Grand Blvd., Ste. 400
Detroit, MI 48202

Minnesota

Bethany Christian Services
3025 Harbor Ln.,
Ste. 223
Plymouth, MN 55447
(612) 553-0344

Crossroads, Inc.
4640 West 77th St.,
Ste. 105
Minneapolis, MN 55435

Forever Families International
Adoption Agency
2004 Hwy. 37
Eveleth, MN 55734

Hope International Family Services,
Inc.
4940 Viking Dr., Ste. 388
Edina, MN 55435

New Horizons Adoption Agency
Frost-Benico Bldg., Hwy. 254
PO Box 623
Frost, MN 56033

Wellspring Adoption Agency, Inc.
1219 University Ave. SE
Minneapolis, MN 55414

Mississippi

Bethany Christian Services
2619 Southerland Dr.
Woodland Hills Bldg.
Jackson, MS 39216

Catholic Charities
748 N. President St.
PO Box 2248
Jackson, MS 39205

Catholic Social & Community
Services
PO Box 1457
Biloxi, MS 39533

Mississippi Children's Home
Society
PO Box 1078
1801 N. West St.
Jackson, MS 39205

New Beginnings of Tupelo
PO Box 7055
Tupelo, MS 38802-7055

Missouri

Adam's Child Placement &
Counseling, Inc.
600 Broadway, Ste. 430
Kansas City, MO 64105

Adoption Advocates
4901 Wornall, Ste. 10
Kansas City, MO 64112

Adoption Option
200 S.E. Douglas
Lee's Summit, MO 64063

Bethany Christian Services
7700 Clayton Rd., Ste. 205
St. Louis, MO 63117-1346

Catholic Charities of Kansas City
1112 Broadway
Kansas City, MO 64111

Catholic Services for Children &
Youth
4140 Lindell Blvd.
St. Louis, MO 63108

Children's Home Society of
Missouri
9445 Litzsinger Rd.
Brentwood, MO 63144

Family Network, Inc.
9378 Olive St. Rd., Ste. 320
St. Louis, MO 63122

James A. Roberts Agency
8301 State Line Rd., Ste. 216
Kansas City, MO 64114

Jewish Family & Children's Services
9385 Olive Blvd.
Olivette, MO 63044

Love Basket, Inc.
4472 Goldman Rd.
Hillsboro, MO 63050

Lutheran Family & Children's
Services
4625 Lindell Blvd., Ste. 501
St. Louis, MO 63103

Missouri Baptist Children's Home
11300 St. Charles Rock Rd.
Bridgeton, MO 63044

Provident Counseling
2650 Olive St.
St. Louis, MO 63103

Universal Adoption Services
124 E. High St.
Jefferson City, MO 64101

Montana

Catholic Social Services
25 S. Ewing
PO Box 907
Helena, MT 59601

LDS Social Services
2001 11th Ave.
Helena, MT 59601
Lutheran Social Services
PO Box 1345
Great Falls, MT 59403

Montana Intercountry Adoption,
Inc.
109 S. Eighth
Bozeman, MT 59715

Nebraska

Black Homes for Black Children
115 S. 46th St.
Omaha, NE 68132

Catholic Social Service Bureau
237 S. 70th St.,
Ste. 220
Lincoln, NE 68510

Jewish Family Service
333 South 132nd St.
Omaha, NE 68154

Nebraska Children's Home Society
3549 Fontenelle Blvd.
Omaha, NE 68104

United Catholic Social Services
3300 N. 60th St.
Omaha, NE 68104

Nevada

Catholic Community Services
808 S. Main
Las Vegas, NV 89101

Catholic Community Services
PO Box 5415
Reno, NV 89513

Jewish Family Services Agency
3909 S. Maryland Pkwy.,
Ste. 205
Las Vegas, NV 89101

LDS Social Services
513 S. Ninth St.
Las Vegas, NV 89015

New Hampshire

Adoptive Families for Children
26 Fairview St.
Keene, NH 03431

Child & Family Services of
New Hampshire
99 Hanover St.
PO Box 448
Manchester, NH 03105

Lutheran Child & Family Services of
New Hampshire
85 Manchester St.
Concord, NH 03301

New Hampshire Catholic Charities,
Inc.
215 Myrtle St.
PO Box 686
Manchester, NH 03103

New Jersey

Adoption & Infertility Services
43 Main St.
Holmdel, NJ 07738

AMOR Adoptions
12 Grenoble Court
Matawan, NJ 07747

Bethany Christian Services
1120 Goffle Rd.
Hawthorne, NJ 07506

Black Adoption Consortium
5090 Central Hwy., Ste. 6
Pennsauken, NJ 08109

Casa del Mundo
260 Hwy. 202/31, Ste. 300
PO Box 2141
Flemington, NJ 08822

Catholic Family & Community
Services
476 17th Ave.
Paterson, NJ 07501

Children of the World
685 Bloomfield Ave., Ste. 201
Verona, NJ 07044

Children's Aid & Adoption Society
of New Jersey
575 Main St.
Hackensack, NJ 07601

Golden Cradle
1101 N. Kings Hwy., Ste. G-102
Cherry Hill, NJ 08034

Holt International Children's
Services
2490 Pennington Rd.
Trenton, NJ 08638

Homestudies, Inc.
1182 Teaneck Rd.
Teaneck, NJ 07666

Spaulding for Children
36 Prospect St.
Westfield, NJ 07090

United Family & Children's Society
305 W. Seventh St.
Plainfield, NJ 07060

New Mexico

Catholic Social Services
138 Park Ave.
Santa Fe, NM 87507

Chaparral Maternity & Adoption
Services
1503 University Blvd. NE
Albuquerque, NM 87102

Child-Rite/Adopt a Special Kid
(AASK) of New Mexico
PO Box 1448
Taos, NM 87571

Rainbow House International
19676 Hwy. 85
Belen, NM 87702

Triad Adoption Services, Inc.
2811 Indian School Rd., NE
Albuquerque, NM 87106

New York

Abbott House
100 N. Broadway
Irvington, NY 10533

Adoption & Counseling Services,
Inc.
One Fayette Park
Syracuse, NY 13202
Bethany Christian Services
105 Lake Hill Rd.
Burnt Hills, NY 12027-9507

Brookwood Child Care
25 Washington St.
Brooklyn, NY 11201

Catholic Charities of Syracuse
Family Division
1654 W. Onondaga St.
Syracuse, NY 13204

Catholic Family Center
25 Franklin St.
Rochester, NY 14604

Catholic Home Bureau
1011 First Ave.
New York, NY 10022

Child & Family Services
678 W. Onandaga St.
Syracuse, NY 13204

Children's Village
Dobbs Ferry, NY 10522

Community Maternity Services
29 N. Main Ave.
Albany, NY 12203

Episcopal Mission Society
18 W. 18th St., 10th Floor
New York, NY 10011-4607

Family Focus
54-40 Little Neck Pkwy., Ste. 3
Little Neck, NY 11362

Harlen Dowling Children's Services
2090 Seventh Ave.
New York, NY 10027

Hillside Children's Center
1337 E. Main St.
Rochester, NY 14609

Jewish Child Care Association
575 Lexington Ave.
New York, NY 10022

LDS Social Services of New York
2 Jefferson St., #205
Poughkeepsie, NY 12601

Little Flower Children's Services
186 Remsen St.
Brooklyn, NY 11201

Lutheran Service Society of
New York
2500 Kensington Ave.
Buffalo, NY 14226

Miracle Makers, Inc.
33 Somers St.
Brooklyn, NY 11233

Mission of the Immaculate Virgin
6581 Hylan Blvd.
Staten Island, NY 10309

New Alternatives for Children
37 W. 26th St.
New York, NY 10010

New Beginnings Family &
Children's Services, Inc.
141 Willis Ave.
Mineola, NY 11501

New Life Adoption Agency
117 South State St.
Syracuse, NY 13202-1103

Parsons Child & Family Center
60 Academy Rd.
Albany, NY 12208

Voice for International & Domestic
Adoptions (VIDA)
345 Allen St.
Hudson, NY 12534

North Carolina

Association for Guidance, Aid,
Placement, & Empathy
(AGAPE)
302 Colege Rd.
Greensboro, NC 27410

Catholic Social Ministries
400 Oberlin Rd., Ste. 350
Raleigh, NC 27605

Children's Home Society of
North Carolina, Inc.
740 Chestnut St.
PO Box 14608
Greensboro, NC 27415-4608

Christian Adoption Services
624 Matthews-Mint Rd., Ste. 134
Matthews, NC 28105

Family Services, Inc.
610 Coliseum Dr.
Winston-Salem, NC 28226

Lutheran Family Services in the
Carolinas, Inc.
505 Oberlin Rd.
PO Box 12287
Raleigh, NC 27605

North Dakota

Catholic Family Service
2537 S. University
Fargo, ND 58103

Christian Family Life Services
1202 12th Ave. North
Fargo, ND 58102

LDS Social Services
PO Box 3100
Bismark, ND 58502

New Horizons Foreign Adoptions
Service
2823 Woodland Place
Bismark, ND 58501

Ohio

Adopt a Special Kid (AASK) of
the Midwest
1025 N. Reynolds Rd.
Toledo, OH 43615-4753

AGAPE for Youth, Inc.
906 Senate Dr.
Dayton, OH 45459

Bair Foundation
325 N. State St., Ste. 2
Girard, OH 44420

Baptist Children's Home & Family
Ministries, Inc.
1934 S. Limestone St.
Springfield, OH 45505

Beech Brook/Spaulding for Children
3737 Lander Rd.
Pepper Pike, OH 44124

Berea Children's Home
202 E. Bagley Rd.
Berea, OH 44017

Catholic Community League of
Canton
625 Cleveland Ave. NW
Canton, OH 44313

Catholic Social Service of
Southwest Ohio
100 E. Eighth St.
Cincinnati, OH 45202

Catholic Social Services, Inc.
197 E. Gay St.
Columbus, OH 43215

European Adoption Consultants
9800 Boston Rd.
North Royalton, OH 44133

Family & Community Services of
Catholic Charities
302 N. Depeyster St.
Kent, OH 44240

Family Counseling & Crittenton
Services
185 S. Fifth St.
Columbus, OH 43215

Family Service Agency
535 Marmion Ave.
Youngstown, OH 45502

Family Service Association
PO Box 1027
Steubenville, OH 43952

Family Service Association
1704 North Rd. SE
Heaton Square
Warren, OH 44484

Family Services of Summit County
212 E. Exchange St.
Akron, OH 44304

Foreign Adoption Consultant
Macedonia Professional Building
8536 Crow Dr.
Macedonia, OH 44056

General Protestant Orphan Home
6881 Beechmont Ave.
Cincinnati, OH 45230

Gentle Care Adoption Service, Inc.
243 E. Livingston Ave.
Columbus, OH 43215

Hannah Neil Center for Children
301 Obetz Rd.
Columbus, OH 43207

HARAMBEE, Services to
Black Families
1466-68 E. 55th St.
Cleveland, OH 44103

Jewish Children's Bureau
22001 Fairmount Blvd.
Shaker Heights, OH 44118

Jewish Family Service
3085 W. Market St.
Akron, OH 44320

Jewish Family Service
Adoption Connection
7770 Cooper Rd.
Cincinnati, OH 45242

Jewish Family Service
2831 E. Main St.
Columbus, OH 43209

Jewish Family Service
4501 Denlinger Rd.
Dayton, OH 45426

Jewish Family Service of Toledo
6525 Sylvania Ave.
Sylvania, OH 43560

KARE, Inc. (Kids Are Really
Essential)
5055 N. Main St., Ste. 150
Dayton, OH 45415

LDS Social Services
4431 Marketing Place
PO Box 367
Groveport, OH 43125

Lutheran Children's Aid & Family
Services
4100 Franklin Blvd.
Cleveland, OH 44113

Lutheran Social Services of
Central Ohio
57 E. Main St.
Columbus, OH 43215

Lutheran Social Services of
the Miami Valley
3304 N. Main St.
Dayton, OH 45404

Lutheran Social Services of
Northwestern Ohio, Inc.
2149 Collingwood Blvd.
Toledo, OH 43620

Mid-Western Children's Home
4581 Long Spurling Rd.
PO Box 48
Pleasant Plain, OH 45162

Northeast Ohio Adoption Services
8031 E. Market St.
Warren, OH 44484

Ohio Youth Advocate Program,
Inc.
3780 Ridge Mill Dr., #100
Hilliard, OH 43026-9231

United Methodist Children's
Home
West Ohio Conference of
the United Methodist Church
1045 N. High St.
Worthington, OH 43085

Oklahoma

Adoption Affiliate
6136 E. 32nd Pl.
Tulsa, OK 74135

Adoption Center of Northeastern
Oklahoma
121 South Creek
Bartlesville, OK 74003

Baptist General Convention
3800 N. May Ave.
Oklahoma City, OK 73112

Catholic Charities
PO Box 6429
Tulsa, OK 74106

Chosen Child Adoption Agency
PO Box 55424
Tulsa, OK 74155-5424

Cradle
7901 Terrace Hill Blvd.
Lawton, OK 73105

Deaconess Home
5401 N. Portland
Oklahoma City, OK 73112

Dillon International, Inc.
7615 E. 63rd Pl. South
Tulsa, OK 74133

Hannah's Prayer Adoption Agency
2651 E. 21st, Ste. 409
Tulsa, OK 74114

Kalamazoo & Baby Too
6506 South Lewis, Ste. 111
Tulsa, OK 74136

Project Adopt
Neighborhood Services
  Organization
1613 N. Broadway
Oklahoma City, OK 73102

Small Miracles International
1380 S. Douglas Blvd., Ste. 101
Oklahoma City, OK 73130-5215

United Methodist Counseling
  Service
1933 NW 23rd St.
Oklahoma City, OK 73106

Oregon

Albertina Kerr Center for Children
424 N.E. 22nd Ave.
Portland, OR 97232

Caring Connection
5439 SE Bantam Court
Milwaukie, OR 97267

First American Adoptions
PO Box 69622
Portland, OR 97201

Heritage Adoptions
516 SE Morrison, Ste. 714
Portland, OR 97214

Holt International Children's
  Services
PO Box 2880
Eugene, OR 97402

Northwest Adoptions & Family
  Services
2695 Spring Valley Ln., NW
Salem, OR 97304

Open Adoption & Family Services,
  Inc.
239 E. 14th Ave.
Eugene, OR 97401

Plan International Adoption
  Services
PO Box 667
McMinnville, OR 97128

Pennsylvania

Adopt-A-Child
6403 Beacon St.
Pittsburgh, PA 15217

Adoption Alliance
859 Stirrup Ln.
Warrington, PA 18976

Adoption Horizons
403 Roxbury Rd.
Shippensburg, PA 17257

Adoption International
219 Monroe St.
Philadelphia, PA 19147-4226

Adoption Services, Inc.
28 Central Blvd.
Camp Hill, PA 17011

Adoption Unlimited
2770 Weston Rd.
Lancaster, PA 17603

Bethana
1030 Second St. Pike
South Hampton, PA 18966

Bethany Christian Services
550 Pinetown Rd., Ste. 205
Fort Washington, PA 19034

A Better Chance, Inc.
275 Glen Riddle Rd., H-12
Glen Riddle, PA 19037

Catholic Charities of the Diocese of
  Pittsburgh, Inc.
212 9th St.
Pittsburgh, PA 15222-3507

Child & Home Study Associates
1029 Providence Rd.
Media, PA 19063

Choices: An Adoption Agency
827 E. Glenside Ave., Ste. 14
Wyncote, PA 19095

Concern
1 E. Main St.
Fleetwood, PA 19522

Eckels Adoption Agnecy
915 Fifth Ave., Rear
Williamsport, PA 17701

Love the Children
221 W. Broad St., 2nd Floor
Quakertown, PA 18951

Medical Adoption Services
721 Willow Rum Rd.
Spring House, PA 19002

Option of Adoption
504 E. Haines St.
Philadelphia, PA 19144

Pearl S. Buck Foundation
(Welcome House Social Services)
Green Hills Farm
PO Box 181
Perkasie, PA 18944

Rainbow Project
200 Charles St.
Pittsburgh, PA 15238

Three Rivers Adoption Council
Black Adoption Services
307 4th Ave., Ste. 710
Pittsburgh, PA 15222

Today's Adoption Agency
PO Box G
Hawley, PA 18428

Tressler Lutheran Services
836 S. George St.
York, PA 17403

Wiley House
1650 Broadway
Bethlehem, PA 18015

Rhode Island

Bethany Christian Service
PO Box 618
Barrington, RI 02806

Catholic Social Services
433 Elmwood Ave.
Providence, RI 02907

Children's Friend & Service
153 Summer St.
Providence, RI 02903

Jewish Family Services
229 Waterman Ave.
Providence, RI 02906

South Carolina

Bethany Christian Services
620 E. Washington St.
Greenville, SC 29601

Catholic Charities of Charleston
1662 Ingram Rd.
Charleston, SC 29407

Children Unlimited, Inc.
PO Box 11463
Columbia, SC 29211-1463

Christian World Adoption, Inc.
270 W. Coleman Blvd.
Mt. Pleasant, SC 29464

Southeastern Children's Home, Inc.
155 Children's Way
Duncan, SC 29334

South Dakota

Bethany Christian Services
2100 S. 7th St.
Rapid City, SD 57701

Catholic Family Services
3200 W. 41st St.
Sioux Falls, SD 57016

LDS Social Services
2525 W. Main St.
Rapid City, SD 57702

Lutheran Social Services
600 W. 12th St.
Sioux Falls, SD 57104

Tennessee

AGAPE
(Association for Guidance, Aid,
Placement, & Empathy)
4555 Trousdale Ave.
Nashville, TN 37204-4513

Child & Family Services of
   Knox County
114 Dameron Ave.
Knoxville, TN 37917

Columbus Home, Inc.
114 Hinton St.
Knoxville, TN 37917

Crisis Pregnancy Support Center
1915 Church St.
Nashville, TN 37203

Jewish Family Services, Inc.
6560 Poplar Dr.
PO Box 38268
Memphis, TN 38138

Madison Children's Home
106 Gallatin Rd. North
PO Box 419
Madison, TN 37116-0419

Oasis Center
1219 16th Ave. South
Nashville, TN 37212

Small World Ministries, Inc.
PO Box 290185
401 Bonna Spring
Nashville, TN 37229

Tennessee Baptist Children's
   Homes
107 Franklin Rd.
PO Box 347
Brentwood, TN 37027

Texas

ABC Adoption Agency
417 San Pedro Ave.
San Antonio, TX 78212

Adoption Advisory, Inc.
3607 Fairmount
Dallas, TX 75219

Adoption Advocates
GPM South Tower, Ste. 355
800 NW Loop 410
San Antonio, TX 78216

Adoption Affiliates, Inc.
215 W. Olmos Dr.
San Antonio, TX 78212

Adoption, Inc.
2775 Villa Creek, Ste. 240
Dallas, TX 75234

Adoption Resource Consultants
PO Box 1224
Richardson, TX 75083

Adoption Resource Consultants &
   Counseling
2020 S.W. Freeway, Ste. 3
Houston, TX 77098

Adoption Services, Inc.
3500 Overton Park West
Fort Worth, TX 76109

Alternatives in Motion
20619 Aldine Westfield Rd.
Humble, TX 77338

Care Connection, Inc.
400 Harvey St.
San Marcos, TX 78666

Catholic Charities
3520 Montrose
Houston, TX 77006-4350

Children's Home of Lubbock
PO Box 2824
Lubbock, TX 79408

Gladney Center
2300 Hemphill
Fort Worth, TX 76110

Heart International Adoption
   Services
2951 Marina Dr. Bay
League City, TX 77573

Hope Cottage, Inc.
Circle of Hope
4209 McKinney Ave., Ste. 200
Dallas, TX 75205

Jester Family Service
7800 Northaven Rd.
Dallas, TX 75230

LDS Social Services of Texas
110 W. Jackson Rd.
Carrollton, TX 75006

Life Anew Adoption Agency
2635 Loop NE 286
Paris, TX 75460

Los Ninos International Adoption
  Center
1600 Lake Front Circle
The Woodlands, TX 77380-3600

New Life Children's Services
1911 Tomball Pkwy.
Houston, TX 77070

Quality of Life, Inc.
10242 Crestover Dr.
Dallas, TX 75229

Read Adoption Agency, Inc.
718 Myrtle
El Paso, TX 79901

Smithlawn Maternity Home &
  Adoption Agency
711 76th St.
PO Box 6451
Lubbock, TX 79413

Texas Adoption Service, Inc.
10830 N. Central Expressway
Dallas, TX 75231

Texas Baptist Children's Home
PO Box 7
Round Rock, TX 78664

Texas Cradle Society
8600 Wurzbach Rd., Ste. 1110
San Antonio, TX 78240-4334

Tiad, dba AGAPE Social Service
2212 Sunny Lane
Killeen, TX 76541

Worldwide Adoptions, Inc.
13430 N.W. Freeway
Houston, TX 77040

Utah

Alternative Adoptions
11638 High Mountain Dr.
Sandy, UT 84092

Catholic Community Services of
  Utah
2300 W. 1700 South
Salt Lake City, UT 84104

Children's Aid Society of Utah
652 26th St.
Odgen, UT 84401

Children's House International
PO Box 2321
Salt Lake City, UT 84110

Children's Service Society
576 E. South Temple
Salt Lake City, UT 84102

Families for Children
PO Box 521192
Salt Lake City, UT 84152

LDS Social Services
1001 West, 535 South
Cedar City, UT 84720

Utah Adoption Service
3450 Highland Dr.,
  Ste. 102
Salt Lake City, UT 84106

West Sands Adoption &
  Counseling
461 E. 2780 North
Provo, UT 84604

Vermont

Adoption Center, Inc.
278 Pearl St.
Burlington, VT 05401

Adoption Resource Services, Inc.
1904 North Ave.
Burlington, VT 05401

Casey Family Services
7 Palmer Court
White River Junction, VT
  05001-3323

Friends in Adoption
PO Box 1228
Middletown Springs, VT 05757

Lund Family Center
PO Box 4009
Burlington, VT 05406-4009

Vermont Catholic Charities
351 North Ave.
Burlington, VT 05401

Vermont Children's Aid Society
PO Box 127
Winooski, VT 05404-0127

Virginia

American Adoption Agency, Inc.
9070 Euclid Ave.
Manassas, VA 22110

Barker Foundation, Inc.
1495 Chain Bridge Rd., Ste. 201
McLean, VA 22101

Bethany Christian Services, Inc.
11212 Waples Mill Rd., #101
Fairfax, VA 22030

Catholic Charities of the Diocese of
Arlington, Inc.
3838 N. Cathedral Ln.
Arlington, VA 22203

Children's Home Society of
Virginia, Inc.
4200 Fitzhugh Ave.
Richmond, VA 23230

Coordinators/2
4206 Chamberlayne Ave.
Richmond, VA 23227

Datz Foundation
404 Pine St., Ste. 202
Vienna, VA 22180

Family Life Services
1000 Villa Rd.
Lynchburg, VA 24503

Jewish Family Services, Inc.
6718 Patterson Ave.
Richmond, VA 23226

LDS Social Services of Virginia,
Inc.
8110 Virginia Pine Court
PO Box 638
Chesterfield, VA 23832

Rainbow Christian Services, Inc.
PO Box 9
6004 Artemus Rd.
Gainesville, VA 22065

Virginia Baptist Children's Home &
Family Services
700 E. Belt Blvd.
Richmond, VA 23224

Virginia Baptist Children's Home &
Family Services
Mount Vernon Ave.
PO Box 849
Salem, VA 24153

Washington

Adoption Advocates International
401 E. Front St.
Port Angeles, WA 98362

Adoption Services of WACAP
PO Box 88948
Seattle, WA 98188

Adventist Adoption & Family
Services
1207 E. Reserve St.
Vancouver, WA 98661

Americans for International Aid &
Adoption
(AIAA)
PO Box 6051
Spokane, WA 99207

Bethany Christian Services
103 E. Holly St., #316
Bellingham National Bank Bldg.
Bellingham, WA 98225

Black Child Adoption Program
123 16th Ave.
PO Box 22638
Seattle, WA 98122

Catholic Family Service
611 W. Columbia
Pasco, WA 98301

Children's Home Society of
Washington
West Central Area
201 S. 34th
Tacoma, WA 98408

Family Foundation
1229 Cornwall Ave., Ste. 202
Bellingham, WA 98225

Family Foundation
424 N. 130th
Seattle, WA 98133

International Children's Services of
    Washington, Inc.
3251 107th SE
Bellvue, WA 98004

Jewish Family Services
1214 Boylston Ave.
Seattle, WA 98101

LDS Social Services
220 S. 3rd Pl.
Renton, WA 98055

Lutheran Social Services of
    Washington (Admin. Office)
4040 S. 188th
Seattle, WA 98188

West Virginia

Burlington United Methodist
    Family Services
3983 Teays Valley Rd.
PO Box 370
Scott Depot, WV 25560

Children's Home Society of
    West Virginia
100 4th Ave.
South Charleston, WV 25303

Wisconsin

Adoption Advocates, Inc.
2601 Crossroads Dr.
Madison, WI 53704

Adoption Choice
924 E. Juneau Ave., #813
Milwaukee, WI 53202

Adoption Option
1804 Chapman Dr.
Waukesha, WI 53186

Adoption Services of Green Bay
529 S. Jefferson, Rm. 105
Green Bay, WI 54301

Bethany Christian Services of
    Wisconsin
W255 N477 Grandview Blvd.,
    Ste. 207
Waukesha, WI 53188

Catholic Social Services, Green Bay
PO Box 23825
Green Bay, WI 54305-3825

Children's Service Society of
    Wisconsin
1212 S. 70th St.
West Allis, WI 53214

Community Adoption Center
3701 Kadow St.
Manitowoc, WI 54220

Evangelical Child and Family
    Agency
2401 N. Mayfair Rd.
Milwaukee, WI 53226

LDS Social Services
1711 Universtiy Ave.
Madison, WI 53705

Lutheran Counseling and Family
    Service
PO Box 13367
Wauwatosa, WI 53213

Pauquette Children's Services, Inc.
315 W. Conant St.
PO Box 162
Portage, WI 53901-0162

Special Children, Inc.
910 N. Elm Grove Rd., Off. 2
Elm Grove, WI 53122

Wisconsin Lutheran Child and
    Family Services
6800 N. 76th St.
Milwaukee, WI 53219

Wyoming

Catholic Social Services
PO Box 1026
Cheyenne, WY 82003-1026

LDS Social Services
7609 Santa Marie
Cheyenne, WY 82009

Wyoming Children's Society
PO Box 105
Cheyenne, WY 82003-0105

Wyoming Parenting
PO Box 3774
Jackson, WY 83001

Public Agencies

Alabama Department of Human Resources
(334) 242-1310

Alaska Department of Health & Social Services
Division of Family & Youth Services
(907) 265-7095

Arizona Department of Economic Security
(602) 542-2362

Arkansas Division of Children & Family Services
(501) 682-8345

California Department of Social Services
(916) 445-3146

Colorado Department of Social Services
(303) 287-8831

Connecticut Adoption Resource Exchange
Department of Children & Youth Services
1-800-842-6347

Delaware Youth & Family Center
(302) 633-2655

District of Columbia Department of Human Services
Child & Family Services Division
(202) 727-3161

Florida Department of Health & Rehabilitative Services
Children & Families Program Office
(904) 487-1111

Georgia Department of Human Resources
State Adoption Unit
(404) 894-4454

Hawaii Department of Human Services
Family & Children's Services
(808) 548-4601

Idaho Department of Health & Welfare
Division of Family & Children's
Services
(208) 334-5700

Illinois Department of Children & Family Services
(312) 814-6864

Indiana Department of Public Welfare & Social Services Division
(317) 233-4454

Iowa Department of Human Services
Division of Adult, Children, & Family Services
(515) 281-5358

*Kansas Department of Social &
Rehabilitative Services*
(913) 296-4661

*Kentucky Department for Social
Services*
(502) 564-2136

*Louisiana Department of Health &
Social Services*
Division of Children, Youth, &
Family Services
(504) 342-4086

*Maine Department of Human
Services State House*
(207) 287-5060

*Maryland Department of Human
Resources*
(410) 333-0219

*Massachusetts Department of
Social Services*
(617) 727-8900

*Michigan Department of Social
Services*
(313) 842-7010

*Minnesota Department of Human
Services*
(612) 348-5198

*Mississippi Department of Human
Services*
(601) 359-4500

*Missouri Department of Social
Services*
Division of Family Services
(816) 889-2000

*Montana Department of Family
Services*
(406) 444-5900

*Nebraska Department of Social
Services*
(402) 595-3400

Nevada State Welfare Division
Social Services
(702) 688-2200

*New Hampshire Division for
Children & Youth Services*
Adoption Unit
(603) 271-4451

*New Jersey Division of Youth &
Family Services*
(609) 757-2700

*New Mexico Human Services
Department*
Social Services Division
1-800-432-6217

*New York Department of Social
Services*
(518) 473-3170

*North Carolina Division of Social
Services*
(919) 733-2140

*North Dakota Department of
Human Services*
(701) 328-2310

*Ohio Department of Human
Services*
Adoption Services Section
(216) 621-5775

*Oklahoma Department of Human
Services*
(405) 521-2778

*Oregon Department of Human
Services*
Children's Services Division
(503) 945-5600

*Pennsylvania Department of
Public Welfare*
Health & Welfare Building Annex
(215) 560-2547

*Rhode Island Department of
Children, Youth, & Families*
Division of Direct Services
(401) 457-4708

**South Carolina Department of
Social Services**
Office of Children, Family, & Adult
Services
(803) 734-5670

**South Dakota Department of
Social Services**
Child Protection Services
(605) 773-3227

**Tennessee Department of Human
Services**
(615) 741-5935

**Texas Department of Human
Services**
(512) 450-3011

Utah Department of Social Services
Division of Family Services
(801) 264-7589

**Vermont Department of Social &
Rehabilitative Services**
(802) 241-2131

**Virginia Department of Social
Services**
(804) 662-9131

**Washington State Department of
Social & Health Services**
(206) 364-0300

**West Virginia Department of
Human Services**
Family & Children Services
(304) 558-4098

**Wisconsin Department of Health
& Social Services**
Division of Community Services
(608) 266-0690

**Wyoming Department of Family
Services**
(307) 777-6789

Index

A

AASK Midwest (Adopt a Special Kid), 46
Abused child, adoption of, 16
Adopted children
  baby book of, 6, 172
  decorating room for future, 172
  involvement of birth parents in life of, 7, 10
Adoption
  of abused child, 16
  answering personal questions on, 170–72
  changes in, 4–5
  confidential. *See* Confidential adoption
  decision making in, 4
  foster parent, 63–64
  identified, 58–62
  importance of positive attitude in, 2–4
  independent. *See* Independent adoption
  infants available for, in the U.S., 12–13
  intercountry. *See* Intercountry adoption
  legal risk, 63
  motivation in, 53–54
  national organizations concerned with, 205–7
  of older child, 16–17, 40–44
  open. *See* Open adoption
  options in, 11–12
  private. *See* Independent adoption
  sources for information on, 11, 18–20, 170, 195
  of special-needs child, 14–17, 40–44, 56, 130
  time management while waiting, 166–74
  transracial. *See* Transracial adoption
  types of children to consider, 55–58
  of waiting children, 46–47
Adoption agencies. *See also* Agency adoption
  and choice between open and confidential adoption, 58
  for intercountry adoption, 18, 32, 54, 83–84, 117
  small local, services, 54–55
  working with, 4, 76
Adoption attorneys
  in independent adoption, 142–44
  in intercountry adoption, 18, 122–23
  listing of selected, 185–94
  need for competent, 133–34
  in open adoption, 8
Adoption facilitator, role of, 9
Adoption Information Center of Illinois (AICI), 44–45
Adoption Options of Louisiana, 14–15
Adoption risk insurance, 62
Adoption Services associates, 62
Adoptive Families of America, Inc. (AFA), 11, 18–19, 26, 130

Adoptive homes, physical
    requirements for, 101
Adoptive parents
    counseling for, 9–10
    magazines and newsletters of
        interest to, 210–11
    rights and responsibilities of,
        69–73
Adoptive parent support groups, 22
    affiliation of, 26
    benefits of belonging to, 26
    contacting, 27
    finding, 26, 27–29
    function of, 22–26
    for intercountry adoption, 24
    listing of, 195–203
    for single adoptive parents,
        129–30
    meetings of, 24–25
    services offered by, 25
African-American child, adoption
    of, 14
Agency adoption. *See also* Adoption
        agencies; Private
agencies; Public agencies
    baby broker agencies, 68
    choosing type of agency, 65–66
    comparison to independent
        adoption, 140–41
    creating work space, 30–31
    establishing timetable and plan of
        action in, 33–36
    and identified adoption, 58–62
    of infant born in U.S., 76–83
    obtaining list of licensed agencies,
        31–32
    orientation meeting in, 65
    problems in searching, 36–38
    pursuing, 65–68
    requirements for U.S. infant
        adoption, 51–52
    researching, 32–33
    setting up your files, 36
Agency-assisted adoption. *See also*
        Identified adoption in
        intercountry adoption, 117
Age requirements, in private agency
    adoptions, 49–50

American Indian children, adoption
    of, 14
Arrival announcement, ordering,
    172–73
Assertiveness, in finding waiting
    child, 44–46
Attitude, importance of positive, in
    adoption, 2–4
Attorney. *See* Adoption attorney

B

Baby book, of adopted child, 6, 172
Baby broker agencies, 68
Bethany Christian Services, 54
Birth mother
    and choice of adoptive parents,
        13
    counseling for, 9–10
    decision to keep child, 9, 12–13
    demand for active role, 5–6
    following lead on, 23–24
    and identified adoption, 58–62
    involvement in adopted child's
        life, 7, 10
    magazines and newsletters of
        interest to, 210–11
    networking in finding, 148–49
    obtaining medical and social
        history on, 144–46
    reasons for choosing private
        adoption, 140
    rights in independent adoption,
        137
    and use of open adoption, 6–9
    writing letter to, 152, 157–63
Birth mother video, making, 163–64
Birth parents. *See* Birth mother

C

Casa del Mundo, Inc., 132
Catholic Charities, 47
Child-care classes, 168
Children Awaiting Parents (The CAP
    Book, Inc.), 45
Committee for Single Adoptive
    Parents, 129
Confidential adoption, 7, 11–12
    versus open adoption, 58
Costs. *See* Fees

Council of Three Rivers, 46
Counseling
  of adoptive parents, 9–10
  of birth parents, 9–10
  in identified adoption, 59
  in open adoption, 9

D

Denominational agencies, 47–49
Designated adoption. *See* Identified
  adoption
Direct adoption. *See* Parent-initiated
  adoption

E

Education, in open adoptions, 9
Employment of mother, as adoption
  restriction, 52

F

Families Adopting Children
  Everywhere (FACE), 25–26
Fast-track adoption. *See* Identified
  adoption
Federation for Children with Special
  Needs, 17
Fees
  in baby broker adoption, 68
  computation of adoption, 51
  for home study, 88–90
  in identified adoption, 62
  in independent adoption, 133,
    138–39, 141
  in intercountry adoption, 17,
    123–24, 184
  for private agency, 48–49, 50, 51
  for single parent adoption,
    133–34
Foster parent adoption, 63–64

H

Home study, 13, 46
  costs of, 88–90
  definition of, 85
  documents needed for, 90
  getting information on, 106
  handling nonapproval in, 92–93
  in infant adoption, 77

  for intercountry adoption, 2–3,
    83, 88–89, 114–16
  length of time for, 88
  need for, 13, 85
  obtaining references in, 93
  paperwork in, 86–87
  questions asked in, 94–100
  role of public agency in, 46
  role of social worker in, 100–102
  successful completion of, 91–92
  update of, 88
Home study report
  copies of, 102
  example of, 102–106

I

Identified adoption, 58–62
  costs in, 62
  counseling in, 59
  risks in, 62
Illien Adoptions International, Ltd.,
  54
Immigration and Naturalization
  Service (INS), U.S. and
  eligibility of child for adoption,
    109
  paperwork for, 113–14
  requirements of, in intercountry
    adoption, 17
  service district offices, 204
Independent adoption, 4, 18, 135,
  141
  comparison to agency adoption,
    140–41
  costs in, 133, 138–39, 141
  decisions in, 147
  definition of, 137
  example of one couple in, 149–51
  final thoughts on, 165
  in intercountry adoption, 122–23
  legal issues in, 138–39
  listing of agencies for, 212–36
  locating birth mother in, 147–48
  myths in, 135–36
  networking in finding birth
    mother, 148–49
  newspaper advertising in, 144–57
  obtaining information on birth
    parents, 144–46

preparing résumé in, 152–54
process in, 136–38
reasons for choosing, 139–40
role of attorney in, 142–44
single parent adoption of infants
    through, 131–32
state laws on, 138
writing a dear birth mother letter,
    157–63
Indian Child Welfare Act, 14
Infant adoption
    agency requirements for, 51–52
    process of, 76–83
Infants
    availability for adoption in U.S,
        12–13
    single parent independent
        adoption of, 131–32
    U.S., with special needs, 14–16
Infertility, questions on, and private
    infant adoption, 50, 51
Insurance, adoption risk, 62
Intercountry adoption, 4, 107–8
    adoption attorneys in, 18
    agencies for, 18, 32, 54, 83–84
    anticipated changes in, 125–26
    availability of children for, 108–9,
        110–11
    choices in, 116–17
    documents needed for, 114–15
    ensuring legal, 124
    fees in, 17, 123–24, 184
    getting advice on, 124–25
    home study for, 2–3, 83, 88–89,
        115–16
Immigration and Naturalization
    Service requirements for, 17,
        113–14
    independent adoptions in,
        122–23
    initiating process for, 112–13
    parent-initiated adoptions in,
        117–22
    preparing for, 173–74
    as privilege, 84
    reasons for, 112
    requirements for parents in, 108

sample local service agency
    contract and financial
    agreement for, 69–75
by single parents, 132–33
support group for, 24
type of child eligible for, 109
International Concerns Committee
    for Children (ICCC), 19, 45,
    125
Interstate Compact on the
    Placement of Children (ICPC),
    33, 77, 85, 115, 139

J

Jewish Family Services, 47
Journal, recording adoption process
    in, 167

L

Latin American Adoptive Families
    (LAAF), 19–20
Latin American Parents Association
    (LAPA), 118
Legal risk adoption, 63
Letter, writing to birth mother, 152,
    157–63
Library of Congress, Handicapped
    Hotline, 17
Life book, making, 164–65
Light House, 48
Local service agencies
    adoptions through, 54–55
    sample contract and financial
    agreement for intercountry
    adoption, 69–75
Lutheran Social Services, 47

M

Marriage length, as adoption
    restriction, 52
Medical insurance, coverage for
    adopted child, 173
Motivation, in adoption, 53–54

N

National Adoption Center, 45
National Adoption Exchange, 45

National Adoption Information
  Clearinghouse (NAIC), 6, 19,
  27, 138
National Association of Black Social
  Workers (NABSW), stand on
  transracial adoption, 13–14
National Council For Adoption, 20
National Information Center for
  Children and Youth with
  Disabilities, 17
National Information Clearinghouse
  for Infants with Disabilities, 17
Nebraska Children's Home Society,
  50
Newspaper advertising
  in independent adoption, 154–57
  sample ads in, 155
Nondenominational agencies,
  49–50
North American Council on
  Adoptable Children, 20, 26–27

O
Older children, 130
  looking for, 40–44
  single parent adoption of, 130
Open adoption, 6–9
  benefits of, 8
  versus confidential adoption, 58
  counseling in, 9
  definition of, 7
  education in, 9
  problems with, 9–10
  renegotiation of terms in, 7–8
  risks in, 10
Open Door Society, 25, 125
*OURS: The magazine of adoptive
  families*, 11, 173

P
Parent-initiated adoptions, in
  intercountry adoption, 117–22
Parents, characteristics of, who
  adopt quickly, 2–4
Pediatrician, finding, 168–69
Picture, including, with résumé,
  130, 153–54
Postadoption services, availability
  of, 59

Private adoption. *See* Independent
  adoption
Private agencies, 5, 47
  computation of fee, 51
  denominational agencies, 47–49
  fees in adoptions, 48–49, 50
  nondenominational agencies,
  49–50
  sample application, 78–82
Pro-life agreement, denomination
  agency requirement for, 48
Public agencies, 39–40
  looking for older children and
  children with special needs
  through, 40–44
  process of adopting, 41, 44
  requirements for adopting
  waiting children, 46
  sample application, 42–43

Q
Questions, answering personal,
  170–72

R
Reading, 170
Résumé
  including picture with, 153–54
  in finding birth mother, 148–49
  preparing, in independent
  adoption, 152–53
  sample, 151
Rocky Mountain Adoption
  Exchange, 45
Room, decorating for future child,
  172

S
Semiopen adoption, 7
Single parent adoptions, 127–28
  of babies, 131–32
  of child from other country,
  132–33
  fees in, 133–34
  getting information on, 128–30
  of older child, 130
  of special-needs child, 130
  of young child, 131
Single Parents Adopting Children
  Everywhere (SPACE), 130

Social worker, role of, in home
    study, 100–2
Special-needs adoptions, 14–16
    fees in, 50
    looking for child in, 40–44
    medical problems in, 56
    by single parent, 130
Substance abuse, and confidential
    adoption, 12
Support groups. *See* Adoptive parent
    support groups
    finding, 26, 27–29
    for single adoptive parents,
    129–30
Support system, building, 167

T
Targeted adoption. *See* Identified
    adoption
Time management, in adoption,
    166–74

Transracial adoptions, 13–14. *See
    also* Intercountry adoption
Travel advisories, in intercountry
    adoption, 119

V
Volunteer work, 169–70

W
Waiting children
    assertiveness in finding, 44–46
    classification of child as, 40
    requirements for adoption of,
    46–47
    in U.S., 16
World Association of Children and
    Parents (WACAP), 54

Y
Young child, single parent adoption
    of, 131